JOEY
THE HITMAN

THE AUTOBIOGRAPHY
OF A MAFIA KILLER

by

"JOEY"

WITH DAVID FISHER

SERIES EDITOR CLINT WILLIS

Joey the Hitman: *The Autobiography of a Mafia Killer*

First Edition

Copyright © 2002 by David Fisher and Joey
Introduction Copyright © 2002 by David Fisher
Adrenaline® and Adrenaline Classics® and the Adrenaline® and Adrenaline
Classics® logos are trademarks of Avalon Publishing Group Incorporated,
New York, NY.

An Adrenaline Classics Book®

Published by
Thunder's Mouth Press
An Imprint of Avalon Publishing Group Incorporated
245 West 17th Street, 11th Floor
New York, NY 10011

A Balliett & Fitzgerald book

Book design: Paul Paddock

Library of Congress Cataloging-in-Publication Data is available.

ISBN 1-56025-393-2

Printed in the Untied States of America

Distributed by Publishers Group West

CONTENTS

INTRODUCTION

As I watch actor James Gandolfini's Tony Soprano move with anger, angst and tempered joy through his daily life, I can't help but remember "Joey Black," the Mafia hit man with whom I worked to write this book almost three decades ago. "Joey" killed people. It was one of the ways he made his living.

Before I met Joey my knowledge of the crime world was a conglomeration of half-digested facts and feelings gathered from "The Untouchables," *The Godfather*, newspapers, a few books, magazines, rumor and the six o'clock news. When I was first approached to work with "a mob killer," I admit to having felt some apprehension. But the strongest emotion was curiosity. I had no idea what an honest-to-goodness, 100-percent-guaranteed, double-your-money-back killer would be like, and I wanted to find out.

I met Joey for the first time outside the office of Playboy Books' editorial director Ed Kuhn. He stepped into the room dressed smartly in a black leather jacket half-zipped covering a white V-neck T-shirt. His black hair was neatly slicked back 1955-style. Physically he was a bit shorter than the stereotype, but his huge shoulders, deep chest and muscular arms were what I expected. "Whattya say, kid," he boomed, and stuck out his hand. "Sorry I'm late, but I was trying to find a barber. Mine got killed last week." Those words did nothing to make me more comfortable, but he went on to add that a drug addict had done the job in the midst of a mugging, which relieved me some.

Eventually Joey began to tell me his life story. For me the story went on day after day for a number of months. I gathered bits and pieces in New York, Los Angeles, a day in Chicago, and over numerous lunches and dinners, through countless recording sessions. The result was this book.

"My book," as he referred to it, was never meant to be another in the long list of startling exposés which promise to name names and reveal where the bodies were buried. There are real names here and violent events but in, I hope, a different context. The book was intended to portray the day-to-day operation of organized crime; how a gambling operation is set up, how to place a bet, pick a number, find a shylock, smuggle narcotics, hijack a truck, "A Consumer's Guide to Organized Crime," Joey once joked.

It is also an American success story. The autobiography of a killer. Joey's story. When you finish this book, you will have an understanding of how his mind worked. How killing can become a business, and be separated from other parts of his daily existence. In these pages Joey detailed his past and present, his loves and hates, his frustrations and successes. Only his fears are missing—from the first day we met he consistently denied allowing himself any.

Over the months Joey and I became friends. At times I would listen to him spew forth tale after tale of "hitting this guy in the head" or "threatening to make a crowd out of that guy" and lose all patience. But I began to separate the man I knew, and liked, from the violent man we were dispassionately dissecting. Watching him play with my young nephews, I found it hard to believe that he was capable of the things he was telling me.

But there were other moments. In a Los Angeles restaurant, we were with some friends of mine and one of them, a man about my age, asked him what he would do if somebody doubted he was who he said he was. Joey picked up a sharp fork and jammed it against my friend's neck, driving his head uncomfortably upward. "I'd ask him to say it again." It was a nasty moment.

But those moments were rare. I began to believe that this book was meant to serve as Joey's penitence. He saw it quite differently, of course.

He expressed many reasons for wanting to do the book. None of them were entirely convincing, none of them were entirely beyond belief. "Members of organized crime have been made out to look like animals," he told me in his Bronx accent, "and actually we're not such bad people. We are the caterers of society. We just give people what they want. We don't set out to hurt anybody. I want people to understand that."

At another point he spoke of retiring. "I think maybe I've had enough, I'd like to get out."

I think there were other reasons for his wanting the book. Joey saw the traditional mob structure crumbling around him. The traditional oath of silence was being broken every day, and he wanted to get his piece of the action, even though publicly he could never admit his mob identity. In one of his most chilling publicity appearances' he was interviewed on television by the late David Susskind, wearing a bag over his head with eye holes cut out, to protect his identity. (Susskind hosted hundreds and hundreds of shows, but his interview with "Joey the Hit Man" remains one of the three most requested shows he ever did.)

Finally, this book is Joey's monument. It testifies to the fact that he was here and he survived. It was ego-fulfilling, and Joey had a very big ego.

The words and thoughts in this book are his. We worked with a tape recorder, and I did my own transcription and editing. I have been careful to keep my feelings out of Joey's mouth. There are many things in this book I don't agree with. At one point, for instance, he says, "The mob never created an addict." I don't believe that at all. We argued about it, but in the book it is precisely as he said it.

I also knew only those things about him that he wanted me to know. I cannot count the hours we spent together, yet I never knew his real name, where he lived, who he hung out with, what his wife looked like, where he went after he left my apartment. I do know that he was everything he said he was. My introduction to him was through a highly regarded crime reporter, a man who has known Joey for years. Other experts on the world of crime brought in during the vetting process confirmed that Joey was, in fact, the "real article."

Although we disagreed over almost everything, from politics to organized religion, I found myself more amazed than upset by this man. He was one of the more complex individuals I have known. He was a vicious killer, but he was also outgoing, affable, gregarious, funny, egocentric, sometimes unreasonable but usually friendly. In a macabre moment, I dubbed him "The Happy Hit Man," which is what he was.

The facts in the book are also here as Joey related them to me. At the very beginning he explained he didn't believe anyone could really be an expert on the subject of organized crime. "There's too much going on," he said, "and no one can see it all or know all the facts. There are things that go on that even Carlo Gambino doesn't know about.

"I'm only an expert in those areas I've worked in. The mob deals in stolen securities, for example, but I never have, so I don't know anything about that area. Anything I told you would be hearsay, and this book is going to be fact." I questioned some of his facts. At one point he told me there was a $50-million shylocking outfit operating in New York City. I didn't believe it. A few months later the police broke up a ring which had more than $75 million on the street. And, when I expressed my doubt about his ability to find someone quickly in a big city with very few clues, he offered to prove his ability to me.

A friend of mine was going to Detroit to visit his wife's family. Joey and I made a friendly bet. I "hired" him to locate this man in Detroit. All I told him was when he would be arriving. We didn't reveal his wife's maiden name, where they were married, or any other data I considered useful.

The night he arrived in Detroit, Joey called him to say hello.

As an undergraduate at Syracuse University, I was friendly with a basketball player, at first an open, bright, warm kind of guy. As soon as he became the star of the team he changed. He molded himself to fit the role he believed other people expected him to play, that of campus hero. Joey did the same thing. He would play anything from Edward G. Robinson to George Raft. His language ranged from pure gutter to ivy-covered. Similarly, the reader may find the book written in different styles. But they're all Joey's.

Like the fictional Tony Soprano, the real Joey swaggered through life, trying to live the fiction that he was just an ordinary kind of guy with a very extraordinary occupation. And maybe he even believed it. I never really knew.

—*David Fisher*

JOEY
THE HITMAN

THE AUTOBIOGRAPHY
OF A MAFIA KILLER

CHAPTER *1*

JOEY—WHAT YOU'D CALL MY EARLY YEARS

F uck *The Godfather.*

For years movies, television, books, newspapers and magazines have been portraying mob members as something they are not. If anyone believed half of what they saw on the screen or read about us, he would have to conclude that the mob consists of a bunch of tough guys who spend most of their time threatening delicatessen owners in Bronx-Italian accents, screwing beautiful broads, meeting famous people and shooting each other.

Nothing could be farther from the truth: Actually very few mob members even have Bronx-Italian accents.

The other things aren't quite true either. A lot of mob people are not very tough, many of the broads tend to be plump and have skin trouble, the people we meet and deal with are very ordinary, most of us stay home at night and watch TV, and we only shoot each other when absolutely necessary. In fact, the entire image of life within the mob that has been created by the mass media has very little to do with reality. I know, because I have lived and worked within the organization for the past three decades.

Organized crime is very loosely organized but highly structured. We have our own social system and, because we can't use the regular legal system, we've had to construct our own police force to deal with internal problems. That's where I fit in.

Every member of organized crime is capable of doing many different things, but each is an expert in at least one area. Some guys are great bookmakers. Others are wonderful smugglers. Me? I kill people.

My official title is "hit man" and I have 38 "hits" to my credit: 35 for money and three for revenge. But all 38 have been members of the organization. I have never killed an honest man. I may have messed up a few reminding them to pay their debts, but every one of my 38 was a mob member.

There are levels or categories of membership within the structure of crime. If you are a runner, for example, you take bets, that's your category. Or you might specialize in fencing stolen goods, or "shylocking" (lending money at very high interest rates). Because I have no compunctions about doing anything, because it is a well-known fact that I will pull the trigger, I fit into a much higher, more respected category.

I don't even call it murder. To me it's a way of making a living. It's a job. It's my profession. But it's not all I do.

I also smuggle narcotics and cigarettes; hijack trucks; bootleg perfumes, records and eight-track tapes; run card games; work the numbers; do a little muscle work; book some bets; make pornographic movies; put people in contact with shylocks; fence some stolen goods; and now and then scalp some tickets. But my specialty is killing or, as we put it, hitting people in the head. I am one of the most feared killers in this country today. I have a reputation of being able to get the job done, quickly and efficiently, no matter what unexpected problems pop up. The reason is simple: I don't care if I live or die.

If I live, I live; if I die, I die. I have been through it all. The ability to make that statement, and mean it, is what makes me a dangerous man. Violence does not faze me because I have lived with it all my life. I got into this business because I found it could let me live the way I wanted to live. I could earn the kind of money I wanted to earn. I have no regrets. Crime has been very good to me. Crime does pay, and anybody who says it doesn't is crazy. I'll tell you, right now there are more of your so-called criminals walking around with a pocket full of money than there are guys sitting in the can. The guy who goes to prison is the stupid jerk who tried to mug some old man or rape a broad or hold up some nickel-and-dime grocery store. He goes up. The professionals in this business rarely get time. Why? Because we go out of our way not to antagonize the honest citizen. We let people come to us.

I would estimate that, in my lifetime, I have earned roughly four million dollars. That is a lot of money. And if I paid taxes on $300,000 I paid taxes on a lot. As far as the Internal Revenue Service is concerned I am a mediocre traveling salesman handling a line of women's cosmetics. A friend of mine keeps me on his books and every week I sign a check and give him the tax difference. Nobody would know I've made that much money, certainly not my neighbors. I don't live big, I don't live ostentatiously. I don't ride around in flashy Caddies. I ride around in a comfortable, late-model car. I don't go to nightclubs. What I do like to do, unfortunately, is bet. I bet big, and most of the time not too well. I'm a terrible handicapper. I'm lucky if I get a horse that lives. So there isn't much of that money left.

I'll tell you who still has a chunk, my wife. In this business, there are two things you learn: Take care of your wife and never lie to your lawyer, because these are the two most important people in the world. Every time I make a good score I give some to my wife. I know she's gonna salt it somewhere. I don't know where she's gonna put it, but she's gonna put it. This money goes for the day when I get my head blown off, or I die of old age. Or if I have to go away for a while I want to know she's protected. Also, if I need bail money she'll be able to put it up.

Sometimes you get to know your lawyer better than your wife. In my three decades in this business I have never been convicted of a felony. I have been questioned in 17 murder cases (for the record, I was guilty in three of them). I have been brought before a grand jury seven times; four times I was released and three times I was held for trial. I have spent time in jails all across this beautiful country waiting to go on trial. But I have never lied to my lawyer. And I have never been convicted.

So organized crime has been good to me. If I had to do it all over again

I'm not sure I'd change a thing. I've had an exciting, interesting, profitable life. Nobody stuck a gun into my ribs to make me go into it. It's fed me, given me things that I wanted out of life. It has changed me from a very wild, physical type of individual which I was when I was younger, to the thoughtful, quietly violent man which I am now.

I started in crime when I was 11 years old. Not because I particularly wanted to, but because I had no choice. I did not exactly have what you would call a model childhood. I was born in New York City in 1932, the second son of second-generation Eastern European immigrants. My father was a reasonably successful bootlegger and my mother was a very typical Bronx housewife. He was about five foot six and weighed a solid 170, my mother was a little taller and weighed just a little less. When prohibition ended he became a numbers banker. When the money was coming in I remember things being fine. But when I was four years old my father killed two men Dutch Schultz had sent to try to take over his operation. He was arrested and sent to prison and my whole world changed. I didn't see him again for six years.

My mother had never really worked and this was still the middle of the depression. She tried to get a job but couldn't find a single thing. With no money coming in except what my brother, who was three years older than me, could steal we just couldn't make it. She had no choice but to send me to the state orphanage.

I have a difficult time focusing in on the orphanage building itself. That time period seems one big blur. It was a brick building completely stocked with crying kids. Every time you turned around somebody was yelling and crying. I couldn't sleep at night because of all the noise. I went back a few years ago to see the building but it had long since been turned into a parking lot. It was the policy of the orphanage to board out as many children as they could, so I only spent a total of eight months there. My life from the time I was five until I left and went home at age ten was a succession of foster homes.

The foster-home program was successful when a child was put with a family that really cared for him and it failed when the child was placed with people who took him just for the money the state paid. In the five years I was in the program I was with eight different families, just as many good as bad. The real problem was that the orphanage had a policy of limiting any stay to a maximum of one year, so when you finally got comfortable in a place it was time to leave. One of the very best years of my life was spent with a family on the Upper East Side of Manhattan, in a heavily German area called Yorkville. I was placed with a family of German refugees who had a daughter twice my age. In Germany this man had been a professor of mathematics at some university and the family had been wealthy. But when they fled Hitler they lost everything and had to start from scratch here. The old man didn't do too badly. He was smart and he worked hard and he made a decent living.

Every time I think about people in general, what phonies most people are, I think about these people. Even with all their problems they had the ability to take someone in and really care for him. They tried their very best to make me feel like I was their son. They would buy me nice clothes, buy me the toys I never had, take me to baseball games, and even the daughter would stand out in the courtyard and play catch with me. I was happy there, but at the end of one year the guy from the state came and took me away from them.

As I grew older I stayed in contact with these people. I tried to pay them back many times over, but I never could really pay them back. When the old man had a stroke I arranged his hospital care and when he came out I made sure he got the best rehabilitation possible. I would always send them gifts. They never knew what I did, but they knew I was successful. To them I was always a nice little boy who came to live with them for one year.

They were the best. The worst lived across the city, in a rough neighborhood known as Hell's Kitchen. They had a one-bedroom apartment and I slept on the folding bed with their son. We were both seven years old. The first day I was there I caught this kid going through my clothes. These clothes were literally all I had that I could call my own, so I tore into him. I beat him up as badly as one seven-year-old can beat up another. That night the old man, who worked for the transit authority, came home and heard what happened. After dinner he grabbed hold of my arms and held them behind my back while his son pounded away at my stomach. I threw up all over myself but there was nothing I could do about it. It was a helpless feeling. I felt terrible and alone that night. I didn't stay with that family very long. The next day I beat up the kid again and just about every day after that (hiding or running from his old man at night) until they finally sent me back to the orphanage.

I came home when I was ten years old. Home? Not quite. My father had gotten out of prison but he was never around the place. I never saw him. My brother had gotten a job in a warehouse so I only saw him at night. And my mother had gotten sick. She was just in the beginning stages of a long fight with cancer when I came home. She was too sick to really take care of me, my brother or my father, so we all went out on our own. I watched my mother die. At one point she had been a happy, healthy woman of about 160 pounds. When she died she weighed maybe 70 pounds. I lived with horror and brutality all my life, but watching her die in pain was the worst I ever seen. She lived for three years, until I was 14, and made me a believer in mercy killing. Had I been a little older I would have killed her myself.

My father died a year after she did. He had given up a long time before he finally died and one day he just didn't wake up. He knew I had gotten into crime but he never said much about it. I was bringing home the money to support the family and what could he say? "Just do what you think best," was the closest he ever came to advice. I didn't miss him when he died; I missed him while he was alive.

My brother and I became close when I moved back in. There was one incident that stands out in my memory like it was yesterday. It was one of the rare days when we had meat for dinner. I just ripped into mine and finished it quickly. My brother could see I was still hungry, so he took a piece of his meat off his plate and put it on mine. "Here, kid," he said, "you eat this. I'm not hungry anyway." He became my best friend that day, and we've stayed very close ever since. He grew up to be a respected small businessman and has done well. He knows I'm involved with the mob and probably knows that I pull the trigger. We've never talked about it. The closest we ever came took place when I was leaving his house one day. He walked me to the door and as he was handing me my coat he felt the gun

in the pocket. He just looked at me. Finally he said, "Be careful, kid."
That's all.

After our parents died we lived together for over a year in a small
apartment. Then he decided to get married and I found myself a furnished
three-room apartment and moved in. I was totally and completely on my
own. I was 16 years old.

By that time I was an established veteran in the local numbers organization. I had started working just after my 11th birthday. A guy by the
name of Joe Bagels, who felt sorry for me because my family had nothing,
introduced me to my first boss, Sammy Schlitz. Sammy asked me if I
wanted to take numbers and I told him I'd love it. At this point my family
wasn't just poor, we were destitute. I wasn't missing any meals—I was just
postponing them. So when the offer came I had no choice but to accept it.
And, I admit, it sounded like an adventure.

My first "office" was at the intersection of Jennings Street, Wilkins
Avenue, and Intervale Avenue in the Bronx. This was right in the middle
of the neighborhood shopping area. There was a Jewish delicatessen on one
corner, a candy store which was actually a bookmaking office on the opposite corner, and a big drugstore was right next to the candy store. There
were also half a dozen open-air fruit stands within a block.

I was living on Freeman Street, which was one long block away from
this corner. My first morning on the job I got up around 5:45 A.M. and put
on my two warmest shirts. It was late September and I didn't own a jacket.
Finally I stuck a pad and some pencils in my pocket and started lugging a
bridge table and a wooden chair, my "office," to the corner. By the time I
got there and got set up it was almost 6:30.

My very first customer was the owner of one of the fruit stands. He
put a nickel on number 013, I remember it perfectly, and then saw I was
shivering. He took his jacket off and gave it to me. He would do that every
morning: He would wear the jacket to work, I would wear it while I was
sitting there, and then he would wear it home. That went on for about a
month, until I bought my own coat.

I spent a lot of hours at that table. It was decorated to look expensive
and there was a big picture of Buckingham Palace printed on it. I would

leave it at the fruit stand when I was done working so I wouldn't have to lug it back and forth.

My customers were the people who worked in the stores, the people who passed me on the way to work or on the way home, plus the housewives who would come down in the morning to bet.

Of all my customers there is one man that stands out. He was a little black guy, he couldn't have been more than five foot three and he had a clubfoot. He worked as a ragpicker. I once asked him what he would do if he won, and he just looked at me. I don't think he ever considered it possible that he could win. But every day he came hobbling along, laid his three cents down and said, "You gonna get me a winna today, sonny?" And every day I would answer, "I think today is going to be your lucky day." It never was, though. Right up until the day I became controller he would come up and lay his pennies down.

The first day I was there I took in $100 and change from people on their way to work. In those days people didn't bet like they do today— they were betting two cents, three cents, a quarter was a big bet. I also learned the most important fact of life that day: You do not operate unless you have a contract.

A contract is an agreement to do something, from bribery to murder. It's strictly oral, for obvious reasons, but in this business your word is your bond. You live and die on it. If you give me your word and take my money, I expect you to do something; if I take your money or give you my word, you have the right to expect me to do something. The penalty for breaking your word ranges from very bad to much worse.

At eight o'clock that first Monday morning, the cop who walked that beat showed up, stood there, made sure nobody bothered me, and then left. I never found out what that cop was getting, or exactly who was paying him off, but he never took a dime from me. From that morning on, with the possible exception of my time in the army, I never did what you would call an honest day's work in my life.

Besides numbers I was getting involved in all sorts of things when I was still a kid. I began working the Office of Price Administration on 57th Street in Manhattan with a bunch of guys. Because I was small I could slide in over the transom and grab ration stamps that were sitting there waiting to be destroyed. We got tons of them: sugar stamps, gasoline stamps, canned goods stamps, everything. And after we grabbed them we would go uptown and sell them to your so-called honest citizens.

One guy we knew had a truck with a 50-gallon gas drum on the back. We would pull up alongside parked cars and siphon gas out of them into the drum. Or we would jack cars up and steal the tires. We did just about everything we could and, at the tender age of 11, I was making between $75 and $100 a day. When you're as poor as we were you develop a simple attitude: You'll do anything to get something.

It was no secret that I was the local numbers runner; everybody in the neighborhood knew. Who did they think was taking their money? The same hypocrisy I complain about now existed then too. Some of these people would say, "Isn't it terrible, this boy is getting involved with hoods by taking numbers," and then they would hand me a nickel or a dime or a few pennies and make their daily bet. Without those pennies and nickels and dimes and quarters I couldn't have been a runner; I would have had to find something else to do. I'll never forget those people. They all said, "You shouldn't be doing this," but not one of them, not one, said, "Listen, can I teach you a trade? Can I help you get a job where you can learn something?" They never told me that. So I learned my own trade.

Age 14 was a big year for me. Besides doing well with the numbers I had my first sexual experience. The girl's name was Margie and she was 19 years old. Actually she was pretty decent-looking. She had short brown hair and a cute face and really huge tits. As I later realized she wasn't really interested in me as a person, she just liked being with someone who had a reputation of being a so-called tough kid. There are a lot of women like her around. There is something about being with a hoodlum that really turns them on.

Margie and I had gone out a few times, but nothing had ever happened between us. It might have—I really wanted to get my hands on those tits—but I didn't know how to go about it. One night we went to her apartment to listen to Bob Hope on the radio. Her parents had gone on vacation for a few days so we had the place to ourselves. After the show was over I decided to take a shower—we never had hot water at our apartment—and when I stepped out of the shower she was standing there holding a towel for me. It was the first time in my life any woman except my mother had seen me naked. I tried as hard as I could to be cool—I let her dry me off, then I went inside and she took a shower.

I had just started getting dressed when she walked into the bedroom. She was totally naked. Except for magazines, this was the first time I had ever seen a nude woman. We laid down on the bed and she began rubbing her hand all over my body. At this point everything I knew about sex had come from rumors, but I didn't get scared or anything. Finally she stuck her tongue in my ear and drove me up a wall. Then we made it—just barely.

I saw her on and off for about a year. She was a great teacher.

By the time I reached my 15th birthday I was already punching people in the mouth for money. It was about that time I started working as the controller of my numbers area and making what seemed to me a small fortune. As controller I had to go around to all the different runners in the area and collect their money. I didn't even have a driver's license but I had a nice car and I used to drive around all day picking up other people's action. I also kept my dollar customers from Jennings and Wilkins, but I put somebody else on the corner for the small customers. I had 40 runners working for me and I was collecting 10 percent of their action, plus 35 percent of my total take (the rest went to the button man and on to the boss) for a *daily* income somewhere in the neighborhood of $500. At 15 years old.

In return for my ten percent of the runner's take, I was responsible for the runners. I had to handle the police contract and, if any of my men ever got picked up, I had to split the lawyer's fee with him.

I worked as a controller for almost two years, finding time along the way to kill my first man, my numero uno I'll tell you about later, and then my entire career came to an abrupt halt. Three Italian guys from Fordham saw that I was doing all right and that I was young and they walked up to me one day and decided that, all of a sudden, the four of us were going into business together. My business. I could have gone to the office and told them that I was having trouble, but if you do they start to look at you funny, they think you can't take care of yourself, and you don't move up so fast. They'd protect me, but my chance of ever really going anywhere wouldn't be so good.

I certainly didn't want to lose that $500 a day. I couldn't afford to. I was spending every penny of it. It was just going through my hands. What I wasn't giving to my father I was gambling and getting rid of in every possible way. So I told these three guys, "Go fuck yourselves, I don't need no partners."

One guy says, "You got a fresh mouth," so I smashed him in his.

"Let me tell yas somethin'," I said. "If I ever spot yas, I'll hurt yas. Don't come near me. Stay away from me." Unfortunately they didn't believe me. About two weeks later I was walking along and I noticed that I had company walking across the street following me. I stopped off at this Davega sporting goods store and bought a 32-ounce Louisville Slugger. I walked out of the store and walked directly across the street and started swinging. I never said a word, just laid the wood on them. I always had a nice level swing, with good power down the left-field line, and I was doing a very good job. I broke arms, I broke legs, I broke heads, and then—just my luck—a cop came along. This is known as felonious assault.

When we got to court these three guys wouldn't open their mouths, but I had a pretty bad reputation and the cops had caught me in the act. The judge had me as a juvenile and he gave me a choice of four years at a state center in Elmira, New York, or going in the army. I like to say that I'm the only guy in the world who needed the recommendation of a judge and 12 jurors to get into the army. That day, for all practical purposes, was the end of my "childhood."

I liked the responsibility the army gave me. In fact, I liked it so much that I made sergeant four different times, one less than the number of times I made private. I went up and down the ranks like a yo-yo. They would bust me for the stupidest things. For example, they gave us some forms with a long list of organizations and finally asked, "Do you belong to a party that is trying to overthrow the government of the United States?" I put down "Yes," and, sure enough, they called me into the colonel's office. I told them, "I'm a Republican and we're trying to get Truman out of there." Looking back, I have to admit it seemed funnier then.

One thing I will give the army credit for, they taught me a trade. I was an infantryman and when I got out of the service I knew how to use more weapons than I'd ever need. The army also taught me to think, not just to jump but to carefully plan every move and how to follow through on that plan.

I was stationed at Fort Dix, Fort Benning and finally Korea. I fought my first real battle at the Choshin Reservoir. We were the diversionary action for the First Marine Brigade. They had been trapped up there and we jumped in and held the gooks at the Yalu for something like five days, until we ran out of ammunition. I will never forget the minute they told us to clear out. I had about five cartridges left and was looking around for a Thompson submachine gun when our officers started telling everybody to clear out quickly. I took off running down that road like a rabbit. I don't mind fighting, but you can't fight a man who has a loaded machine gun with an empty rifle. I'm running south as fast as I can when I see this guy just crapped out by the side of the road. As I go steaming by, arms pumping, legs churning, he screamed at me, "That's right, kid, dazzle 'em with footwork." I started laughing so hard I fell right into a ditch.

The army also taught me something about loyalty. Right at the beginning of basic training I hooked up with two other guys. One was a kid from Boston who had been a thief all his life, and the other was a tough, quiet kid from Ohio. We became a trio. We hung around together all the time, we fought the whole world together and we took care of one another pretty good. On our very last mission, the kid from Boston was killed by some gook. I could have left almost anybody in the world out there but I couldn't leave him. I had to bring him home. Me and the kid from Ohio took turns carrying his body 70 miles, that's seven-oh miles, and we were a few days behind everyone else getting back. It's not that I value life, he was dead anyway, but the three of us started together, we figured to end together.

I was never really scared in combat, but I was wary. This is a trait I have managed to retain. I really do act very cautiously when I'm not 100 percent positive of everything that is going on around me.

I didn't mind the army too much. In fact, I came very close to making it a career. God, what the world of crime would have missed! My buddy and I were coming back from a raid and we came upon this colonel being prodded along by three North Koreans. They had done a pretty good job beating up on him and were taking him down the road to repeat this nasty behavior. We prevented this by killing them. Since this guy couldn't walk so well, we had to carry him back. It was only about 15 miles but ducking gooks and all, it took almost six days and we got to know each other pretty good. He was a West Pointer, but a really good guy. When we got back to our lines we went our separate ways.

When I came back from Korea I was sent to Fort Ord and put in a separation company. I wasn't there but one day when I was ordered to report to the battalion commander. "Jesus," I thought, "I haven't been here long enough to get into trouble." The commander turned out to be that colonel. From that point on I was golden boy: I drank his booze, drove his car and banged his secretary. I could do no wrong. He told me, "You stay in the army and I'll get you into warrant officers' school and you'll never have to work again as long as you live." I was young and full of piss and vinegar and I just wanted out. I got out, and the colonel eventually retired as a major general.

The first thing I did when I got out of the army was go home and get very, very drunk. Then I went back to work and learned how to operate in the world of organized crime. What I learned is what the rest of this book is all about.

CHAPTER *2*
THE GANG'S ALL HERE

I was sitting in Patsy's Pizzeria reading the New York *Daily News* not so long ago when a numbers runner I know sat down at my table to ask if I wanted to bet with him. The headline of the paper stated that the police had caught the men who had kidnapped, and presumably killed, Carlo Gambino's nephew. He shook his head sadly, "Those guys are in some trouble."

I said, "No, they ain't, they're safe. It's the law that's got them. Carlo's wife and brother called the FBI when they got the ransom note."

He again shook his head sadly. "Ain't that a sorry situation when Carlo Gambino has to call the cops. This business is in a bad state."

This business. Our profession, organized crime. Organized crime is indeed a business. A business that happens to be illegal, but still a business. It is run better than the United States government or General Motors and makes a bigger profit than United States Steel, Chrysler Corporation and Standard Oil combined. It is run very smoothly: We have no union problems, we don't pay overtime, we have no pension plan and we have enough work to keep everybody busy. Our profit-sharing plan is the best in the business world, and our customers usually are satisfied and happy. We—and by "we" I mean the 100,000 or so men in this country who can honestly claim they belong to the nationwide crime organization—we exist simply to serve the public. We give them what they want, we cater to their desires. We do things for our benefit, of course, but in doing them we give people what they want.

And what they want is a chance to make a bet, get some narcotics, borrow some money quickly and quietly, or the opportunity to buy first-class merchandise, from cigarettes to stockings, at good prices. We supply these things to your so-called honest citizen. We deliver on time, we stand behind our merchandise and we pay off when we lose.

Occasionally we use violence—but when we do, it is generally confined to people in the mob. Very rarely do we step out of our own realm to hurt somebody. The only people outside the organization who do get hurt are people who borrow our money and don't pay us, or bet with us and don't pay us, or make an agreement and don't pay us. These people are going to get hurt, no question about it. But the honest citizen has nothing to fear from us; we are not out to hurt him. Violence is expensive, killers cost a lot of money, musclemen command good fees, and so violence is only used as a last resort. The real money comes out of gambling and shylocking and narcotics and merchandising.

Most of the money made by organized crime today is made in areas that are legal in other countries—gambling and prostitution, for example. If there is one thing I'm going to stress in this book, it's that you cannot legislate morals; don't try. The people want prostitution, let them have prostitution. They want to gamble, get ready to take their money. As long as you let people do what they want, as long as they don't bother anyone else, then who is being hurt? Let man be the master of his own fate. The minute you tell a man he is not allowed to do something, you've just created a brand-new business. Because I'm gonna be there to help him do it—just as often as he can afford.

Prohibition is the best example of what I'm talking about. The bluenoses came in and said nobody drinks anymore. Boom. Organized crime was born. You made millionaires out of people who never figured to earn more than ten dollars a week. Today some of your most respected people are former bootleggers. The people who founded the "21 Club" in New York, bootleggers. Toots Shor was a bootlegger. These people made bathtub gin, or they ran the stuff in from Canada. Bootleggers spawned everything from shylocking to murder. Yet these people are idolized in the restaurant business today. What kind of morality is that?

The stupidity of the people in this country never ceases to amaze me. I'm supposed to be an evil man. I'm supposed to be eliminated so people can walk on the streets at night. Not only is that bullshit, that's the worst hypocrisy I've ever heard. Without your so-called honest citizen I would cease to exist. He's my customer and my employer. All the organization does is act as his supplier; whatever he wants, we get. As soon as the average American decides he's willing to pay the full price for merchandise, willing to follow all the laws, willing to stop gambling and playing around on the side, I'm gone. I can't survive.

But it will never happen. People are going to continue doing exactly what they want, and I'm sick and tired of being blamed for their faults. I used to work in the Cincinnati area in one of the most beautiful bust-out joints this side of Las Vegas. When I say bust-out joint I don't mean it was crooked, it was not. A real bust-out joint is a place where you come in and they take you up one side and down the other. This place was called the West Riviera Club, and you got as fair a shake there as you would anywhere else in the world. I was working there for Meyer Lansky, making sure nobody was pocketing his money. One night I met a customer from Omaha, Nebraska. He was the deacon of his church. I know because he kept telling me. Yet here he was 6 or 700 miles from home, shacking up with a broad he never saw before, drinking like gangbusters. So I said to him, "Listen, instead of coming all this way, why don't you just legalize it in your community?"

He says, "What! Are you crazy? I wouldn't subject my family to this!"

"If you're such a great family man," I asked him, "what the hell are you doing messing around with a girl young enough to be your daughter?" I mean, if he's gonna do it, what the hell difference does it make where he does it? This type of hypocrisy makes me sick. And that is another reason for this book.

I'm not saying that the mob is a branch of the Sisters of Mercy. These are men, some of them, who will kill you if you cross them. But the majority of the people who make their living in crime are simply out to provide for their families. They don't want to hurt anybody. There are a lot of people in the mob who will not pull the trigger, who will not break legs, who will not swing a pipe because they just don't have it in them. I mean, they're larceny-hearted, they're not violent.

But the only people who get to the top, as far as making good money, are the people who don't give a fuck, people who would just as soon blow your brains out as look at you, break your leg if it's a necessity, if you deserve it. Me, for example; I have no compunctions about doing anything. If there is money involved, I will do it. And, because of that, because of the fact that I do not flinch when I pull the trigger, I am a respected mob man.

Organized crime was well organized long before I got involved. The roots of crime as it is organized today were planted hundreds of years ago in Sicily, when the Italian people turned to a secret organization for protection from the land barons and feudal rulers. The first initials of the name of this society spelled out Mafia, which is why the group was called that. At first the Mafia was very popular with the Sicilians but then *it* began to get powerful. Eventually it was more powerful than the barons had ever been, and controlled everything from the stores to the Church. They even began to offer protection from the Mafia itself, which is how the extortion business got going.

The first Mafiosi came to America in the 1880s. Most of them left Sicily because the police were after them there. They figured what worked in Sicily would work in America. They were right. These Italian immigrants were very superstitious—they considered it bad luck to be beaten up—and the protection rackets started. Eventually the Mafia controlled a great deal of the illegal activities in the eastern United States.

At the same time the Italians were arriving other immigrant groups were streaming in too. The Irish and the Jews saw what the Italians were doing in their community, so they began doing it to their own people. At this point there was absolutely no organization. The Irish couldn't touch the Italians, and the Italians left the Irish alone. Everybody had their own territory and did their own thing.

That all changed when Prohibition began.

The original base of organization within crime came from an uncle or cousin of Al Capone's named Johnny Torrio. Torrio left Brooklyn and formed a crime cartel in Chicago, dealing in numbers, bookmaking, prostitution, things like that. When bootlegging became important he needed somebody to run the Chicago operation for him and he sent for Al Capone. A few years later a rival gang almost killed Torrio, and he decided he needed some fresh air, in another country, and Capone took over. That's when everything really started: the fight for territory, control, power and money. Your gang wars started here. (Eliot Ness. The so-called Untouchables.) Capone modernized mob thinking. He realized that communication and cooperation with other major mobs was not only necessary for business purposes, it was a good thing in general. As the years went by the old-timers, the people who had started it all, the Mustache Petes, had to go because they were stagnating, and your young turks began rising. By the mid 1930s almost every major city was controlled by a single mob which had outlasted and outfought its competitors. The city of Detroit was predominantly controlled by the Jewish mob. Cleveland was Jewish. The Irish owned the docks, and the Italians had part of New York and most of the East Coast. These people realized that Capone was right, they had to work with one another or be destroyed, so the organization was created. We organized because we finally realized we were all in the same business, and if engineers could organize and real-estate operators could organize, so could we, the people who worked in crime. Today people of almost every race, creed and nationality work in or for the organization. It is truly an American business.

It's funny, people blame all of organized crime on the Italians. They think that the Mafia is the same thing as organized crime. Not true. The Mafia is just part of the entire nationwide structure of the organization. Unfortunately for the Italians, they are the people who always get the publicity. But just to make sure the Italians don't get *all* the publicity, many Italian hoods, when they begin to make a name for themselves, make sure it's an Irish name. Jimmy Plumeri became Jimmy Doyle, and Thomas Eboli became Tommy Ryan, for example. I don't know why they do this, the Irish certainly don't need any help. *Today*, even, you have a strong Irish mob. You have a strong Jewish mob; Jews practically control gambling. You even have Chinese mobs. But everybody blames everything on the Italians. Now I don't want to take any credit from them away, they've done their fair share, but the hardest people to deal with, the most vicious killers in organized-crime history, were the Jews. It was Jews who founded and worked for an outfit called Murder Incorporated. This was originally started by a Jew named Abe Reles and had members like Louie Lepke Buchalter and even Bugsy Siegel.

Nobody thinks of the Chinese as members of organized crime and, in reality, they are not. They have their own gambling, their own money-lending, their own narcotics. This is all Chinese, no Caucasian in the world is going to get in there. If a white guy tried to get into New York or San Francisco's Chinatown mobs he would be blown away. I know these people. There's one guy in New York, a little old Chinaman by the name of Wu. This man controls fan-tan, Mah-Jongg and narcotics down there. He runs an organization comparable to any mob in the country. And he makes a lot of money because the Chinese are great gamblers, they'll bet on which of two cockroaches has more legs. The Chinese have their own political clubs, their own collections, their own connections. You do not dictate to them. They got their own setup and that's it, pal. People in the organization respect them because they went out and put their own thing together, they organized themselves, like everyone else did.

On a national scale organized crime, or the syndicate, or the mob, the hoods, the boys, whatever you want to call them, is actually very loosely organized. Each area is broken down into certain specific territories, and each of these territories is under the direction of a boss. You cannot operate within another man's territory without the permission of that boss. Let's take an area like the north Bronx. This area is controlled primarily by the Carmine Tramunti mob. The people in this area, the book makers, the shylocks, the numbers runners, any activity you want to mention, are beholden to him. Carmine has established this area as his domain. This will probably run from the tip of the north Bronx right to the end of Westchester County, as far south as the Parkchester area, approximately, and anyone doing business within these boundaries is doing so with the consent and protection of Carmine Tramunti.

In return for that permission and protection a percentage of every dollar made in that area goes to the so-called family. In New York there are five major families which control the city and all surrounding areas.

Internationally there is no worldwide crime oganization like television and the movies would have you believe, but there is a certain amount of cooperation between groups. Consider narcotics. We have to get it from somewhere. The trade was originally controlled by the Corsicans, but now most of it comes from South America by way of Europe and Asia. There are international working agreements, but there is no organization in the American sense of the word.

As far as American-built organizations expanding into other countries, you can forget that. The way we have successfully built an organization is by knowing how to operate within the American system—we know where we can do it, we know how we can do it, we know with whom we can do it. Other countries have totally different systems, and it would be impossible to adapt to them.

Only one Western country can say today that it doesn't have organized crime and that's England. They have crime there, spectacular crimes like bank holdups, train robberies, stuff like that. Gambling has been knocked off by being legalized, prostitution has been knocked off—it's not legal but they don't bother you—and the government's narcotics program has taken most of the profit out of that. England also has a very tough legal system to beat. They have uniformity of laws. There is no such thing as a law in London and another law in Manchester—each law is for the entire country. And finally, over there, from the time you are arrested to the day you go to trial, it's never more than three or four weeks. In other words, it's very difficult for a man to do a dishonest day's work in England.

Now take a look at a map of this country. Almost every state is broken up into areas like the north Bronx, some bigger, some smaller, but all organized the same way. A man gets to be boss of an area because he has been smart enough or strong enough to organize a group of people, which the newspapers will call a family. A family can consist of anywhere from 20 or 30 men to a few hundred.

The boss delegates some of his authority to certain men who will act as his lieutenants, or button men, as they're known. Let me explain a button man. A button man is an individual who will control a certain area, maybe a few blocks, maybe a whole neighborhood, for a boss. He is liable to have as many as 40 to 50 men, "soldiers," working under him in a specific area. The button man is responsible for making sure everything in his area runs smoothly and those people who are beholden pay their dues. All the money that comes from that area, after his people get paid, he will split right down the middle with the boss. This money will include receipts from shylocking, bookmaking, numbers, all illegal money. Legal activities might include food stores, bowling alleys (which are very big), bars and social clubs. (Social clubs are usually storefronts or apartments where you can always find a bookmaker, a shylock, a card game and a fence with almost any kind of stolen merchandise.)

As far as loyalty within a family there is not an extreme amount of it. Money has a very big mouth; it not only talks, it screams. Under normal circumstances, though, a man is loyal to a boss because (1) he is treated well, or (2) he is afraid of him or (3) he can earn a lot of money working for this particular individual.

A few big bosses command loyalty simply because they treat their button men and soldiers very well. A man like that will be able to ask his men to do anything for him. When I worked for Jack Dragna in California, for example, if he told me to go to hell I would have taken a shovel and started digging. I literally loved that man. He showed me how to make money, he showed me how to live good, he got me out of trouble when I stepped into it. He stopped me from drinking and taught me to control my violence. When I did something wrong he didn't yell and scream at me, he talked in a nice quiet voice, and explained right and wrong. And how to do wrong better.

At his peak Jack ran southern California. To put it bluntly, you couldn't take a shit in southern California unless Jack got a piece of the toilet paper. I don't know how he got to be a mob boss because he was in power when I first met him. But I assume he got there the same way everybody else did: by being a little tougher and a little more ruthless than anyone else around.

Physically he was about five foot eight, a little paunchy, and spoke with an Italian accent. He was what a mob boss should be: loved by his employees and feared by his enemies. He issued orders in a cold, calculating way and never left any room for discussion. The party was over when Jack said it was over.

One night the party took place in a little restaurant called Alex's or Alexander's in Los Angeles. Mickey Cohen had gotten out of jail and he wanted to reorganize bookmaking and various other activities so he could regain some lost power. So he called a meeting with Jack and about 20 other hoods. I went along as Jack's protection.

The food was wonderful. We started off with antipasto, shrimp cocktails and baked clams. Then they brought in the macaroni, spaghetti and ziti. Finally the main course, veal and chicken, was brought in. The restaurant I don't remember, the meal I can't forget.

Jack never did like Mickey or any of his associates very much, and he was quite happy with the status quo, so he was not fond of Mickey's reorganization plans. He waited until the dinner was over, until Mickey had made his proposals, and then he got up and began speaking. "You makea nice speech and you serva me nice meal and I'ma thankin' ya. I'm thankin' ya by tellin' ya somethin'. If I find anybody who'sa going south of LA on their way to Mexico, or they goin' west on a way to Arizona and they stoppa for anything but to take a piss and a cuppa coffee and gasoline, I'm a gonna kill 'em. Good-night, gennelmen." And then we left.

I originally met Jack through some people in New York. I was running muscle with Joey Gallo, just two young punks on the way up, and we had to go see a man about some money. This guy had an office on the first floor of the Strand Building, which was on Broadway between 47th and 48th. The guy started to give us a song and dance, and I just grabbed him and threw him over my shoulder. I figured I would just slam him around a little—unfortunately I threw him right out an open window. I said to Joey, "I think we had better take leave of this place," and he agreed. The guy wasn't really hurt, but a lot of people had seen him become a hit on Broadway.

We went back to see the guy who hired us, and the next thing I know I'm in a car going to Chicago. I had no idea why they wanted me out of town, but they were paying the bills so I agreed to go. They put me in the Maryland Hotel for four days and just kept sending up broads, booze and food. I figured, "What the hell, if I'm going to die, I might as well have a good time."

Eventually a man named Eddie Marlowe came to see me and gave me a plane ticket to Los Angeles, $100 and the address of a bar in San Pedro. I arrived, went to the bar and sat around waiting. I still didn't know what was supposed to happen. Inevitably I got into a fight with a guy at the bar. In those days I fought with just anybody. I didn't know any better. I had just finished opening up this guy's head with a beer bottle when Jack Dragna walked in. He smiled and told me who he was and explained that I would be working for him. The first thing he did was take me to a men's shop and buy me six new suits. Then he got me an apartment and a car. The first place I worked for him was in a bucket of blood, a whorehouse in Tijuana, Mexico, a place called the El Matador. Eventually he brought me back to LA to run certain things for him; smuggling, numbers, whatever came up. We had a wonderful relationship, he treated me more like a son than an employee. When Jack died—of an overdose of his own heroin—I felt like I lost my father. To this day I miss that man. As far as I'm concerned he was the finest mob boss who ever lived.

The Boss also has people he is responsible to—the Board of Directors. This "board" consists of all the bosses in a large area. The Commissioner is called the Boss of Bosses (in New York, for example, this is Carlo Gambino, who earned it through time, respect and survival). This board meets whenever an emergency arises, whenever somebody important has to be killed, or concerning a territorial dispute. It is up to this board to say either, "Yes, you can control this if you're good enough," or "No, you cannot step over into this territory." There is enough territory to go around, and to try to abuse someone else is only going to hurt everybody, so the board keeps control. Every major city, with the exception of Los Angeles which is almost mob-free today, is set up like this. If you wanted to do something in another city you would have to first obtain the permission of that city's Boss of Bosses. And that goes for Carlo Gambino as well as for me.

I have earned my right to do a lot of different things within the structure of the mob, but anything I do I'm still completely beholden to it. If I want to start an operation within an area I still have to contact the man who runs the area, tell him what I have in mind and take him in as a partner. A boss's territory is his own, and he directs everything that happens in it.

There is no single national leader, no one man who runs the whole show. Even Capone, at the height of his power, all he controlled was Cicero, Illinois. He didn't even really have the city of Chicago. There is no way in the world a man in organized crime could take over the entire country. It is just a physical impossibility. He would have to have the loyalty of more than 100,000 people; he would have to be the Fuehrer, a complete dictator. It can't be done.

The one man who has come closer to being a national boss than anyone else is Meyer Lansky. He is the man that the mob has more respect for, that the mob owes more to, than anyone else in the world.

I worked for Meyer for almost eight years. He is patient, easy to work for and brilliant. I firmly believe that if he had decided to be the president of the United States he could have made it. Instead he went after the world, and he made that. Meyer appreciates when you do things right. He lets you know it with a pat on the back, extra money, a broad, whatever you want. And he is the one man who has the total loyalty of the people who work for him.

Wherever you go in this country Meyer is known as "The Old Man." In this case this is a term of respect and affection, as well as a nickname. As the movies and print media have shown, nicknames add a great deal of glamour to the inhabitants of the world of organized crime. Not everybody has a nickname, of course, some people pick them up as they go along, others never get one. Me, for example, I've had a lot of aliases, but I've never had a real nickname that was mine and mine alone.

The nicknames themselves come from everywhere. Some of them are based on an individual's real name, like a guy named Joe DeStephano becomes Joey Dee, or if his name was Frankie Zeno he would probably be Frankie Z. If a guy's first name is Frank he may become known as Cheech.

Other people get their names from their looks. Carmine the Snake got his name because he looked like a snake. Charlie the Bull was built like a bull. Alex the Beard had a beard. If a guy has a big nose he might become known as Big Nose.

Other people pick up names because they are directly opposite what they are supposed to be. Fat people are called Skinny, skinny people are known as Fats (so are some fat people, of course), and bald people are called Curly.

A physical handicap might be the basis for a guy's nickname. An individual with a bad arm would be known as Wingy; a bad leg, Gimpy; and a cross-eyed guy would be called Cockeye. There was one famous cross-eyed guy (actually he became famous when he went to the electric chair) by the name of Cockeye Dunn.

Some people are known by their ethnic background: Nick the Wop, Alex the Greek, Yiddy Stein. Others by the services they perform: One guy who used to work on the docks was called Charlie the Hook. If he didn't like you he would pick you up with his longshoreman's hook. A guy that's good with a knife may become The Blade. One guy I used to know who ran a string of flophouses was known as Louie Flophouse. A guy who is good with his muscle, a slugger, would probably be called The Club or something like that.

Others get their names from where they come from. Johnny Odo came from the Bathbeach section of Brooklyn, so he was Johnny Bathbeach. A guy from Pittsburgh was called Louie Pitt.

Certain names have very specific meanings. A man whose last name is Black represents death. He is either a hit man or he sets hits up. Just like the man who uses the name Costello is probably a gambler. It's just an association: Costello equals gambling. Also a guy whose name is Peppy would probably also be in the gambling phase. It's just something that's known, that's accepted.

A few guys got their names from their habits. This guy Funzi I know likes to eat pizza all the time, so everybody calls him Pizzaman. There was one guy who was always sniffling, so he was named Jimmy the Sniff, and I know one guy who used to take at least nine showers every single day and douse himself with bath powder after each one. He would put his hat on first, so he didn't get any powder in his hair. His nickname? Baby Blue.

If a man has one unusual thing happen to him in his career, that might be the basis of his nickname. Joey Gallo became Crazy Joey when he tried to plead temporary insanity to a burglary rap. Lucky Luciano became Lucky when they found him ventilated with bullet holes, but somehow still alive.

Finally, some people are so good at what they do that they are given a special nickname, and everyone knows them by that name. It's as much a term of respect as it is a nickname. The Fixer, for example, was Frank Costello, which was a tribute to his tremendous political connections. Gil Beckley was known everywhere as The Brain because, when it came to figuring out odds, he could outthink a computer. When Frank Erickson was alive he was The Bookmaker's Bookmaker because people all over the country would lay off their action on him.

When you begin in the mob, you start right at the very bottom. Let's say you see that the numbers runner in the neighborhood is making a good salary and you decide that's what you want to do. First thing you do is find some people who want to start playing the numbers. You talk to these people and ask them if you can handle their action. For your own health you'd best make sure these people are not already playing with somebody else. After you have your customers you have to find a controller. A controller is the individual who runs the business end of a specific operation. They're not difficult to find, just ask your local bartender to put you in touch with his runner, almost every bar has one, and then explain the situation to the runner. He'll make the proper introductions. You tell the controller you got some customers you'd like to pick up for him. So now you've got a little franchise and you start progressing from there.

If you're sharp you look around for deals in which you can make money for the mob. You find out who's shying, who's booking, and you start bringing them customers. Of course, you're responsible for the people you bring in. From that point on it's just a matter of how ambitious you are, how much initiative you have. Eventually if a hit comes along and the mob feels you are capable of making it—you've shown you have muscle and are not afraid to use it—you may be approached, or you may even let the word out that you're interested. You can go as far as your balls and brains will take you.

What makes a good mob man? A lot of things. He's got to be an individual who can take the consequences of what he is doing without belly-aching; an individual who can show complete loyalty to the people he is with. Most of the people who have been at all successful are fairly intelligent. They have learned how to think, how to keep their mouths shut and how to observe. They learned, as I learned, that if you're not sure of something, or someone, you just pass on that particular job or deal.

Physically, a good organization man will be tough, a guy who isn't really afraid. Most people are afraid of jail, violence, death—but the guy who is really a hard case, the guy who can legitimately say he doesn't give a damn, he's the guy who is gonna move.

What keeps a man out of the organization? You'll find that junkies do not work in the organization. Dummies do not work in the organization. Loudmouths do not work in the organization. We don't want people with emotional hang-ups, because they cannot be trusted, people with sex problems, like homosexuals, because no one wants to work with them, and the bleeding-heart sentimentalists who are going to worry about what happens to the other guy.

Today it is difficult to pick the average mob guy out of a crowd. He looks like any other businessman or blue-collar worker. In the old days you lived the mob. Everything you did centered around the mob and mob business. That's not entirely true anymore. Today you got a lot of people like me who either work freelance or have their own small thing going and don't spend that much time with other people in the organization. If we go out among ourselves, which we don't do too often, it is generally for dinner and then to a sporting event, usually the fights. But the center of attraction is the food. Mob people are among the best eaters in the world. They just love to put it away.

Food and business go hand in hand. I would say 95 percent of all the business meetings I ever attended have taken place over a dinner. The choice of restaurant, as well as the honor of paying the bill, always belongs to the individual doing the inviting. I would say that the most popular restaurants in New York City, as far as my friends are concerned, are Patsy's Pizzeria on 118th Street and First Avenue, Delsomma's on West 47th Street, Rao's on 114th Street and Pleasant Avenue, Walsh's Steak House on East 23rd Street, and Manny Wolf's Chop House on East 49th and Third Avenue when it's not burned down.

I was in Patsy's one night for a busines meeting. I went with a friend of mine who runs muscle by the name of Rocco. I had to go in back and see somebody, so I told Rocco to stay out front and have something to eat on me. I figured he would have a nice dinner, but when I came out his bill was $23. Twenty-three dollars in Patsy's is like $100 somewhere else. I asked the waiter, "What the hell did this guy eat?"

He consulted his check. "A dozen baked clams, two orders of ziti and clam sauce, veal, a pizza pie, some wine and six bottles of soda."

I looked at Rocco. "Had enough?"

He burped. "That'll tide me over until I get home."

My wife is a decent cook—she does all right with steaks and chops—but I'm the real chef in the family. Though I'm not Italian, I am an excellent Italian cook, an art I learned in self-defense. When I was doing a lot of collecting I was on the road all the time. One day in this city, two days in another, a few hours somewhere else. There was never enough time to discover the decent restaurants, so I would end up walking into some greasy joint and ordering a steak. The cook would throw it on the grill and it would slide off and onto the floor and he would pick it up, dust it off and put it back on the grill. This turned my stomach a little, so I went out and bought some cookbooks and taught myself. This is how I won Rocco's allegiance, incidentally. We were staying in a motel in Akron that had a little kitchenette, and I did my little thing with veal and a salad. After we finished Rocco laid down on the bed, burped, and said, "You tell the boss. Wherever you go—I go!"

I think the social aspects of mob membership began to fade when the organization became professional, when the old customs started dying. Funerals are a good example. Take Joey Gallo. A very small funeral. In the old days Joey would have rated dozens of big black flower cars and tens of limousines. But the people got smart, they realized funerals like that attracted a lot of attention, so they were dropped. We don't try to attract attention, we get enough without trying.

That doesn't mean we're heartless. We do go to funerals, but we just don't make a big deal out of it. I went to a funeral in 1971 for an acquaintance of mine who died of lead poisoning—he was shot full of it. This man will remain nameless, but it was a very nice service. The priest really eulogized this guy. He said things that were just unreal. Finally he says, "This man should not have died in the prime of life."

"If this guy was as good as that priest said he was," I told the guy I was with, "he would *not* have died in the prime of life."

In the old days the mob was much more family and community oriented. One family—and by that I mean a group of men working under a boss, not only blood relations—might include brothers and cousins and uncles and brothers-in-law, and they would be tied together by blood as much as by choice and money. When the boss died his son would be there to pick up the reins. Not anymore. Today a "family" is just a business organization. Generally you'll find that when a man is strong enough to hold it together, his kid ain't got the guts to pick up a rubber ball and throw it against a wall. A lot of bosses don't keep their children in the business; for the most part they try to keep them away. Albert Anastasia, for example, was extremely powerful when he died. Yet his son, Al Junior, couldn't do a thing. Joe Colombo's son is having a very hard time holding it together too.

Another way things have changed for the worse. In the old days mob people used to live in the same area in which they worked, and they used to work out in the open, on the streets. I'll tell you something: In those days the streets were safe. Until the Kefauver Committee started attacking the mob, which took the runners and shylocks off the corners, you could walk the streets at night without being afraid some punk was going to come along and mug you. The mobs did not want people being hurt in their domain. People who got hurt were people who could not come out to bet or buy. So these punks were simply not allowed to operate. As tough as I was as a kid, if the man who worked on the corner told me to get home, my only question was how fast. Wherever the mob operated, the streets were safe for honest people. Even today you're safer in Little Italy in New York City than you are in your mother's arms. That is the way almost all big cities used to be.

Yeah, things have changed in the last 15 years. The mob has become modernized, more professional. A lot of the excitement, the so-called romantic aspects of crime, have gone the way of the famous "Kiss of Death." I have to admit missing some of the old stuff, but, on the other hand, business is both better and safer than ever.

I've seen the changes take place and I've been able to adapt to the changes. I used to make the major portion of my income from physical work: muscle jobs, hits and protection. Now most of my money comes from more sedate things like running card games, smuggling cigarettes, bootlegging different items and, just to keep it interesting, an occasional hit.

I learned a long time ago that it is vitally important to keep up with the times. That's the first lesson any good businessman learns.

CHAPTER *3*
THE NUMBERS

'm never gonna forget one day I was standing on a corner in the Bronx and I see this numbers runner actually running down the street and there was this little guy chasing him. A few days later I bumped into the runner and I asked him what that was all about. "What happened," he says, "is that this guy has been playing the same fucking number for five years. He left a message for me at the bar where I usually meet him that I should come to his house. He left five dollars with his wife to play the number. What am I, a plumber? I ain't got time to make house calls so I say fuck it, and sure enough, his number comes in. He was so fucking mad he woulda killed me if he coulda caught me." I've heard of this happening a few times, which makes me wonder if that's not where the name "runner" comes from.

If there is one business that most mob men cherish above all others, it is the numbers. The numbers is easily one of the most beautiful things ever invented. It is simple to set up, simple to run, almost risk-free, and incredibly profitable. Like me, most mob members look upon the numbers with nostalgia, because it is the first thing they ever did in crime.

THE NUMBERS

Sometimes it gets a little rough. Like a runner finds too much of his customers' money in his pocket and, like they say, succumbs to temptation. That means he takes off for Montreal or Kansas City a rich man— and nine times out of ten a dead man a few days later. My hit number 23 was a guy like that, the victim of his own greed.

Customers love the numbers too. For them it is the easiest and cheapest form of gambling. All they have to do is pick a number between 1 and 999 and if that number hits, the "bank," or the people who are running the operation, pays off at 600 times the amount bet. The bettor receives 500 times what he bet, and the runner, the man who collects his bet, gets 100 times the amount.

There is really no way of figuring out how many people bet the numbers six days a week, 52 weeks a year, year after year. The game is centered in the East, particularly in the ghetto areas of your big cities. In these areas, forget it, everybody plays every day. To these people the numbers is more than a game, it's a dream. They all think that someday they're going to hit the number and be able to buy everything they have ever wanted. Once in a while somebody does hit a number big, and every runner in the area knows it the next day—all his customers add a little extra to what they normally bet. The numbers isn't played too much in California or the Far West, and I don't really know why. I would guess that it's because the people live too far apart to make it really worthwhile for a runner or a bank to operate. The profit from numbers is in numbers—you need thousands of bettors to make the operation successful. Jack Dragna had an operation running out there, it never was the gold mine it is in the big cities.

But who needs California? I would guess, and this guess is based on my experience as a runner, that there is at least $25 million bet a day or about $150 million per week. That comes to about seven and a half billion dollars a year, which if you haven't noticed is a lot of money. That is why there are a lot of people buried in unspecified places. They tried to get a piece of it and weren't strong enough to make their bid stand up. Anybody who tries to take more than he earns gets hurt. That includes runners who steal, runners who have been cheating for years and finally get caught, customers who make false claims and assorted other people who make mistakes.

There are a few different ways to play the numbers. First of all, you are allowed to bet anything from a penny up, although some runners won't take anything less than a dollar. In New York you bet either the New York or Brooklyn number. The Brooklyn number consists of the last three digits of the total mutuel handle for the day at whichever New York track the thoroughbreds are running at. (If they're not running in New York a Florida track is generally used.) That means that all the money bet that day at one specific track is added up, and the last three numbers of that total are the Brooklyn number. All a numbers player has to do is look in his daily newspaper and he can immediately see if he has hit the winning number.

The New York number is much more difficult to figure out, which is why the Brooklyn number came into being in the first place. The New York number is derived from adding up the total mutuel payoffs for the first three races and taking the first number to the right of the decimal point. That is the first digit of the winning "number." Then you add up the second three races and again take the first number to the right of the decimal point. That's the second digit of the number. Same thing for the last three races, and the third and final number. For example, in the first race you got a $5.80 win, $3.60 place, and a $2.80 show on the winner, then you got a $4.40 and $2.60 on the place horse, and the third horse paid $3.80. You add that all up. You do exactly the same thing for the second race and exactly the same thing for the third race. Then you add up all three totals, which comes out to maybe $78.65. The first digit of the New York number would be 6, because it is the first digit to the right of the decimal point. Then you just do the same thing for the second three races and the third three races until you have the New York number.

Both the New York number and the Brooklyn number are used every day. When the runner writes up his ribbon, which is what his figure sheet is called, he writes down either 381B or 381N, depending on what his customer tells him. Now this number, this 381—B or N—can be played in a variety of different ways. The customer can make a straight bet, which pays off at 600 to 1, or he can make a combination bet. Naturally a combination bet pays off less than a straight bet. Let's say the customer wants a 10-cent combination, which is a 60-cent bet because there are six possible combinations of the three different numbers. If he plays 381 he can win on that number, on 831, 138, or any other combination of 1, 3 and 8. But that 60 cents, which would pay $300 on a straight bet, will only return $50 on a combination because, in reality, he has only bet a dime on each number.

The customer can also play what is called "leads." That means the bet is placed on just the first number, the second number, or the third number. The payoff is 8 to 1. This is a good bet for the bank because the odds are 10 to 1 against the bettor, so the bank is pocketing 20 percent even before the game begins. If a guy bets the 5 for $10 and wins, he wins $80. And he will get paid the very next day, which is one reason numbers is the most popular lottery there is.

People pick the number they are going to bet on by every possible (and crazy) method. They have a dream and they see a number, or they almost get hit by a car and bet the first three numbers on the license plate. They bet on birthdays, weights of kids, ages of friends, the date of an anniversary, a national holiday. Anything. And when they find one number that has a good feeling, that they believe is a winner, they will stick with it for a long, long time. When I was a runner there were people who bet the same number with me for months. I never knew their names, I just knew them by their number. Of course it was even, they didn't know my name either. But they knew the mob well enough to know that, if they won, they would be paid.

The numbers is wonderful because everybody makes money—sometimes. When the customer hits, and the law of averages says everybody is gonna hit if they keep at it long enough, he makes enough money to keep him happy, and betting, for a long time. The beauty of winning at the numbers is that when a man hits he gets to keep every cent of his payoff. There are no taxes to worry about because no one is going to report him to the Internal Revenue Service. I know a guy who won $15,000 on a $30 bet. That's not the biggest payoff I've ever heard of, but it's the biggest anyone I know personally has actually won. Even I hit the number a few times. My biggest payoff was a few hundred for 714, the number of home runs Babe Ruth hit, which I bet on the opening day of the baseball season. It's the chance to bet and the thrill of opening the newspaper to see if you've hit the number, as well as the payoff, that keeps people coming back day after day.

The customer knows he will be paid off if he wins. Even if the runner who took the bet disappears, which happens occasionally, if the bet has been filed, the office will pay off. Very few customers make false claims, and very few runners try to cheat, but when you're dealing in so much money and so many figures, people are going to make mistakes. Usually the office will notify a runner if any of his customers hit, but sometimes they overlook one or two. A guy who thinks he hit the number and hasn't been paid will make his claim and the runner will check with the office.

When I was running, in order to protect myself and my customers, I would write up a carbon when I wrote my ribbon; that way I had one for myself and one for the office. So if one of my customers walked in and said, "Hey, I hit you yesterday and didn't get paid," I could immediately check my copy. If his number was there, I could call the office and give them the page, the column and the number that this hit was listed in, and have them send the money right over to me. You never want to keep a customer waiting if you don't have to, but mistakes are made. A clerk may miss a hit because he has to check thousands of lists every day.

As long as the office, the bank, has a lot of customers, it can't lose. Since the payoff is 600 to 1, and the odds are 999 to 1 against the bettor, the bank has a built-in cushion. And rigging, or fixing the number, is almost impossible. I say "almost" because it did happen at least once I know of. A group of people wanted to take over a large number of banks and they figured it would take a disaster to open the way for them, so they created this disaster. They knew a large number of superstitious patriotic Americans bet 776 on the Fourth of July. So they controlled every betting window at the track, I don't know how, and they rigged the number: 776. After the banks got finished paying off all their customers these guys just walked in and took over.

A lot of runners do nothing else but take numbers, and they do very well. The runner pockets 25 percent of all the action he takes in, plus he gets 100 times the amount bet if one of his customers hits the number, plus as a rule every customer will give him anywhere from five to ten percent of his winnings as a tip. (There are a few offices opening up now that are paying the customer 540 to 1 and giving the runner only 60 times the bet.) So a good runner can make a nice living. One guy I know works as an elevator operator in a high-rise office building. He makes maybe $80 a week from his job and yet he drives to work in an $18,000 Rolls-Royce. He can afford it because he has been using his elevator as his office for years. While he's going up and down all day he is taking numbers from somewhere between 800 and 1000 people, which means he's making a minimum of $250 every day!

The most unusual runner I've ever known was a man I brought into the business myself. We were in the same unit in the army. He was tough and quiet and I was tough and noisy. We were a perfect pair. We went through a good portion of Korea together and when the time came to get out he had nowhere to go. He had no family, no job, no responsibilities waiting for him, so I decided to teach him a trade. I brought him to New York City and I taught him the numbers. He was about six foot three and weighed 220 pounds, so the fact that he was quiet and even a little shy didn't hurt him. He had never seen so much money in his life. When I got in trouble and had to leave New York I spread the word that he was to be left alone and took off.

When I finally got settled in California (working for Jack Dragna) I called him and told him to come out. Jack immediately put him to work running, and everything went well. Then, about eight months after he arrived, he came to me one day and said he wanted to quit the business. I said sure, if he wanted to quit, why not? But I wanted to know his reasons. "Aren't you making money?" I asked.

He said money had nothing to do with it. "You know," he told. me, "I've always played it pretty straight. I don't drink, I don't smoke, I don't curse."

"I noticed that," I said, "but I thought you were just a little peculiar." He laughed and then he broke his big news, he wanted to get married to a girl he met in New York. "Wonderful," I told him, "but I still don't see how that interferes with the business."

"That's not all I have to tell you." He took a deep breath and told me the complete truth. "I'm going into the ministry."

I couldn't believe it. A good kid like this. "You're kidding, right?" Wrong. He was serious, and after I got used to the idea I didn't think it was such a bad idea. We started to set the whole thing up and had no problems until one of the controllers said he wasn't going to let him quit. I asked him why not.

"Because he knows too much!"

"Whattya been doing, dummy, reading too many gangster novels?" I threatened to mess this guy up, and we're screaming at each other when Jack walked into the room. He wanted to know what the fighting was about.

I told him my man wanted to quit the business and get married and become a minister. Jack considered this for a moment and said, "That'sa nice occupation. Good, steady employment. And you gotta a good boss. When are you getting married?" My man told him. Jack reached into his wallet and pulled out ten $100 bills and handed them to him. "This is your wedding present. Do me one favor, though. Forget everything you seen here."

So "Preach," as he was nicknamed, that day went to UCLA on the GI bill and eventually became a Presbyterian minister. He has his own church in California today, and I stop by and see him occasionally.

For tax purposes most runners are listed on a payroll somewhere and, like I do, they pay the man who lists them whatever he has to pay the government in taxes.

Working as a runner is not a particularly easy job. You've got to keep hustling the whole time because the more places you cover the more money you'll make. Some runners work all night long. They catch the bartenders, the cabdrivers, the waiters, the waitresses, the truck drivers, the newsstand dealers, the hustlers, the pimps and the prostitutes. They start at maybe nine o'clock and work till six or seven in the morning. You get a guy who works like this and he can make himself more than $100 a night. I know because I did. When I was running numbers after I got out of the army, I used to make about $150 a day. All I did was just go around and see my people. I had all the thieves, and these guys didn't play nickels and dimes. I earned a good living that way.

A good runner works his operation like any other small business. He gets to work on time every day or every night, he provides extra services (introductions to people in other areas of organized crime, for example) and he even takes a yearly vacation or two. The only thing most runners don't do is bring their kids to work to see what daddy does.

Most runners are honest businessmen just looking to make a good living, but like in any other business there are a few bad apples. These are the runners who hold back an extra $10 to $12 every day from the boss, figuring the number won't come in. This is fine, but if they get caught they're gonna get a leg broken, a sure way to stop them from running. And, if a number that they held back hits and they can't pay off, the rotten apple is going to have his core taken out.

When I worked as a controller I looked for family men to do my running. I preferred a guy who wasn't a big gambler, who had some stability and didn't have any great ambitions, because this was the type of individual I could usually trust. But even when I had this type of man, if there was a big payoff, say three or four thousand dollars, I would tell the runner to have his customer meet us and I would give him the money personally. I would give the runner his end, but I wouldn't let him handle the entire payment. There was just no reason to put that temptation in front of him.

Not every controller was as careful as me, however, which is how hit number 23 came to be. Normally I never find out why a guy is being hit, but I knew this guy was a runner and I knew his boss wanted his head very badly. It was public knowledge. I got a message one day asking me to meet some people up at Patsy's Pizzeria on 118th Street in Manhattan. I went up there and in the middle of Patsy's crispy pizza they asked me if I was interested in going out of town to make a hit.

It turned out they wanted me because I knew the intended and they wanted to make sure they got the right man. His name was Angie, and one thing I remember about him is that he had the worst complexion in the world. Nobody had to go to the moon to see craters; all they had to do was go over to Angie's house. He had been running for someone, and one day two customers hit the same number. He had a seven-dollar hit, three five-dollar hits and a ten-dollar hit. This is where the controller made a mistake. He gave the money—more than $19,000—to Angie to make the payoffs. I guess Angie saw red rats, which means he went temporarily crazy, because he decided to grab the money and take a hike.

If he had gone to some small town in the Midwest somewhere and never written and never phoned he probably would have gotten away with it. But he couldn't change his habits, he just couldn't stay away from the action. It proved fatal.

As soon as they got the word he had left town, the numbers operation paid off all his customers and began looking for him. They called people in all the big cities and gave them his description. They bribed the mailman to let them look at all out-of-town letters his family was receiving. They wouldn't open them—that is a federal offense—but the controller knew his handwriting. They didn't expect him to put any return address on the envelope, if he wrote at all, but there was nothing he could do about the postmark. The operation could have tapped his phone, but they didn't bother. They would not bother his family. That's an ironclad rule and people who break it end up dead. Every mobster is fair game, but nobody touches his family.

Finally his face gave him away. Somebody spotted him in Chicago about eight months after he left New York. They gave me his address and wished me luck.

This was not a very difficult assignment. He had fallen into a pretty regular routine. He got up every morning about ten and went to a small coffee shop for eggs, a roll and a cup of coffee. Then he went to a pool hall and stayed there all afternoon. He had also started running numbers for a small outfit there—that's where he was seen—and his collections took most of the later afternoon and early evening. After dinner he would go play cards in a small house near a factory-warehouse. That's where I decided to take him.

Actually it was a perfect setup. He made a point of arriving at the game a few hours late, so I didn't have to worry about the other players seeing me. The game itself was protected, so there was no law around, and the house itself was so isolated there were no neighbors for 500 yards. I got there early one night and checked to see if his car was there. It wasn't. So I put my car in a dark spot and waited. And waited. And waited. When I saw him coming I got out of my car and walked over to the spot he parked in every night. I hid behind a tree until he parked. Then I sprang on him. I didn't even give him time to get out of his car. I just shot him in the head two or three times. I was back in New York City spending my $15,000 the next day.

If a runner works hard, and hustles, and proves himself, when there is an opening he might be promoted to controller. The controller is the man who acts as the go-between between the bank and the runners. He is kind of like a franchise owner. His responsibility is to hire runners and take care of them when they get into a jam, make the police contacts and contracts, go around and pick up the money from his runners every day and make the payoff to the runner when his customer hits. He, in return, receives ten of the gross taken in by all his runners, plus, if he has his own customers, which he will invariably have, he gets 35 percent of what they bet instead of the normal 25 percent.

When I became a controller I met with each of my runners and told them very simply, "Fuck with me and I'll go after you," and they believed me. Even though I was only 15, I was strong as a mule and probably a little crazier. I can break a leg with one kick, and a jaw with one punch, so I never had any trouble with my people.

The last people to make money from the numbers, the real big winners, are the police. In order to operate a numbers game, you have to have the police and usually some politicians on your side. You simply cannot be in business for more than 24 hours without the police knowing about it, so the normal operating procedure is to make your contracts with them before you take your first number. I had to pay ten dollars per week for each of my 40 runners when I was operating, to make sure they were protected. I made this payoff to a cop who worked out of the Bronx borough office. He would come around each week in a squad car, and I would be standing on a corner waiting for him. The police car would pull up to the curb, and I would reach in and put the money in his little bag. The money went to the borough, the division, the precinct and even into the commissioner's office. In other words, everybody got a share.

For the record, numbers is either a misdemeanor or a felony, depending on the amount of money they catch you with. I know only one numbers runner charged with a felony, and that was only because he made a very stupid statement when he got arrested. A cop asked him if he was working with protection. This wise guy says, "If I didn't have no protection would I be working in the middle of the street?" Unfortunately he happened to say that in front of a police inspector from the commissioner's office. End of argument. He refused to elaborate any further on payoffs in front of a grand jury and, as a result, got four years.

Under normal circumstances (you can't plan for big mouths like this guy), the payoff guarantees that (1) my men will have no trouble operating and (2) people who were not paying off would not be able to operate. The cops do make arrests because they don't know every runner on sight and therefore don't know who is on the pad (payoff list) and who isn't. When any of my runners were picked up all they had to say was, "I work for so and so"; the cop who made the arrest would take the name and check it with the man who holds the pad and, if the runner's name was on it, he would be let go. Occasionally you would catch a maverick cop who would make a bust and hold the work, or the list of who bet how much on what number. (If the word got out that a runner lost his ribbon you might get a hundred claims and have no way of checking them out.) The cop would contact the controller and tell him how much he could buy the list back for, and the controller has no choice but to go along with him. The other cops shrug their shoulders and say there is nothing they can do about it. It's just all part of the game.

Numbers was the first thing I got back into when I got out of the service, because it doesn't take too long to build up a good list of steady customers and earn a good living. Although I personally have always worked for somebody else, there are people, small guys, who operate one-man shows. They go out and take their numbers and make their own contracts and take their own payoffs. I would guess they have to average about $700 a day gross, and the odds are pretty good in their favor that they won't get clobbered.

With luck, at the end of the year they can walk away with maybe $150,000. Of course, these are pretty tough boys, guys who can take care of themselves.

Because there is so much money involved, there is a good amount of violence involved in numbers. Since the beginning of time guys have seen what a good thing this is and tried to muscle in. Violence on the inside has always been a part of numbers, especially when it first started booming during the depression. The Dutchman, Dutch Schultz, became very, very big with numbers. He would walk in and tell a guy he was taking over his operation. If the guy didn't consent, Schultz would kill him. The numbers first got popular during the depression because nobody had any money. A guy could take a nickel and win maybe $25, which would feed his family for a couple of weeks, so everybody played. Many of the people really powerful in the organization got their starts in numbers during that period.

Nobody has been able to figure out how to stop the fighting. I know of one runner who decided he was going to take his own customers and open a small game of his own. The boss found out about this and told him, "We can settle this in one of two ways. I can give you five hundred dollars and tell you to stop taking numbers from my customers or I can pay somebody two hundred fifty dollars to break your leg." The guy took the $500 and was never heard from again.

Sometimes it gets a little more complicated. A few years ago a friend of mine had a small operation going and was doing very well. One afternoon a couple of goons walked in and announced they had just become his partners. My friend called me and told me he would rather give me half the operation than take these guys in. I accepted his offer and got ready to defend my business.

I went down to his place and I was waiting for them the next time they showed up. I shot one of them in the rib cage—I just wanted to hurt him, I didn't want to kill him—and told them to get the fuck out and never come back. Four days later four of them showed up. I shot a couple more in the rib cage, in the legs, in the arms, and told them that the next time anyone bothered us we would probably be forced to get violent.

Boom! The phone rings. It's Meyer Lansky and he says, "What are you trying to do, start World War Three?" I said no, just finish it. He asked me what we wanted, and I told him we just wanted to be left alone and, if he wanted the game that badly, he could buy it . . . the price was one million dollars. After he got through laughing he asked me what the bank was doing. "The bank is grossing about fifty thousand a week," I told him. I lied, we were doing maybe twenty, but I wasn't going to tell him that.

He laughed and said, "You're a liar, kid, and you know it and I know it." I said okay, but the next time anybody showed up I was gonna shoot them where it might do permanent damage. Meyer said we wouldn't be bothered again, and we weren't.

The biggest single numbers operation I ever heard of operated in New York City under the direction of Fat Tony Salerno, or Tony Fats as he's called. If I had to guess how many runners he had working for him I'd say at least 2000. When I first started on Jennings Street I used to bring my collections to his office (Sammy Schlitz was one of his controllers), which was located in the basement of a funeral home on 116th Street. I would bring the money in and lay it right on the stone slab. I remember one day he had a body on one slab and about $100,000 in cash on a second slab. It was really eerie.

Like all the other people who reached equally high positions, Tony got to be a big boss by being totally ruthless. He destroyed anything that stood in his way, anybody that tried to stop him, anybody who looked as if he might be a problem. Tony got there because he was big enough and strong enough to hold on to what he took, and I admire him for it.

THE NUMBERS

On the other hand there was Richie Schivone, who was not strong enough to hold on to his own game. He is dead now, and the story is that he fell and hit his head. I'd like to believe it. Richie took over an area in the north Bronx, shylocking, bootlegging, narcotics—he had everything, including a big numbers operation. He lasted about a year and then, supposedly, got drunk and fell and hit his head. I think it's very possible he hit his head on the back of a baseball bat. Whatever it was, after one year he was gone.

A lot of states in this country are finally beginning to wake up and realize that people like to bet, so they are going into the lottery business. A couple of states are even talking about having daily lotteries now, which would be exactly the same as numbers except that the customer would not be allowed to pick the amount of money he wants to bet, or the particular number he wants to bet it on, and, if he wins, he would have to pay taxes from his winnings. Good luck.

There is no doubt in my mind that the numbers should be legalized. If you do it, though, you're going to have to change your entire tax structure. As long as the man who wins is going to have to pay taxes on his winnings he's going to come to me to play. So the states are going to have to run their games the way we do—no taxes. They'll still make their money. Think about this the next time you hear how the city or state has no money: If you legalize numbers and pay off at 900 to 1, you're still going to be making $99 out of every $1000. Now, even with payoffs, you're still not going to lose money, that I will guarantee you. You'll have lines around the block waiting to get down on a number.

Those of you who weren't aware of the wonderful world of numbers until now, and just can't wait for your state to wake up, are probably wondering how to find your local neighborhood runner. Go into any all-night restaurant and there'll probably be one sitting there. Or go to a cab garage or gas station that's open at night, they'll know. I used to play cards late at night with a dispatcher at a cab company who also worked as a runner, but we had to give it up because there was a continual stream of people walking in off the street to give him two dollars or five dollars. He just sat on his ass, checking in the cabs when they came in (and taking numbers from the drivers), and he was making maybe $250 a day. So somebody must have been finding him.

If you can't find a runner, forget it. Your number ain't never going to come in. Or, even better, perhaps I can interest you in starting a small business of your own . . . as long as you can count to 999.

CHAPTER **4**

THE PROCESS OF
ELIMINATION

've dabbled in just about every area of crime, but my specialty, the thing I do best, is kill people. I am to mob rubouts what Leonard Bernstein is to music. I am one of the most feared killers in the United States today. I'm proud of that reputation; I've worked long hours and in dangerous places to earn it.

I don't make that claim braggingly, but truthfully. I have sent 38 deserving men to their early graves. I can remember each man that I hit. I can give you the order. The details. Even the weather on the day I made the hit. Number 18, for example, was a gambler who was discovered informing on the mob. He had been arrested quietly and made a deal in order to keep himself out of a jackpot. Certain things began to kick back, and some people checked and found out my man was the source, so he had to go. I caught him in a small bar and I just walked in and blasted him with a .38. It was dark, and I was wearing a dark shirt and dark pants and when I started shooting everybody scrambled for cover. I remember him. I remember them all. You never really forget.

But it doesn't bother me, not one bit. This is my job. It is my business. I shoot people and that's it. I never think in terms of morality, although that may be hard for a lot of people to believe. I know the difference between right and wrong. By most standards of morality what I do would be considered wrong. But this doesn't bother me. I also know the difference between eating and starving. Between having a new pair of shoes and stuffing newspapers in an old pair to keep my feet from freezing. Believe me, I know.

So I don't worry about it. Because I have the ability to pull the trigger I can do what I like to do, go where I want to go, live comfortably, eat well, be what I want to be. I have no second thoughts. No recriminations. I don't even think about it because, if I did, and if I was an emotional person, I could not live with it. It would destroy me. So I do my job like a guy lays brick, a guy tends bar, a guy cuts hair.

At home, I'm not really that much different from your average bricklayer, bartender or barber. I take out the garbage four nights a week, worry about my wife when she's out alone at night, clean the outside windows every few months and complain about those ridiculously high telephone bills. Believe it or not, I'm a human being. I laugh at funny jokes, I love children around the house and I can spend hours playing with my mutt. Only one thing, I never cry during sad movies. I've only cried for one person in my life, my first wife. The day I found out she had been killed, I cried. Then I changed. So my eyes weren't even damp at the end of *Love Story*.

I've had my chances to get out of the business. One night, in I think 1966, my wife and I were driving back from spending the weekend with some relatives and there was a car pulled over to the side of the road. Regardless of my profession, when I see somebody in trouble, I stop. I pulled over, took my cannon out of the glove compartment and handed it to my wife. "If there's anything wrong," I said, "just pull the trigger."

There was a woman sitting alone in the front seat, and her husband, who turned out to be a well-known, very wealthy businessman, was sitting in back with his leg in a cast. He had broken it so he was helpless, and she didn't know the first thing about cars. I couldn't get their car going, so we drove them back to town. This guy asked for my phone number and, when I told him I didn't give it out, he gave me his card and asked me to call him.

About three days later I did call, and he invited me to his club for lunch. We really got along well, and when he asked me what I did for a living I told him straight out. "You're too nice a guy to be in that business," he told me. "How would you like to work for me?" He offered me good money, and I almost said yes. But I finally turned him down because I knew I would go out of my mind. So I stayed in the old business, doing the same old thing, killing people.

There are three things you need to kill a man: the gun, the bullets and the balls. A lot of people will point a gun at you, but they haven't got the courage to pull the trigger. It's as simple as that. I would give you odds on almost anybody you name that, if I put a gun in his hand, he would not pull the trigger. I mean, some people will go ape for one minute and shoot, but there are very few people who are capable of thinking about, planning and then doing it. To carry out an execution with the cold knowledge of what you're doing, you have to believe in nothing but yourself. That I do.

I killed my first man when I was 16 years old. The hit was offered to me by a mob guy who protected the numbers organization I worked for. The thought of killing a man had never occurred to me before. I had been a violent person and I had laid guys out, but actually killing a man just hadn't entered my mind. I was sitting on a stoop one day, and he walked over and sat down next to me. Very casually, without even looking at me, he asked if I was interested in making a hit.

I stared at him and said, "You got to be kidding." He said he was serious. I said, "You must have fifty guys that can do the same job."

He nodded. "We understand that. Just let me know tonight."

At some point you become a man or you fade. For me, this was the point. I had to make the decision whether I wanted to be dirt or accomplish something. I was very young, but I decided I wasn't going to be a piece of shit. I wasn't going to let people walk all over me. I was going to be a man.

So when he came back that night I told him okay. I had no idea what the guy I was going to kill had done. I was handed a gun, and this guy was pointed out to me. He could have been anybody; once I made the decision I knew I would stick to it. I had to plan the job myself and I wasn't too damned thorough. I waited for him one night. When I saw him on the street I just walked up behind him and blew the top of his head off. He was dead before he hit the sidewalk. Then I turned and walked away. I didn't run, I walked.

I had to get rid of the gun, but I didn't know exactly how. The first thing I did was go back to my apartment and get a little saw and I sawed the gun barrel into four quarters. Then I took the gun and the shells and got on the subway. I rode it all the way down into lower Manhattan, the Wall Street area, and I started throwing the shells down the sewers. I wasn't taking any chances, one shell to one sewer. When I finished doing that I went over to the river and heaved the pieces of the gun as far as I could. Then I went home and went to bed.

I never really got to sleep. I just tossed and turned for a few hours, going over the whole thing in my mind about a hundred times, making sure I didn't make any mistakes. I held my breath for about two days until I was positive there were no witnesses. Nothing happened.

Then the realization came to me that I was a made individual. I was a force to be reckoned with. A lot of people who had looked at me as being a snot-nosed wise-ass kid would now be speaking to me in different tones. The job paid $5000. Five thousand dollars! It seemed like a billion. My older brother was working ten hours a day in a warehouse and bringing home $24 a week. Five thousand dollars, that's how it started.

Contrary to legend, there is no great celebration after you make your first hit. I mean, nobody throws a party for you or anything. But you are made. The word is out very quickly that you are a capable individual. That you are a heavyweight, a gunsel, a torpedo, a cannon, a hit man, a boy who will do the job. In *The Godfather* they said, "Make your bones." Now I never heard that before, but it has the same meaning.

After this first hit my career was interrupted by the army, which taught me the proper way to handle a gun—I beg your pardon, a weapon. They taught us this rhyme I remember. You had to hold your rifle and point one finger at your prick and repeat, "This is my weapon [the rifle], this is my gun [the prick], one is for shooting, one is for fun." My only problem was I never could figure out which was for which.

After I got separated from the service I kicked around in New York for a while and then went out to California and began working for Jack Dragna. Jack knew I was a wild man, but he didn't know how wild. He wanted to test me and offered me a hit.

"Sure," I told him, "why not?" After my experience in Korea I figured what difference would another guy or two make. I never did find out what number two had done either. Jack just showed me his picture and handed me a gun. He told me what kind of car this guy drove, gave me his license-plate number and explained that the guy always collected some payoffs in a certain shopping center on Monday afternoons.

The following Monday afternoon I drove over there in a stolen car and found his car parked towards the back of the parking lot. I found a spot almost directly across from his car and pulled in. I got out and sat on the trunk of my car for almost three hours, doing nothing but watching for him and listening to a transistor radio. Nobody paid any attention to me; for all anybody knew I was waiting for my wife. Finally I saw him walking down the aisle toward his car. I looked around and there wasn't another person within 70 yards. Lucky for me—unlucky for him. If I had seen anybody else I would have got in my car and trailed him and waited for another opportunity. I waited until he started to edge between his car and the car parked next to him, then I took a few steps across the driving lane and hit him. Nobody saw him go down. I put three bullets in him, then I got in my own car and drove away.

There are many reasons an individual is killed: He may be a stool pigeon, he may be too greedy, the man he is working for might suspect he is taking too much, the man he is working for might think he is too ambitious, he might be blown away because he has not lived up to an agreement he made, the job might be planned by an underling trying to take over from a boss, the target could be a mob member who has become a junkie and is therefore unreliable, it might be part of a gang war and it could even be payment for an attempted double cross. There is always a good reason and it always involves doing something you shouldn't be doing as a member of organized crime.

Innocent people, civilians, are very rarely hit. You recently saw the reason for that in New York City. You had half a battalion of mob guys killed after the Colombo-Gallo business and nobody did much of anything. But when two innocent meat salesmen in a restaurant were mistaken for mob men and killed accidentally, the commissioner almost declared martial law.

We leave civilians alone. We don't hurt them and we don't work for them. As a matter of fact, if a civilian wants to buy a hit he might be able to get someone who has done a few, but I doubt he could get anyone connected with the mob. Chances are, whoever he got, the civilian would just be taken for his money. The hit will never be made. What's he gonna do about it? Who's he gonna complain to?

Mob guys very rarely take outside work because they can't trust civilians. The police lean on a civilian and he is going to fold. He has never been battered by questions, he has never been mentally assaulted, so he's gonna quit on you. The police are experts, they can turn you up one side and down the other with their questions. And who needs to depend on a civilian?

Not me. And not any professional hit man that I know. I just don't want to mess with your so-called honest citizens. As a rule you just can't trust them.

I did come close once. Tony Bender asked me to see a civilian about doing a job for him. Tony had done me some favors, so I said I would. The civilian was a wealthy New York City socialite type. I figured maybe somebody was leaning on him businesswise. Generally civilians want other civilians hit to settle personal scores, and I certainly don't want to get involved in that. But this guy didn't want that, he wanted a broad hit in the head. I found it very unusual for a man to want a girl killed so I asked him about it. He said he had been shacking up with her and things were getting complicated.

Before giving him an answer I started doing a little investigating on my own. I found out the reason he wanted her hit in the head was that she had the nerve to get pregnant on him. I figured maybe she wanted a lot of money, but I was wrong. All she wanted was to make sure the kid was properly cared for. She didn't want no big amount of money, she wasn't looking to shake him down, and she didn't want to get involved with the Social Register. Two hundred fifty dollars a month for the kid was what she wanted. My blue-blooded friend was terrified someone would find out about the baby and it would embarrass his family. After considering the facts I decided I did not like this socialite's idea of the proper way to treat children.

I went back and I told the guy, "I am going to give you some very bad news. For one, you're gonna give this girlfriend of yours one hundred thousand dollars. And then you're gonna give her two hundred fifty a month until that kid is old enough to take care of itself. And if you don't, motherfucker, I'm gonna put a bullet in your head and I'm gonna let the whole world know why you got killed." He went running to see Tony Bender. Tony told him he couldn't interfere. Actually he could've, but he didn't want to. This guy finally gave her the money. She eventually found out the story and what I did for her. After that she left town and had the kid. Today she is married and lives out in the Midwest. I heard from her a couple of times, but I'm a part of her life she would rather forget.

But you see the problem you get into when you deal with civilians. I like to stick to my own. It's easier.

Every hit begins with a contract. If you're working independently, as I usually do, the people who need your services get in touch with you. A meeting is set up, and details are discussed. I'm told what the job entails and how much it pays and occasionally what the beef is. I'm not told who the party is, but that's not important. The details will probably give me a good idea who he might be, but I will very rarely ask for a name until I decide to take the job. If I figure I might know the man, or the people he hangs with, I'll probably say "pass." If I figure it's okay I'll do business. On certain jobs I'm told who it is right away, like with Joey Gallo, for instance, because the word was out all over anyway.

There is no set price for a hit. It depends on who the man is, how difficult the job and what the results (who will gain what) will be. It usually averages anywhere between $10,000 and $25,000 and could go higher. The largest contract I've ever heard of was an open offer of $250,000 payable to anyone who could get to Joe Valachi. But nobody would take the job. If the mob could have gotten to Valachi nobody would ever talk to the police again because it would have completely destroyed the confidence of anybody who thought about becoming an informer. (There's a story that Valachi was causing problems in prison and word was sent to Attorney General Bobby Kennedy. "Tell him to stop it," Kennedy supposedly said, "or we'll let him go.") The most I've ever been offered was $50,000 and I've been offered that a few times. That was the price I was quoted on Joey Gallo.

A contract is always a verbal agreement, but these contracts are as strong as any written agreement in the world. You don't have to sign a paper, you're guaranteeing it with your own life.

The money is paid in advance. The full amount. After the contract is out, the man who put it out can rescind it, but none of his money will be returned. Once I take your money I'm going to make the hit—unless you tell me you've changed your mind. That's fine, but you pay the full amount for that privilege.

There is a guarantee in the contract covering the unlikely situation that I'm caught. I will not talk. Not a word. Not a sound. Not a peep. In order to ensure that, the party with whom I've made my deal must pay all legal fees, support my family the entire time I'm in jail, and have something waiting for me the day I get out. When I came out of the Tombs (that's the Manhattan House of Detention) after sitting there for almost a full year, I was handed $50,000 for keeping my mouth shut.

That may sound like a lot of money, but it's worth it to the mob. Knowing my family is being supported and I'm earning while I'm sitting, there's no reason for me to talk. The only alternative the mob has is to try to kill me and that's stupid because, if they did, no professional would ever work for them again. Amateurs, like Jerome Johnson who shot Joe Colombo, don't get this sort of deal because no one has any doubts that, when caught, they would reveal everything. Their payment is inevitably a bullet in the head. But amateurs are very rarely used.

If you happen to be a full-time employee of a particular organization, rather than a freelancer, the contract procedure is a little different. If you're on salary and they tell you somebody has got to go, he goes. Makes no difference who he is and how close the two of you might be. He's gone. A new soldier for that big organization in the sky.

THE PROCESS OF ELIMINATION

Under any circumstances, if I take your money the job is going to be done unless you decide differently. Once I take a penny, I've guaranteed that contract will be fulfilled. And so I want to make sure it gets done quickly and correctly. That's where experience comes in.

Planning a hit is not difficult. There are only a few simple rules you have to be aware of: You do not kill a man in his own home; you do not kill a man in front of his own family; you do not harm his family; you do not hit him in a church or near a church or any other place of worship; you do not torture a man (we're not his judges, just his executioners); and you do not rob him. Other than that, he's all yours.

There are three basic ways to plan a hit. The hit man will be given his intended's routine, or he'll study the man and pick up his routine himself, or the party will be brought to him at a preselected spot. I like to do as much as possible myself. I like being in total control and I'll spend as much time as necessary making sure everything is exactly the way I want it. I once clocked a man for ten days before I hit him. This guy was a numbers controller who was fingering other controllers to be robbed. He used to park his car in a gas station overnight, and I decided that the gas station would be the place. I waited in my car, which I parked in a shadow, until he showed up. When he did I walked up to his car. He didn't realize what was about to happen until I pulled the cannon. Then he realized—I'm gonna die. He started to beg, but I didn't give him a chance to get five words out of his mouth. He knew why, and it wasn't my job to sit there and give him a lecture. That gas station was the perfect spot: closed, quiet and dark.

The safest way is to have the party brought to you. If I'm told the hit is being set up this way, I get to the location early and check it out carefully. If I'm not completely satisfied with it I may not do the job. After all, it's my head in the noose. I got sent to St. Louis once on a loan. They had the thing all lined up and needed an outside gun. When I got there, I said, "You guys don't mind if I take a couple of days and see if I go along with the plan, do you?" I wouldn't care if the FBI had checked it out in advance, I wanted to check it myself. They agreed, and I found their schedule was perfect and the spot they picked likewise. Only then did I agree to pull the trigger.

After you're satisfied that the proper plans have been made you can

54

begin the execution. There are actually very few preparations that have to be made. I normally get the gun I'm going to use as soon as I agree to take the job. The gun can come from anywhere. It might be stolen off the docks or I might get a hot gun from a friend. There is a tremendous market in hot guns. Wherever I get it, the first thing I'll do is file the serial number off to make it as untraceable as possible.

If there is any chance people will see me leaving after I've done the job, I'll use a stolen car. I'll steal the car myself two or three days before the day I'm going to make the hit and just stash it away. I'll check it over carefully to make sure it's going to start when I need it to start, and if the battery looks the slightest bit worn I'll put a new one in.

Up until the time I intend to make the actual hit, my day will be very normal. I'll give you an example.

A mob guy dealing narcotics had started using them himself. He had turned himself into an addict, and the man he worked for wanted him eliminated. I agreed to do the job.

His boss gave me a pretty good idea of what his schedule was like, and I followed him for a few days just to verify my information and pick the spot. He did different things each night but always ended up at this girl's apartment. She lived in a brownstone way over in the West Forties, which is a good area to make a hit because it's dark and, in the winter, when this all took place, there are few people on the street late at night. He also parked his car in front of the same fire hydrant every night.

I got up about 11:30 the morning the job was going to be done. I made myself some coffee, and my wife and I sat down to watch the television program "Jeopardy," which is one of my favorite shows. If they would let me go on as a contestant I could win a lot of money. The only categories my wife can beat me in are "show business" and "literature."

After "Jeopardy" ended I went to a pool hall and spent most of the afternoon shooting with a buddy of mine. My days aren't what you call structured. I really never know what I'm going to be doing; it depends on what I feel like. I might go to the track, go bowling, play cards, visit some friends, see a broad. I might even stay home. But it was cold outside, so I stayed in and shot pool.

THE PROCESS OF ELIMINATION

From there I went to a small Italian restaurant in the East Village named Sonny's and had dinner with some friends. I left there about 9:30 and just drove around the city till about midnight. I went over the plan in my mind a few times, but I didn't really concentrate on it. Sometimes when I've got a job to do I'll spend the night at home watching television or even go to a movie, but this night I just felt like driving. I did stop in a few different places to say hello to some friends, but I didn't stay anywhere very long.

Finally I drove up to this block and parked about three car lengths behind the fire hydrant. I looked for his car and it wasn't there, so I knew he hadn't shown up early. I have had people do that on me, which earns them an extra night of living. The only things I brought with me were a transistor radio, a thermos of coffee and a blanket. I use the transistor because I don't want to run down the battery of the car. I rarely mind the cold because it keeps you awake and alert, but the blanket is there in case it really freezes up.

This guy showed up right on time. I saw him coming in my rear-view mirror and I kind of laid down across the front seat so he wouldn't see me. While he was parking I slid out of my car and hid so he didn't see me and take off. When he turned his engine off I began the casual walk toward his car. I hit him in the head as he started to get out. Two bullets. I knew he was dead.

I walked back to my car and drove home. I was asleep within a half hour.

I usually work alone, but when you're just starting out in this line of work a backup man is normally sent along to make sure everything goes correctly. Once you're established you go out by yourself or, at worst, with a single driver. The only exception is when you're hitting someone in a crowded area and you think there is a chance you might be chased. Then you use a getaway car and a crash car. The crash car is set up to block traffic after the job is done and, if somebody tries to follow you, to "accidentally" crash into them. Under any circumstances you're only going to use the getaway car to go a few blocks. Then, depending on where you are, you're going to get out of your vehicle and lose yourself as quickly as you can in a crowd, or take some public transportation, or ride a cab, or even take another car that you have waiting.

The most important thing is to try to isolate your victim. I may be sitting in his car waiting for him and as soon as he gets in I'll blast him, or I may have made arrangements for him to be picked up by someone he trusts and brought to a destination where I'll be waiting. If possible, it's best to catch him late at night. But catching him alone is really the important thing because, if you don't, innocent people might get hurt and you don't want that, no way.

I've never had a problem with innocent people because I've always been very careful about picking my spots. But if I was on a job and an innocent person got in the way, he would have to go. I know I wouldn't feel too good about doing it, but I know I'd kill him anyway. It's part of being a professional. Other people don't take as much care as I do. Little Augie Pisano, for example, was with a girl when he received a phone call and was told to come to a meeting. The jerk brought the girl with him. Now it is a clear violation of the rules to bring a civilian with you to any business meeting. So, when he showed up, his killers were waiting for him. They had no choice—the girl had to go too. And she did.

Sometimes, though, it's almost impossible to get a guy alone. Maybe he has too many bodyguards, or maybe he's very careful. Then you have to hit him in public. On a job like this the important thing is to be cool. If you're careful there is actually very little to worry about. I've walked into restaurants in which my man was sitting and I've calmly walked over and calmly pulled the trigger and then I turned around and calmly walked out. I didn't run. I just make sure, in a situation like this, that I use a gun that's going to make a lot of noise because I want everybody in that place diving under tables. I was fortunate enough to see the police report on number 14, which I did in a restaurant. I was described by 11 different people in 11 different ways . . . and not one of them was totally accurate.

Like every professional hit man I've ever known, I've always used a gun. Always. All 38 times. I am a good shot and I know where I'm going to hit you and you are going to die. No one has lived yet. I have steady hands, a sharp eye—I don't wear glasses—and a great amount of confidence.

I prefer to use a .38 revolver whenever possible because it's not too big and I know it's not going to jam unless I have a bad cartridge in there or the hammer's busted, and I always check to make sure this is not the case. If I catch the guy by himself I use a silencer. That way the gun doesn't make any loud noises, just a small pfffttt. You always try to catch a guy in the head with your first shot because that ends the argument quickly.

A magnum, which is a very big gun, is nice to have around if you're putting down a revolution, but you're not going to use it in my work because it's too heavy and you need fluidity when you're doing a job. It's also not that accurate a weapon because, when you pull the trigger, you get a severe kickback. If you hold it at hip level when you fire, by the time you get through you'll be pointing at the sky.

At one point drowning was a popular way of killing people, but no more. Why go through all the trouble of taking somebody and dragging them to a spot where there is water and then drowning them when you can shoot them much more easily? Because you want it to look like an accident? Bullshit! You *don't* want it to look like an accident! You want people to know why a guy was hit. It serves as a warning to others.

The weapon I carry every day was especially made for me by a friend who is an excellent mechanic. (A mechanic is our term used to describe anybody who is great at anything.) It's a "gun" about two and one-half inches in length and about an inch wide. It's about half an inch thick and, in general, looks just like a cigarette lighter. It is actually a trigger mechanism. I have buckshot cartridges that have been designed for this weapon. I simply screw the cartridges in and pull the trigger and, at 30 feet or less, I can make a long-division problem out of you. I can have cartridges made up for any bullet I want. As far as I know there are only about five weapons like this in existence, all made by my friend. They're great guns because there is absolutely no recoil and no markings are left on the slug or shot.

I've heard of people who have used knives, hatchets and icepicks, who'll strangle you and garrotte you, and every once in a while someone'll use something exotic like a blowtorch. I've also heard of one guy who uses garlic. He rubs the bullets he's going to use with it. This guarantees that his target is going to die—if the bullets don't get him, the garlic will cause a slow, agonizing death by blood poisoning. I've also been told of one guy left hanging on a meat hook for three days until he died, and another guy who was heated slowly with an iron, but I don't go in for anything like that. I don't want to spend that much time with my targets, I don't want to watch them suffer. That's not my job. Of course, some people have different tastes. A midwestern hit man used alcohol and a truck. His target was a stool pigeon, and the organization did not want the police to know they were on to this guy. The guy was a heavy drinker to begin with, so the hit man and his driver kidnapped him and brought him to a small apartment. They put a gun at his head and a glass of whiskey in his hand. "Drink," the hit man said, and the target did. He kept drinking until he was completely drunk. Then they brought him down to the highway, parked his car nearby and pushed him in front of a truck. Even if the police suspected anything there was nothing they could prove.

Lately I've been hearing about a new weapon. It's a certain type of gas that you spray in someone's face. Not only does it kill him immediately, it leaves the same aftereffects as a heart attack. I got a hunch the two men who were involved in the trial of Newark Mayor Hugh Addonizio were killed this way. It's very strange that two important witnesses should die of heart attacks behind the wheel of their cars within a short time of each other.

I'm a traditionalist. I like using a gun. I feel comfortable with it. I doubt I would ever use anything else because I don't like to get too close to my man. I'm not looking to be sophisticated, I'm looking to do a job and not get caught, and so I never get closer than two or three feet.

Hell, if I'm within two or three feet of him, he's dead. It's important to set it up so the guy never really has a chance to move or try to protect himself or run away. The furthest I've ever had to chase a guy was about 30 yards and that was someone else's fault. This guy was brought out to a field in the middle of nowhere. He thought he was going to a business meeting. The idiot driver let him get out of the car before I was ready; he saw me and took off. I chased him on foot and, when I got close enough, I pumped four bullets into him. End of story.

He was one of the few who had that much time. Very few of the 38 ever knew what was about to hit them. I was the last thing they ever saw. I never said a word to any of them. What am I going to say? A lot of times you'll get ready to hit a man and he'll realize briefly what's happening and make the sign of the cross, or he'll start screaming, "No!" But before he can get too much of anything out it's usually all over.

Let me give you an example of a perfect hit. Number 27. At the time I was working for a particular organization, and it was decided that a man was going to die because he had become too ambitious. He was trying to move up too quickly. I was contacted and told there was a contract I was to fulfill. I had no choice in the matter. The price, I was told over pizza, was $20,000.

"Do I set up my own deal or do you set it up for me?" I asked. My employer told me I was on my own, and I began studying my man. I took about a week and by the end of it I knew what time he left his house, where he went, who he saw, what business he conducted on what days and, finally, who he was sleeping with. I noticed that this man continually drove through an isolated area and I studied this area carefully, trying to find a good quiet spot where I could pick him off. I couldn't find exactly what I wanted so I looked for another place.

I discovered he had a girlfriend who he visited on the nights he made his gambling collections, and I picked one of these nights. I used a driver but I made sure he parked about a block away so he couldn't actually see what I was doing. That way he couldn't testify to a single thing. He wasn't about to hear the shots because I was working with a silencer.

When my target came out of his girlfriend's house about six in the morning, I was standing there leaning against a lamppost. I hit him as he walked to his car. Three shots and he went down. I walked over and put another one in the back of his head. My driver dropped me off at my own car and I got in and drove home. The first thing I did that morning was get rid of the gun.

Most professional hits are similar to that one. The only time it's really different, as I said, is when a boss is involved. There are two ways to kill a boss. The easy way is to get to his bodyguard or the top man in his organization and make a deal with him.

Now the tougher way. If the bodyguard does not agree to the hit he has to go too. I was working for Meyer Lansky at one point, and some representatives of Vito Genovese invited me to a meeting. They had decided that Meyer was to be hit. An offer was made and I said no thank you. Maybe some people don't, but I believe in being loyal to an individual who helps you earn. But by saying no I made myself a target.

The only reason I wasn't killed right on the spot, after I turned them down, was because I had a gun in my hand. Whenever I go to meet somebody on business I always wear a pair of pants in which the pocket has been cut out and I can reach through to a gun I have strapped to the inside of my leg. In this particular instance we were sitting in a restaurant, me with my back to the wall. After I said no the guy said, "I'm sorry to hear that."

I pulled my cannon out and laid it on the table. "Now why is that?" I asked. He said, "We'll be seeing you," and got up and left. I made one mistake after that—I didn't tell Meyer. It almost cost me my life, but I thought I could handle it.

I couldn't. I was coming out of a bank in Miami Beach and three guys opened up on me. It's a very strange thing to be hit by a bullet. For a second there is a tremendous burning sensation, then shock takes over. Then you go into what I would call limbo—everything moves in sort of slow motion. You can feel the impact, but not the pain, when you're hit again, but you're not exactly sure what you're doing. That's when your reflexes take complete control. The next thing I remember, I had a gun in my hand and I was using it. I remember hitting one guy and seeing his head explode. I remember shooting the second guy. I never saw the third guy, he took off.

The lawyer I had gone to the bank with managed to get me into a cab. The next thing I knew I was lying on a slab in a warehouse and a doctor was cutting bullets out of me. One week later I was on a boat to Brazil where I stayed, well supported, for almost a year. So they didn't get me and they didn't get Meyer.

A few years later I was sitting in an Italian restaurant and a man walked up to me and said, "You don't know me, but I was almost your executioner." This was the third man. We talked about it. I understood. Business is business.

THE PROCESS OF ELIMINATION

Normally a boss is very careful where he goes and rarely travels without a bodyguard. One mistake is all any good hit man needs. I'll give you an example. I was out in California recently and I went to visit a friend of mine who has a bakery shop. Whenever I'm out there I go see him because he's probably the only person west of the Mississippi who makes good cannoli. Of course, I'm not the only guy who knows this.

We talked in his back room for a little while, and then I got up to leave. As I walked out from the back of the place who's standing by himself at the counter but one of the biggest mob bosses in the country. He took one look at me and his face went white. His eyes opened to about the size of a silver dollar. I looked at him and smiled. "Take it easy, babe," I said. "If I was here to see you, you wouldn't have seen me." Then I reached under the counter, handed him a chocolate-chip cookie and walked out. I guarantee you he won't go to the bathroom by himself for the next five years.

In any case, whoever the victim, the first thing you do after making a hit is dispose of the weapon. Once the weapon is out of your hands, and can't be traced back to you, it's almost impossible to get pinned with a crime. No weapon, no murder raps. I break up every gun that I don't leave on the spot. I have a friend who has a little machine shop and he takes the gun and melts it down. Or I'll bring it to a junkyard and flip it into one of the compressors. Good-bye, gun. As soon as the barrel is destroyed you're safe. Once that's gone there is no way of matching the bullet to the gun.

As I said, sometimes I leave the gun right on the spot. I'll do this if it's a stolen weapon and it's completely clean. There's really nothing to worry about. The handle of the gun has ridges and won't pick up fingerprints (unless you're stupid enough to use something like a pearl-handled revolver and if you do you deserve to get caught). The hammer has ridges too, and there is always a line right down the middle of the trigger. Sometimes I'll wipe the gun anyway, just to be certain, because fingerprints can kill you. One guy blasted a target with a shotgun and left the shotgun there. Fine, except he also left fingerprints on it, so his employers decided he had to go too. Can't have him being traced back and caught, because then it gets too hot for the people who hired him.

After I make a hit, and get rid of the gun, I follow my regular schedule.

I remember going directly from a hit to a wedding reception. I just forget about it.

One thing I never do is plan an alibi in advance. To me that is really stupid because, by planning, you've got to get other people involved. If you ask them to front for you they know you're going to be doing something. But if I do the job right, who's gonna know I'm there? If I have to I can always set up an alibi. I can get 18 guys to swear they were playing cards with me. Or I can get the owner of some restaurant or movie theater who owes me a favor to swear I was there. No problems.

The police don't usually bother you too much. Number one, a cop is not going to knock his brains out on a mob hit because history shows they are not going to be able to get corroborating testimony, even if they know who did the job, which they do in a lot of so far "unsolved" cases. Don't underestimate the police. They do a good job. But when a mob guy is hit by another mob guy . . . well, let's say they're not overly disappointed and don't work as hard as they might under other circumstances.

You can almost forget about witnesses. There have been very few people willing to testify in cases involving organized-crime members. Not so much because they tend to disappear, but because your average individual is a family person and he is terrified someone in his family will get hurt if he gets involved. And, second, he's just not that socially conscious. They think just like the cops, what the hell, he only killed another gangster, what's the difference. Let 'em all kill one another.

Who can blame them? The newspapers, television, movies, magazines and books have done our job for us. The newspapers in particular love to turn simple rubouts into full-scale pitched battles. I personally never check the papers after I've done a job. There is no reason for me to, I'm not interested in the publicity, and I decided a long time ago it would be a poor idea for me to keep a scrapbook. Besides, the event the papers report is not going to have too much in common with the one I remember. I quit looking after my fourth hit. It was simple and quick, I just put three bullets in the guy from close range. The papers made it sound like a whole platoon of hit men had ventilated him with submachine guns. They didn't even have the number of bullets right.

THE PROCESS OF ELIMINATION

All that the communications media have succeeded in doing is scaring the hell out of people. Let me ask you a question: After seeing *The God-father*, would you testify against Don Corleone? Shit. After seeing *The Godfather*, would you even testify against Marlon Brando?

Even when the occasional silly soul comes along and claims he has seen a crime being committed, he usually changes his thinking before the trial begins. That is exactly what happened to me—but before the witnesses realized their mistake I spent almost a year in the Tombs in New York.

The district attorney claimed he had two witnesses who had seen me pull the trigger. They were a man and a woman in their late twenties and they had been parked in the shadows near the docks making out.

Four cops came to my door to arrest me. They stood right there in the hallway and read me my constitutional rights. My wife didn't take the whole thing very seriously at first. "Now what have you done?" she kind of scolded.

"Nothing," I said. "I don't know what these gentlemen are talking about." The only person I ever discussed this with was my attorney. I sat in the Tombs for almost a year, and we finally went to trial. Amazingly enough, the DA couldn't produce his witnesses. He asked the judge for 24 hours to produce them.

The next day he came into court and he was fuming. "Your honor, the witnesses have disappeared. But the state believes the defendant had something to do with their disappearance!"

"Your honor," my attorney protested, "my client has been sitting in jail for almost one full year. He could not possibly have had anything to do with the disappearance of the DA's alleged witnesses. We're ready to go to trial. If the state isn't ready to proceed, after all this time, we ask that you dismiss the charges." Case dismissed.

I don't know what happened to the witnesses. All I can guess is they had a sudden attack of honesty and decided to go on a long vacation.

Witnesses sometimes need help to understand that things aren't always what they appear to be. In 1963 I was hired to provide that help.

A man claimed he had seen a member of a particular organization shoot down a guy in cold blood. The police put him under full protection:

a squad car outside his apartment building, a cop in the lobby and a third cop in his living room. I was offered $20,000 to prove to him that the cops couldn't protect him.

I watched his place for a few days and made my move one night. Dark, no moon. I didn't want to use the fire escape because I couldn't take the chance on making noise and having someone look out their window. So I went to the roof of another building on the block and climbed across to his roof. I brought a rope—with plenty of knots tied in it to rest my feet on—and a grappling hook. I dug that hook into the roof and lowered myself down. It was only two stories.

This was in the middle of the summer and his window was wide open. I climbed in very quietly. Then I put one hand over his mouth and put my gun in my other hand, and shook him gently.

"Don't make a move or a sound," I said. "There's a cop right outside your door and if he comes in here you're both gonna die. All I want to do is show you that the cops can't stop us. Wherever you go, whatever you do, we're gonna find you. We don't want to hurt you, but we think you should consider it carefully before you squeal on our mutual friend. Just do the right thing by him and you won't get hurt, I promise you. Now I'm gonna leave you. You go back to sleep. If you make a sound and I get caught, you're dead." Then I climbed back up the rope and went home.

We didn't want to kill him because that would have created a lot of heat for us. It worked out very well, he just had a sudden loss of memory. I made $20,000 and I didn't even have to pull the trigger.

Neither witnesses nor informers are hurt unless they have to be. Abe Reles, who informed on Murder, Inc., had to be. He just knew too much. He was supposedly under police protection when he "fell" out of a window and was killed. The story was that he had tried to get away from the police by tying sheets together and climbing out. The mob got to somebody and he was thrown right out the window. I assume the police who were supposedly guarding him were paid a great deal of money.

One stool pigeon who died was Arnold Shuster, the kid who fingered Willie Sutton. Arnold just had a case of bad luck. Nobody cared about Sutton, he was a freelance bank robber and meant nothing to the organization. But one day Albert Anastasia happened to turn on the television and some sort of interview was on. He looked at Shuster and said, "Kill that motherfucker. I hate stool pigeons," and a few days later Shuster was blown away. If Anastasia had not turned the television set on, Shuster would never have been hit. As it turned out his death served as a warning to other potential informers, but it also led to Anastasia's death. It was a totally unnecessary killing and it brought a lot of heat down on the mob. The other bosses never forgave Anastasia for this.

About the only thing you have to think about, after the gun, the witnesses and the police, is the body. Most of the time it's best to leave it where it falls, but some people prefer to have victims simply disappear off the face of the earth. No body, no police. What the hell, they're paying for it. One organization brings its leftovers to a junkyard that has a compressor and makes them part of next year's Lincolns. Another uses a furnace in the backyard of a New Jersey estate. And there are still some undiscovered farms with lots of shallow graves fertilizing the plants. I suppose the most popular places are construction sites. The organization finds an area where concrete is about to be poured and they put the body in there. Some guy comes to work the next morning and, what does he know, he pours the concrete. Here's a helpful hint, though—always pour lime over the body or, when it starts decomposing, it's going to smell just terrible.

This point was proven just a few years ago by some people in the Canarsie section of Brooklyn. They had the bodies of two recently departed individuals on their hands and they did not want them discovered by the police. These victims had been linked to a business everyone thought was legitimate, and the mob didn't need that. So they made an early deposit in what was going to be a bank. They showed up one night in February and stuck the bodies in the foundation. Unfortunately, they neglected to cover them with lime. This was fine in the winter, because the bodies froze and nobody knew they were there. But by the time the bank opened in August the bodies were decomposing and nobody could walk in or out of that place without losing lunch.

I've only broken one rule in my career. I have killed three men for revenge—and I made them suffer when I did it. Normally you're supposed to get permission, but I didn't bother. When I think back on it, it seems like a plot for a bad motion picture. I remember in *Nevada Smith,* Steve McQueen tracked down the three guys who killed his parents and, when he found the third one, he just couldn't kill him. That's the difference between real life and pictures. There wasn't a man on this planet who could've stopped me.

It was 1958 and I had made a private deal to bring narcotics into the country from Mexico. My cut was supposed to be $40,000, but instead of paying me the party thought it would be a great deal cheaper to kill me. Unfortunately, when he sent his goons to my house I wasn't there. My wife was there and four months pregnant at the time. They came into the house looking for me and when they realized I wasn't home they got abusive. One of them kicked my wife in the stomach and they left her lying on the kitchen floor. She started hemorrhaging. She was dead by the time our neighbors got her to the hospital.

They caught up to me in Reno, Nevada. I had just come out of one of the casinos—at this point I didn't know what happened to my wife—and I started to cut through this alley over by some railroad tracks. The lights blanked out. I was smashed over the head with a blunt instrument.

Ten days later I came to, paralyzed from the neck down, in the Washoe Medical Center. The doctor manipulated my vertebrae and managed to restore some feeling in my body. The next day some friends came by and they told me what had happened to my wife.

That was the day I stopped caring whether I lived or died. That was the day I lost all fear of death. All I had within me was hatred. I would not have gone after the three men for what they did to me—business was business—and I would have simply settled with the head man. But they were dead the moment they kicked my wife.

We had only been married a few months. When we got married I didn't know if I was going to stay in this business or not. I certainly never would've stayed in as a hit man if she had lived; I even like to think I would have quit. You talk about your life changing around because of a woman . . . mine did. She was a real clean kid. And she was mine. For the first time in my life I had found someone who made me completely happy. Until that point, I didn't know what happiness was. All my life I had been a taker, everything I owned I had had to grab. Finally I had found someone who was willing to give simply because she liked me. There were never any threats, any wild shows, any violence; she liked me just because I was me.

Then my whole world exploded. It just came apart. It changed me radically. Before this I was sometimes wild and crazy, but I just wasn't mean. This made me mean. As soon as I could move I got on the telephone and called the guy who had set the whole thing up. He picked up the phone. All I said was, "You made a mistake, fuck. I'm still alive."

I laid in the hospital for eight months, and one day the doctor walked in and said I could either lie there like a vegetable for the rest of my life or risk an operation. I asked him what my chances were.

"Even," he said. "You'll either walk out or be carried out." I didn't give a damn either way, so I told him to start cutting. Seven months later I walked out of that place. And went after the three men who had killed my wife.

I started to hunt them down. I carried .22 long-range flat-nosed bullets because I wanted them to suffer. At short range they won't kill you, but they will smash your bones and make you bleed. I found the first one in California. I killed him very slowly. I had trapped him in a garbage-filled alley and he started swearing he had nothing to do with it. There was no way I was going to listen. I just started to pump bullets into him methodically. First into his legs so he couldn't move. Then into his rib cage so he would bleed. Then into his shoulders and then I shot his ears off. I just kept reloading the gun; I was having a good time. Then I left him there to die.

I found the second one in Mexico and killed him the same way. I had never known anything as sweet as these killings. They were wonderful sights. And I could smell the fear. If you've ever wondered why an animal attacks someone who's afraid of him, it's because the fear just pours out of him and creates an odor. I saw it. I smelled it. I loved it.

I had to chase the third one completely across the country. He knew I was after him and he tried to hide. It took me almost a year to find him, but I did, in New York City. He went down just like the first two. Then I got on the phone to the boss. I said two words, "You're next," and then I hung up. But before I could get him he was arrested on a narcotics charge. That bust saved his life. I guarantee it. And, if he lives through it, the day he walks out I will be standing there waiting for him. I swear it.

Why do I do it? Why do I kill people? There are a number of reasons. Obviously, the money. I like money. I like what money can buy, what it can bring you. I remember when I didn't have it.

I like the status it brings. I'm somebody. Straight people like to associate with me. They like to be able to brag that they know a real live killer, or that this guy can "do things" for people. And girls, when they meet me, they want to find out what it's like to be with an individual who has killed people. They want to go to bed with you. Don't ask me why, but they do. They feel you're going to be different than anybody else. You're not, and they're disappointed when they find out, but the idea of being with an animal really appeals to a lot of people. Believe it or not, there are "hit man groupies." I like women being attracted to me. I didn't have what you would call a normal social life when I was younger; I didn't do too much dating. And I know I'm not the best-looking guy in the world either, so if it's being the tough killer that turns women on, I'll play that role. I'll be as tough as they want. Usually, though, after they ball you, they get sick. They feel they've corrupted themselves.

I also see killing as a test of loyalty and courage.

In business terms the ability to pull the trigger is vitally important. If you expect to progress in the organization you have to be able to do it. I would say almost every man who has ever become a boss has pulled it somewhere along the line.

And, finally, I guess I do it because I enjoy it. I like having the power of knowing that I am it, that I can make the final decision of whether someone lives or dies. It is an awesome power.

Don't try to analyze me or any other hit man either. I would guess there are maybe 1000 men still working at it throughout the country. But except in New York there hasn't been much work lately, so I guess you could call us a dying breed. The thing about hit men that is so unusual is that they are so usual. A man that is sadistic, that is crazy-wild, that is a troublemaker, that has strange habits or stands out in a crowd, he can't make it. He'll be disposed of.

Hit men differ in a thousand ways. Some are friendly, some moody, some tall, some short, some bald, and, lately, some even have long hair. You would never be able to pick one out of a crowd but, then again, you won't have to. A hit man is only known to those people who have to know who he is.

What makes a good hit man? Pride and confidence. A good hit man goes out, does his job, comes home to his family and can sit down and eat his dinner without any problems. After all, no one likes to bring his work home with him.

CHAPTER 5
THE SHY'S THE LIMIT

y favorite television commercial is the one for bank loans which promises, "You have a friend at Chase Manhattan." That is true. I got a friend at Chase, you better believe it. Every time an individual needs money badly and my friend at Chase Manhattan turns him down, he has got to come to me, or someone like me, to make the loan. The guy needs the money or he wouldn't have gone to the bank in the first place. Just because they wouldn't give it to him doesn't mean he isn't going to still need it. Because I'm helping him out quickly and quietly, and because I'm taking a chance on someone a bank considered too risky, he is going to pay very well for my service. Very well indeed. This business is known as shylocking, or loansharking, and is one of the most lucrative of all mob enterprises. And, as in any business in which large sums of money are involved, there is always the threat of violence.

I did a job for a shy in 1967. I usually don't do jobs unless I can do them my way, but he threw in an extra $5000 to have it done the way he wanted it. He set one condition for the hit—I had to take this guy from New York to a small town in Pennsylvania and dump him there. It seems the intended was a collector who had gone to this town to collect a debt and instead of paying the shy his share, he told him the guy had run. When the shy checked up, he discovered the collector was lying.

The shy hired two drivers for me and set the whole thing up. He told his men that we would be picking the guy up and taking him to a meeting. He also supplied us with a hot two-door sedan (so the guy couldn't try to leap out the door if he figured what was happening) with a set of hot plates on it.

We picked the guy up late in the afternoon so it would be dark when we got to Pennsylvania. I sat in the back with him and the two other guys sat up in front. At first we had a very friendly conversation. We were talking about the meeting we were going to and the people who were supposed to be there. Just gossip. We were halfway down the New Jersey Turnpike when he realized something was happening. He must have seen a sign for the town or something. He simply asked, "Did I do anything wrong?"

I said, "I don't know. You tell me."

"This is no business trip, is it?"

"All I know is that we're supposed to go someplace and meet some people."

He was petrified, but he didn't panic. He tried to make a deal with us. "Listen, I'll give you anything you want. Just let me out of here. I've got money stashed and it's yours. I got forty thousand dollars. I'll tell you the location. Just let me out of here."

We just sat there. We didn't say a word. He began to beg. He even went so far as to tell us where he had stashed his money. Finally he realized there was absolutely nothing he could do. He sat there quietly. Then he started crying. I didn't feel a thing for him.

It took us just over two and a half hours to get to the town. Then we rode around until we found a nice quiet area and parked. I told the two guys in the front seat to go take a walk. I didn't need any witnesses. Then I just pulled the gun out and shot him in the head. One shot. He didn't resist at all, I think it's possible he was in a state of shock. As I shot I put my hand on his shoulder to make sure he fell the other way. Sometimes the concussion of the bullet will bring a man forward, and I didn't want him all over me. If you shoot a man in the head with a small-caliber bullet he won't bleed very much.

When the drivers got back in the car I said, "Can you believe that he would commit suicide like that?" There's no way these two guys could swear they saw me do anything. They can assume I did, but they never actually saw me pull the trigger.

We pushed the body out of the car onto the side of the road and drove to Philadelphia. We went over to the dock area, cleaned the car to make sure we didn't leave any prints, and then left it there. We came back to New York on the train and first thing we went to the place where he said he had hidden his money. It was wrapped in an oilcloth and hidden under a deserted dock. We split it up and then went our separate ways.

Your basic shylocking operation can be broken down into three separate areas: banking, finding customers and collecting. The banker is the individual who owns the money, the finder is the one who actually puts it out on the street, and the collector makes sure it all comes back, with appropriate interest. If a man is rich enough and strong enough he can handle the entire operation himself; otherwise he has to have people working for him.

The people who put the money on the streets usually pay back 50 percent of whatever profits they make from it. They can either be regular employees of the shy or individuals looking to go into business for themselves. If they are trying to start their own business, then they in effect have taken the loan out themselves. They are therefore responsible for paying back 50 percent of the interest, whether they have it to pass along or not. Regular employees do as well as they can, but if they can't find anybody who needs money they are not responsible for the interest.

In most cases the man who actually makes the loan also collects it, but when that's impossible and muscle has to be brought in, those people supplying it are usually paid a straight salary. There is absolutely no limit on the number of people a busy shy might have working for him at any one time.

A good shylock can put $100,000 on the street and, at the end of one year, increase the total to $250,000. The profit in shylocking is the vigorish, or the "vig," which is the amount of interest a man pays for a loan. The vig is determined by the length of time an individual will take to pay back every penny he has borrowed. If it is a short-term loan, a few weeks or less, he'll pay a higher rate of interest, usually about five points per week but ranging to as high as 20 percent per week depending on the risk. A point is one percent of whatever money he has borrowed; on a $1000 loan one point would be $10, five points $50. Again, this is five points, or $50, *per week,* not five points on the entire loan. For example, if you borrow $1000 on five points you will pay back $50 a week vig until the total loan is paid back.

You can also borrow money over a longer period of time if you're a good risk. The vig on this type of loan is lower, usually two or three percent per week, because the shy is happy to have his money out and working. The longer it sits in his pocket the less money he makes. Say you take a $1000 loan for ten weeks. Depending on the shy you're doing business with, you're either paying back $120 or $130 a week, every week, because you're paying back part of the principal plus the vig. The interest does not decrease with each payment. On a loan like this the total amount you would have to pay back would be either $1200 or $1300— assuming you don't miss any payments—which is a 20 to 30 percent profit for the shy.

You can also pay back a long-term loan by agreeing with the shy that the total will be some predetermined amount, say $1600. When you do your arithmetic you'll find this is very high, but you are actually buying yourself protection. That is a loan with a closed end, the total you owe is $1600. You might pay $100 a week for 16 weeks or $50 a week for 32 weeks, but once that $1600 is paid off you're done. On other loans it's not quite as easy as that if you have trouble making payments.

If you borrow money and you can't pay back the principal that week, you're still charged the interest. Say you're supposed to pay me $130 a week, $100 being the principal, $30 being the vig. If you can't afford to pay me the total amount, all you do is pay me $30. That is considered a carrying charge and in no way affects how much you owe me; you still owe me the balance of the principal, plus $30 a week until you've paid off the whole thing.

Take the same $1000. Let's assume you make three payments and I come to see you for the fourth payment and you don't have any money. So you give me the $30 vig. But you still owe me the $700 principal and the $210 in interest. Nothing changes, the loan just remains stationary. That's just an extra $30 it has cost you. How long would I let that go on? Years and years and years. Just don't try to leave town.

One guy I heard of borrowed $1000. For three years, *three fuckin' years*, this guy paid the vig and never touched the principal. For three years he paid back $30 a week. That's $1500 a year in interest, and he still owed the principal. He paid back $4500 before he began paying back the principal.

If you give a shy a choice he would probably prefer to loan you his money on points. Take $1000, at five points—at the end of one week he would make back $1050. At the end of ten weeks—during which time he may loan the same $1000 to five different people for short periods—he'll make a $500 profit. Take the same $1000 loaned to one person at three percent per week for ten weeks. The total amount paid back would be $1300, or only $30 a week profit. So, by points the shy is making an extra $20 per thousand every week. Let's expand a little. Say I've got ten guys who I give $1000 apiece to. I give it to them on points. Now my $10,000 is on the street and I'm making $500 a week interest. And my money is still there, safer than in a bank. At the end of a year I've made $25,000 profit or 250 percent interest on my money. Find me a bank that will pay that well.

Needless to say, the vig adds up. If you put $10,000 on the street and keep it working, within three years you will be a wealthy man. Follow this: At the end of the first year your $10,000, loaned out at three percent weekly interest, will earn you $15,000. It's simple multiplication, three percent times 50 weeks is 150 percent. It's only a 50-week year because Christmas is usually considered a grace period and your customer doesn't have to pay back. Now you've got a total of $25,000. You take that money and you put it on the street and it will bring you a $37,500 profit, bringing your total to $62,500. Send that out to earn for you and it's going to bring in a $93,000 profit. That's $93,000, plus the

$62,500 that made it, brings your total to $155,500, which you made in three years from a $10,000 investment. In my business $155,500 is known as a lot of money.

But this would be considered a very small operation by some. The New York City police recently broke up an operation that had $75 million on the streets and was charging as much as 22 percent per week interest.

Who comes to a shy? Practically everybody. Legitimate people as well as people in the organization. People who have gotten in a bad jam as well as people who just want to make a good-sized bet or a down payment on a factory. Black people and white people, men and women, cops and crooks, brokers and bookies. Everybody in this country needs money, and not everybody can get it from a bank.

Individuals who get themselves jammed up gambling are probably the prime users of shylocks. A guy has a sure thing which turns out to be not so sure and he's got to pay off. He doesn't have the money, and his book-maker doesn't believe in extending credit. Where else is he going to go?

Not only do the bookies' customers use shylocks, but bookies them-selves are among the biggest friends of shys. Most bookmakers have a shy, or even several shys, that they work with. If they lose they need a place to get large amounts of money quickly; if they win and their customers don't have a place to get the cash, they can actually sell the customer to the shy and let him do the collecting.

The biggest shy I know is Fat Tony Salerno, the same Tony Fats that ran the numbers outfit I worked for. He is originally out of East Harlem, yet he has a stake in New York and Westchester numbers and has lending representatives in Florida, New York, New Jersey and a few other states. Among Tony's best customers are bookmakers who fizzle and mob guys who make bad bets. He is known for financing bookies when they go tapioca. If your operation has a bad week, say the office loses $60,000 or $80,000, you go to Tony and either borrow on points or you borrow on payments. He gives you as much money as you need, and the interest usually depends on what your action will be the next week.

You go to him and say, "I got wiped out pretty good, I need sixty thou-sand dollars."

Tony says, "All right, how we gonna do this?"

"I don't know," is the usual reply, "let me see how I do next week." So you have a decent week and make $30,000. You would give it all to him. The next week he would get the rest of the principal plus the vig. The idea is to pay him back as soon as possible, even if you have to give him five points, because otherwise you are going to be giving him three percent every week over an extended period of time. And one thing about Tony, he can add real good.

A few years ago he was operating out of a barbershop on 40th Street and Broadway in Manhattan and lending money to bookmakers. In the aftermath of an Oakland-Baltimore football game in which many bookmakers got destroyed, they ran to Tony so they could pay off their customers. I went down to the shop on this particular Monday and the line outside the door was so long you would think it was Bing and Bob doing the Christmas show at Radio City Music Hall. I wait around until most of them are taken care of and then I start talking with Tony on some other business and number 73 or whatever walks in and he's got his face hanging down to the floor. "Whassa matter, kid?" Tony asked him.

"Ah, I had a bad week, blah, blah, blah," the kid says.

Tony turns around to this guy Pat who's holding all the money and says, "Pat, give this kid a thousand." So Pat hands the guy the thousand and the guy walks out the door. "Uh, by the way, Pat," Tony asks, "who was that guy?"

Pat turned white. "How the fuck do I know?" he says. "I thought you knew!" They both take off out the door like a shot. I've never laughed so hard.

As a rule scenes like this, with dozens of losing books, are very rare. Most bookies win—or at least break even—most of the time. But sometimes their customers lose too much and can't pay off and so the bookmaker will deal him to a shy. Say I am a bookmaker and I have a customer who loses and he don't have the wherewithal to pay me. If I have the cash I'll act as my own shylock. I'll ask him, "If you want, I'll arrange a loan for you with a shy." Normally the customer is so happy to go along with me, I won't bother to tell him I'm the shy. If he loses $1000 I'll pay the office its share, usually about half, and he has to pay me $130 a week for ten weeks. So I make a nice $800 profit on him.

Now, if I don't have the resources to shy myself I will sell this customer like a pound of fish.

I'll go to a shy and tell him, "I got a guy who owes me a thousand. I'll take seven-fifty for him, you charge him thirteen." The office is happy because they get their $500. I'm happy because I still pocket $250, I didn't lose on the deal. The shy is happy because he will make $550, and the customer is happy because his bookie is off his back, even if it costs him a few hundred more.

One deal that comes to mind is this guy from the Bronx who lost $3000 and couldn't pay any of it. I went to a shy in Brooklyn and put my customer on the market. "Look," I told the shy, "this guy owes me three thousand dollars. I'll take twenty-five hundred dollars, then you charge him the vig on three thousand dollars." We had a meeting with this guy and the shy, and arrangements were made. I was paid $2500. I gave the office its $1500 and pocketed $1000. I didn't really mind the loss of $500. I don't like to wait for my money and hassle. This particular customer was so slow on the bank draw, the vig came to almost $2000, so he ended up paying $5000 to cover a $3000 loss. But he was still happy because nothing happened to him.

Legitimate people use shylocks. They may be businessmen who overextend themselves and get in a jam where they need $5000, $10,000 or sometimes $100,000 and they need it quickly. They may have had a bad year or dumped a bundle in the market and the bank won't give them any credit. They either get the money or go out of business—so where is the last place they turn? Where else.

A man I know is in the double-knit business. He bought eight machines a few years ago, when the double-knit business was just starting, at $16,000 per. The same guy who sold him the machines financed the deal. The contract said the notes were payable on demand. In other words, the man who sold him the machines could tell him he wanted his money within 24 hours, and if he didn't get it, he could pick up the machines.

Because the double-knit business was slow for a while, my friend was just paying the interest on the notes. Then, boom, the double-knit business got hot. The same machines that cost $16,000 a few years ago were now worth $45,000 or $50,000. So, one afternoon about 3 p.m., after the banks were closed, the phone rings and the guy who holds the note says to my friend, "You pay me back the entire balance due by tomorrow morning or I rip out the machines." He must have had a buyer and he knew he could make a quick $200,000 or so.

Now where is this guy going to be able to come up with $80,000 in the middle of the afternoon? Only one place. Your little old shylock. He happened to come to me. This guy is a friend of mine to start with, and even if he wasn't I don't like to see an honest guy get fucked. He broke his ass for six years to build up a business and he's just starting to see daylight and the bottom is going to fall out. I called Joe Cheese and told him what the problem was. He asked me how much my friend needed and I told him. I explained the situation, that he needed the money long enough to pay this fuck off and show the bank the machines were his free and clear and then he could take a loan. Joe says fine, and that night we picked up the money. We charged him five percent a week, or $4000 a week interest. (Even if you pay back a loan the same day you borrow it, you've still got to pay the interest for the entire week.) We knew it would take him a week or two to get the money from the bank. He got it in two weeks, paid his bill, and everybody was happy except the guy who tried to stick him.

I'll give you another example of a legitimate businessman who needed a shy. A very close friend of mine was in business with a partner building apartment houses, developing real estate and things like that. What happened? His partner put everything in my friend's name, took all the money the business had, and headed for some beach in South America. My friend wakes up one morning and he's in hock for $150,000. They were looking to repossess his house, his car, everything. He had no idea what was going on, he didn't know where to turn. He finally gets in touch with me and says, "I need a shy and I need him right fucking now!" Because he was a close friend I got him the money with no interest. Sometimes we can work things out like this between me and the shy. In return I did a little collecting for him. I wanted my friend to turn me loose on his partner, but he wouldn't do it.

Even famous people and your supposedly very rich use shys. One high-living quarterback borrowed money at one point because he was making and spending so much he couldn't afford to pay his taxes. Unfortunately, he also had a hard time paying the shy back. This hero was told, in plain English, that the money got paid back or the only way he'd walk back on the field would be with the help of crutches. He had to go to the owner of his team to bail him out.

In this case the shy had the guy's body for collateral. The club would be willing to pay just about anything to protect him. I know a woman who used her body as collateral. She is a show broad who had been living well above her head and needed money in a hurry. It was arranged for her to meet this shy, and he loaned her $7500. She was supposed to pay back so much per week for so many weeks, per usual, but this goofy dame couldn't even do that, she couldn't pay anything. So she ended up fucking and sucking this shy every week until she paid him back every cent. This is a broad who is supposed to be a big name, a big star, and he was doing her anytime he felt like it.

The first time I hit big money—about 1953—I was making $7500 a week and spending $10,000. Believe me, it can be done anywhere, but somehow it's easier in California. That's where I was. Every time I stepped out of my apartment I bought something. I had about 60 suits that I paid $300 apiece for. My shoes were a minimum of $50 a shot and I can't even guess how many pairs I had. I was paying a broad's rent, buying her clothes, covering her expenses and giving her presents. And I was gambling on horses, football, basketball, cards.

One day in particular stands out in my mind. Jack Dragna and I were driving out to Santa Anita and on the way I was counting my money. I had about $4000 on me. After the third race it was all gone and I walked over to Jack and asked him for a small loan. Instead of the loan he just hauled off and smacked me in the face. For a minute I felt like killing him right on that spot. Finally he said, "You lissen, you stupid. I make more money in a one day than you make in a year. I'ma bettin' twenties, where you get offa betting thousands?" Always he tried to teach me how to handle money, but I never learned. It just sort of oozed through my hands.

Very few shys have problems collecting their money. A shy is gonna know that a customer is reliable or he isn't going to loan him the money. I know people who work at retail credit agencies, and when I need to know something they'll check for me. Chances are, though, if I'm pushing money I won't lend any appreciable amount to anybody unless he owns a business or is in a managerial position. I'm not going to loan $1000 to some joker who's making $100 a week. I might give him $100, because on that salary he can afford to give me back $20 a week for six weeks or so. A football player's muscles or some Broadway star's body might be good for collateral, but most people's bodies aren't worth the bones that hold them together. I don't want to hurt anybody, I want my money.

What I will often do for collateral, if a lot of money is involved and the individual that is doing the borrowing owns his own business, is have a legal contract drawn up that says I am a partner in the business. Now, I won't exercise that contract at all . . . unless I don't get my money. If I don't get paid I'll move right into that business and take my share. Most shys I know do the same thing and I could not give an estimate of the number of shylocks who have become partners in profit-making businesses.

If the individual does not have a business, I'll ask for some jewelry or furs to hold, kind of like a security blanket. In the final analysis, though, there is muscle. It's there, everyone knows it's there, you don't really want to use it, and the customer really doesn't want you to. So people generally pay back.

When you borrow money from a shy he doesn't ask you what it's for, he couldn't care less. You use it for whatever you want. All he's interested in is how is he going to be paid back, and how fast.

There is almost no limit to the amount of cash you can borrow. The shy's the limit. I know of people who have borrowed a couple of hundred thousand dollars, but these were big financial people, manufacturers and factory owners. They only borrowed the money for a couple of days and they did it because they can get the money quicker from a shy than they can from a bank and there are a lot less questions asked. A big shy can usually come up with whatever amount you need within one day.

One important rule to remember in operating a shylocking business: If you lend money out you'd better be strong enough to collect it. The ability to apply the proper amount of muscle is what separates the amateurs from the professionals. The amateurs try to save money by collecting debts themselves and they really don't know what they're doing. Professionals bring in professionals.

A good muscleman is an individual who never forgets his primary job is to collect a debt, not to beat up some poor sucker. A typical job rarely involves more than a short talk with the slow-paying debtor. Once a customer is convinced the muscle is there he'll almost always pay. It's only when he doubts that it is there that muscle has to be applied.

Almost anybody in the business is capable of running muscle. Strength is not that important, although the tougher an individual looks the less often he has to prove how tough he is. But almost anybody is capable of swinging a baseball bat or an iron pipe.

The most important thing a muscleman has to have is balls. He cannot back down to anyone. I once had a friend by the name of Jack Whelan, who was also known as Jack O'Hara, and nicknamed the "Enforcer," because he was one of the toughest people around. He was an independent muscle. I would estimate he was six feet tall and weighed 240 pounds of rock-solid muscle. He was no fucking weakling. One afternoon Jack and I were having a few drinks and he asked me what I would do if I had to go up against him.

"Go up against you. What else could I do?" I told him. I knew this guy was tougher than me. But how could I afford to back down? The first time a muscleman backs down he's through in the business. The word spreads, and the jobs don't come so easily. There are times a muscleman uses discretion—if a guy's got a gun at my head I'm gonna pay attention to whatever he is saying—but eventually I'm going to catch him without the trigger. I'm no hero, I'll use whatever weapon I can get my hand on, but I can't afford to back down to anybody.

Jack the Enforcer eventually died because he let valor be more important than discretion. He smacked Mickey Cohen in the face right outside the Beverly Wilshire Hotel because Mickey was giving him a hard time about settling a debt. A few weeks later Jack was dead. An Italian guy went away for it, but Mickey set the whole thing up.

My last time out was in 1972. I was hired by a New York shy to collect a $26,000 debt. The customer had been making gargling noises that sounded ominously like "District Attorney" and "Police Department," and I was asked to visit him. I went up to his apartment in the East Seventies and brought along what we call an Arkansas toothpick, which is a knife with a folding blade about an inch long. I knocked on his door and introduced myself and began explaining why he should keep his mouth shut and pay his debts. He was very rude. He interrupted me and said, "I just don't feel like paying twenty percent interest. Under the law that's usury and very illegal."

I agreed that it was illegal. Then I took out the Arkansas toothpick and clipped off a small portion of his right ear. "What I just did is also illegal," I explained. "I'll be back tomorrow. If you pay me you can keep the rest of your ear. If you don't pay me I'll have to take it with me. Then the next day I'll take your other ear. Then we'll start on your fingers."

I could see he was upset but not panicky. "And if you go to the cops we'll skip the little pieces and I'll just take your whole body."

He understood.

There is really no set price for providing muscle. It depends on how large the debt is and how difficult it will be to collect. A good muscleman can make himself $100,000 a year without too much trouble, which is why amateur shys end up attempting to do the job themselves or hire low-cost junkies. A professional will charge you anywhere from $100 to $1000 for breaking a leg. (You're not actually going after one particular leg or both legs, you're just swinging the bat and letting the pieces fall where they may.) But some junkie kid, who needs the money desperately, may do the job for $25. But these are incompetent, unstable individuals who don't have any idea what they're doing.

I personally get $500 for the first swing with a baseball bat. If I'm hired to work somebody over with what we call a shalmin, which is a pipe wrapped in a newspaper (to prevent cuts), I might get as much as $1000. I will very rarely take a muscle job from a civilian shy, because I can't be sure he'll back me up if I'm bothered by the police. I knew a guy named Funzi once who worked almost exclusively for amateurs—he had to because he was so dumb professionals wouldn't touch him. One day I was kidding him about how stupid he was and he got pissed off. He said he was as smart as any man in the social club on that particular day. I asked him what his IQ was.

"Twenty-twenty," he sneered. So help me.

Sometimes an amateur will be smart enough to obtain good muscle and he begins cutting into organization business. When that happens mob muscle is turned on them and they are advised to leave the business. If they don't they are thrown out.

A very unusual thing happened to me in just such a situation. I was hired by an organization shy to convince some amateur he was in the wrong business. I met the amateur and I was very cordial and I suggested he go into another line. About a week later I was informed he had not taken my advice, so I went back to see him. This time I brought my 32-ounce Louisville Slugger with me. I did a job on the guy, nothing permanent, but enough to get the point across. Now this guy got smart. He knew who I was and he was going to get even with me. He was going to hire his own muscle to work me over—and show the mob that he was tough enough to run his own operation. So he called a friend of his and, without mentioning my name, told him he wanted somebody hurt. This friend told him he wasn't interested in the job but would find somebody for him. The price was $1500.

He called me. As soon as he gave me the guy's name I realized what the situation was: I was going to be hired to beat myself up! I called the guy and he told me that he wanted me beat up. Without mentioning my name I made the deal. I told him to give the money to his friend. After he did I went to visit him again. I said to him, "Listen, punk, normally I would destroy you for what you did. But instead I want this to be a lesson to you. It just cost you fifteen hundred dollars to realize that you're too stupid to be in this business." I took $1000 and gave the third party $500.

• • •

Most people I know will pay their shylock before they'll pay their land-lord. Not only because they are afraid, but because they might want to borrow money again. The heavy gambler, for example, needs money to cover his house expenses, or to gamble some more. He'll always pay his shy back, or he'll pay at least the vig, so he can borrow money to gamble again. A legitimate businessman, who may have gotten caught in a switch and needs money in a hurry, he'll always pay you back because he never knows when he's going to need you a second time. And everyone else will pay back because they are afraid.

Not that there isn't any violence connected with shylocking. There is. We usually frown on killing customers as a matter of common sense—you can't get paid by a dead man. Occasionally, though, a very stupid indi-vidual will come along who thinks he can get away without paying. One of these was a gentleman by the name of Frankie Palermo, an ex-boxer who lived in the Bronx. Frankie was a tough kid, but a nice kid. He used to play cards, which is good. He was not a very good cardplayer, which is bad. So he got into hock and he had to borrow a large amount of money from these people up in Fordham and, as time went by, he never made a move to pay them back. He figured, I'm Frankie Palermo and I don't have to pay you back. They asked him for the money a few times, and there were a number of altercations. He was pretty good with his fists, so it was tough to hurt him that way. Finally his creditors got fed up, they figured out they weren't going to get paid, so they killed him. They gunned him down in the back room of a candy store, right in the middle of a Hershey bar. He had warnings, they tried to work something out with him, and then more warnings. When they sent guys over to see him he wound up punching them out. What else could they do but kill him?

About the same thing happened to Frankie Bonavena. Only he took the money and moved. He moved from the Bronx all the way to Brooklyn, which shows you how smart he was. The shy put out a contract for him. One day somebody spotted him at a racetrack and followed him home and never said a word, just blew his head right off. These things happen. You don't cross people, because if you do, you're going to get hurt.

Sometimes a guy is willing but not able. That's okay. If a guy borrows money and there is a legitimate reason he can't pay it back immediately, most shys will work with him. If a man has a problem and it is really an honest one, chances are he won't even be charged additional interest. For example, a guy borrows $1000 and all of a sudden he can't pay because somebody got sick, or he lost his job. We understand this, we won't nail a guy for this. It happens.

A guy I know borrowed $3000 from a shy. The next week he bet $4000 into a bookie operation that worked with this particular shy, and he lost every penny of it. When the time came to pay the bookmaker he says, "Look, I gotta be honest with you. I can't pay. I took a shot with you because I had to. I got this son who has a distorted spine that has to be operated on and I thought I could raise the money for the operation this way."

Now he has $3000 from the shy, which he hasn't touched, and he's down $4000 to this bookie. He figured if he won he could pay the doctor the $9000 the operation would cost. "If my son doesn't get operated on now," he told the bookie, "he's gonna grow up bent."

I was standing there, and the book says, "I'll tell you what, I'm gonna check. If you're telling me the truth nothing is going to happen. But if you're lying you're the one who's gonna end up bent." We took a ride and went up to the hospital and spoke to the doctor, and the guy was telling the truth.

The book—I'm not gonna tell nobody who he is because then people think he's a sucker—paid for the operation, and then cleared this guy's debt with the shylock. He had the guy return the $3000, with no vig; he just told the shy this was one of those things, and the shy didn't say a word. Finally he told the guy, "You don't owe me a thing, but don't ever bet with me again." I felt the book handled the thing right. What did it cost the office? Nine thousand for the operation, plus the $4000 the guy couldn't pay. So, for a total of $13,000, a kid is going to get his shot at life.

Loansharking is illegal, naturally. There are state and federal laws limiting the amount of interest you can charge. The nearest thing to a legal loanshark is called a factor. A factor can charge 20 percent a year interest for your money. What he does is lend businessmen money against what their gross sales are going to be: sales that have already been made, but not paid for. In other words, a factor gives his customer 80 percent of the money owed to him, and then the payments are diverted to him through an agreement. The Tannenbaum people, who used to own Yonkers Raceway, made their money as factors. This is perfectly legal.

But shylocking is strictly illegal. You can wind up in a big jam for shying. You can get two years from federal courts if you cross state lines and an additional stay from most states. But good shys very rarely get caught, because their customers very rarely go to the police.

Enter the occasional joker again, the idiot who figures he can cancel his debt by making one quick phone call and getting the loanshark arrested. This type of reasoning is very bad for an individual's health. When the cops come all a shy has to do is deny that he is dealing in money. Let them prove it. The guy who makes the call figures the cops will get the shy off his back, but he is wrong. The shy will wait six months, a year, whatever it takes, and then nail him. One silly customer went to the cops on a shy I used to work with. The cops came and picked the shy up and charged him with the beef. He had to go for a bondsman, he had to go for an attorney, but he finally beat the case. After the thing had settled down he waited about a year and then he visited this guy and put him in the hospital for two and a half months. When this guy got out of the hospital the shy was standing in the lobby waiting for him. "I'm gonna tell you straight. You are nothing but a motherfucking stool pigeon. I want my money and you are gonna pay me interest for all this time that I didn't get paid. The next time you ain't gonna be lucky enough to go to the hospital." He figured out the amount and it was high. He had the guy working two jobs, in the daytime as a counterman in a luncheonette and at night he had the guy driving a cab. He made this guy live on next to nothing for about two years, until he got every cent he was owed. In my opinion this guy had it coming. When he needed the money he knew where to go, so you figure he's got to know where to go to pay it back.

One of the real advantages of this particular business is that you don't have to pay protection to the police. Cops don't know who you are. I know a guy that's a butcher, for example, as well as a shylock. He makes a hell of a lot more money cutting himself in on mob business than on cutting meat. The money he lends out comes from the mob. But as far as the cops and most of his customers are concerned, this guy is a butcher, period.

Most people would be amazed at how many shys there are in almost every big city. You can find a shy through your local bookie, your numbers runner. If you're a legitimate businessman, chances are one of the people who work in your building, your maintenance men or elevator operators, can tell you where to find one. Most shys don't carry cards that say, "John Jones, Shylock," but a large number also operate legitimate businesses. They may own a luncheonette, a shoe store. One of the biggest guys in New York City operated out of a plumbing supply business. A guy who owns a large dress manufacturing company on Seventh Avenue in New York told me that he would be glad to finance a proposition or two.

The only thing I don't like about this business is it gets lonely. None of your customers are very happy to see you. Either they're borrowing, which isn't fun, or they're paying back, which is less fun.

I'll tell you another thing; nobody cries at a shylock's funeral. His customers are very happy to see him die, because the business dies with him. Who the hell knows who owes who? Most shys have no partners, just employees, so who is going to collect the money? His wife? There's nothing she can do unless she wants to go see somebody and convince them to move in on the deal, and chances are they aren't going to bother. But even though they'll applaud at his funeral, very few customers try to make the death premature. Shys don't get killed by their customers.

CHAPTER *6*

THE BUSINESS OF PLEASURE

There are probably more dirty minds in this country than there are trees. Behind closed doors or in dark, crowded bars and lofts, your so-called honest citizen likes nothing more than to see a pair of big tits or a little fucking, and as long as he is willing to pay to see it organized crime will be there to supply it to him. As the mob learned a long time ago: One man's pornography is another man's profit.

As with just about all other mob businesses, the pornography market was created by a conflict between what people wanted and what the government said they were legally allowed to have.

Recently the Supreme Court changed the marketing picture. By failing to define exactly what pornography is, the court has made just about everything legal. Since the mob was already firmly entrenched in the area it was no problem to take items that had previously been sold under the counter and put them up on top. Although the Supreme Court ruling enabled some legitimate people to get into the industry, it also opened the doors for the mob to make more money.

Probably the best example is the motion picture *Deep Throat*. This is a simple love story about a cute little freckled-face girl who, through a freak of Mother Nature, ended up with her clitoris nine inches into her throat. Therefore she can only have an orgasm by chewing on a particular part of the male body. The movie is well made and funny in places. (My favorite line has a chick asking the man, "Mind if I smoke while you're eating?") And there is no doubt it is completely pornographic. A few years ago *Deep Throat* could only have been shown behind closed curtains at the Elks Club or on some fraternity-house wall. Today it is the attraction in over 80 theaters all across America.

"Certain people" put up $26,000 to pay for the production. The film itself was shot in Florida and took two and a half weeks to make. Normally the people who make these things can expect to gross as much as half a million, but *Deep Throat* just took off. Within the first six months of its release *Throat* has grossed over three million dollars! Seeing the movie has become *the* thing to do. There are lines outside almost every theater showing it. And the people on these lines are not your porno freaks, they are regular, legitimate people: businessmen and secretaries, husbands and wives, boy and girlfriends, boy and boyfriends. In New York a group of United Nations delegates took it all in.

Deep Throat is a perfect example of what I have been saying. You give people what they want and they will pay almost anything for it. Theaters are charging more to see this picture than was generally charged to see *The Godfather*.

Throat is only the first of the porno films to hit big. People will remember and talk about it for years. This is the "Gone with the Windpipe" of dirty flicks. . . .

Organized crime started getting into the pornography market in a big way in the very early 1950s. We have been in soft-cover book importing and printing, playing cards, producing and selling movies, selling sex items like rubber tits and French ticklers, running sex shows and topless and bottomless bars, bookstores, massage parlors, key clubs and even the quarter-per-play peep shows.

The mob has been in both the straight and homosexual markets and, believe it or not, percentagewise, the homosexual market is more profitable because we can charge more money for the same stuff.

Every item in a porno shop is a major profit-maker. A deck of playing cards, for example, the traditional "French deck," can be purchased for as little as a quarter per and sold for as much as five dollars. Still photos are even cheaper and go for a minimum of two dollars each. That's not even mentioning high-profit items like books, films and sex equipment.

There are some real advantages to working in pornography. Number one, you don't need a great amount of cash to get started. Number two, there is little problem with the police. Your privacy is protected by the Constitution of the United States. Even if you get caught, the laws are so hard to interpret or enforce that very few people are ever convicted of anything. Number three, for the same reasons there is no bribery or contracts necessary. Number four, there is little violence in this area because it is so wide open. There is no such thing as "owning an area" because there is more than enough business to keep everyone happy. Number five, once a product is finished, a movie or a book for example, you can continue to make money from it for a long time, rather than a quick hit here and a quick hit there. Finally, this is an area where you are making people happy and having fun yourself. Your business is pleasure.

I first got involved in pornography while I was working for Jack Dragna on the Coast. A friend of his, Charlie the Bull, who had been sent to prison with Lucky Luciano, had gotten out and opened a bookstore in New York. The name of the place was the Busy Bee and it was on 42nd Street between Broadway and Avenue of the Americas. It was a sex bookstore within the confines of what the law allowed in the late '50s, but a regular customer could get any kind of book, magazine, deck of cards or sex item he wanted.

Charlie had come out to California to make arrangements with Jack to get his merchandise smuggled in from Europe to Mexico, transported from Mexico to California and eventually to New York. My job was to take care of him while he was out there, see that his business went well and get him broads, booze and whatever else he wanted. This is how I learned about this industry.

Unfortunately, Charlie got himself into a real jackpot while he was out there. He started banging some 15-year-old broad. When he first told me about her I didn't believe him because Charlie was always bragging about his sexual abilities. In fact, at one point I thought the expression "cock and bull" referred to Charlie's sex stories. Only this time he wasn't making it up. I found that out when he was arrested.

Because I was responsible for him, his problem became my problem. Since he was out on parole at the time he had what you might call a dilemma. I got to the girl's family and explained to them that if they wanted to make a big deal out of it I was willing to help. I would get them all the publicity they wanted. I swore that I'd see to it that their sweet little kid would be blasted all over every newspaper in the country. I don't know if I could have done as much as I threatened, but they believed me. The kid wasn't available when the case was called. Eventually the charges were dropped and Charlie took his books and films and went back East. But some guys can't stay out of trouble. He was sentenced to a year in the can for sending pornography through the mails, and while he was in prison he caught pneumonia and eventually died from it.

As I learned from Charlie, the book business is a consistent money-maker. I can get a copy of a book, bring it to a New York printer I know, and have him print me up as many copies as I need for as little as 45 or 50 cents apiece. Then I can turn around and sell them for between two and five dollars each, depending on the length and whether it is illustrated or not. I'll tell you what I used to do. I would have 20 different books sent from Denmark to Mexico. Then I would make a deal with a printer for about 20,000 copies. I would peddle the books for $3 each or run a giant, super bargain sale and sell the whole set for $50.

With the Supreme Court decisions and the resulting competition from legitimate publishers putting hard sex books on the shelves, our people began looking around for something new to bring customers in. That's when peep shows first came on the scene. These are simply the old-time nickel movie machines, but now they're showing sex films, or parts of sex films. You put a quarter in and see a few minutes of a film. The film usually runs out just as the girl is reaching down to take off her panties. So to see the rest of her action, you have to put another quarter in. These quarters add up. In fact, when the owners of the machines split the take with the owners of the stores, they don't bother to waste time counting them. They get a balance scale and divide the profit by weight.

One of the first people to get into the machine business, a guy named Tex, came to me in 1965 when he was just getting established and hired me for protection. He was putting his machines into a store on Seventh Avenue between 47th and 48th Streets. There were a lot of new companies springing up and competing for business and he expected trouble. He gave me a good price and I took the job.

I was standing in the store when two strong-arms walked in. Fortunately for everyone, one of them was a guy I used to bum with. He asked me what I was doing there, and I told him, "I'm a partner in this firm."

"In that case I guess we have no business to do here," he said, and they turned around and walked out. Tex never had trouble. Eventually he became one of the biggest people in the business. He must have had 750 machines in operation and had to be making a minimum of five and a half million dollars—in quarters—a year. But Tex was also a heavy gambler and he eventually blew the whole wad. I think he's got one store today.

About the same time you had the introduction of live sex shows. These shows advertise "simulated sex," and that's exactly what they give. They get a guy in a jockstrap and a girl in maybe pasties and a loincloth and they go through every sex act known to man—only in simulation. Sounds and everything, but all fake. You'll find there are thousands of yo-yos who will pay five dollars to watch this type of show. An individual I occasionally spend time at the track with had a place on Eighth Avenue between 43rd and 44th Streets. His nickname was "Dirty Morris." "Dirty" would open his show at 11 A.M. and close it at 3 A.M. the next morning. He changed girls about every two weeks, and he never had any trouble finding "actresses" because he paid them about $300 a week. Men had to be replaced more often; even in a jock it was tougher on them. These people got good money and they really earned it, they had to work 16 hours a day, seven days a week. But "Dirty" could afford to pay big salaries. He told me that on a good day he could do close to $2000 worth of business. Say he averaged between eight and ten thousand dollars a week—that's almost half a million a year. So you see why the mob gets involved in this area.

The big pornography market today is still in hard-core porn, usually stag films, or what we call skin flicks. This is the area in which I have personally done the most work. I've smuggled films in, I've sold films and I have even produced one. Joey B. DeMille. There is a great deal of money to be made in movies. You can produce a roll of film, the whole production, for as little as $3000. From that one roll you can make maybe 10,000 duplicate reels which can be sold wholesale for three, four or five dollars a reel. The retailer who buys it from you can sell it, in turn, for as much as $25 or $50 per reel depending on who he is doing business with. I once bought a case of films: 100 reels for $100. I peddled them for $25 each, or a total of $2500. I was making $24 a reel, which is a nice tidy profit. And who was doing the buying? A nice fellow from Pleasantville, another from Larchmont. They want to have a party, they want to have friends in, and they need some entertainment. I'd supply it for them . . . for $25. I even sold one roll to a priest . . . and another one featuring group sex to a policeman.

I also made good money when I had a load of homosexual films. I would walk into a fag bar that the mob owns down in Greenwich Village and tell them I had the stuff with the boys, and they would eat it up. I could charge them anything I wanted to. Today there are both overground and underground markets for stag films. By law legitimate movie theaters are permitted to show *any* film that has "redeeming social value." (Personally, I have never seen a skin flick which could not be redeemed for many times its value.) The key is to make sure the film has some sort of plot. The plot can be almost anything. I saw one full-length feature that consisted of a day in the life of a mailman. All he did was go from one house to another and fuck whoever was home at the time. But this is considered a plot and it would be very difficult for a DA to show that it didn't have "social value." As long as that X rating is shown, there is nothing the police can do to stop the showing of that film.

The underground market consists of direct sales to private individuals. These films need have no social value at all and never do. There are two ways to market a stag film, rental or outright sale. A lot of guys like to rent them, especially the longer ones, but I never did that. I liked to get rid of them quickly, so I always sold. Renting is a problem because then you have to use the mails, and the mails can get you in trouble. Usually no one knows what's in a plain brown package, but if it should be opened by the wrong person you can get in more trouble than it's worth. A lot of people have tried to get around the law by using United Parcel, but that is a lot more expensive and time consuming.

It is easy to produce a pornographic motion picture. What you do is find a guy who has no real qualms about being paid for getting blown and laid with people looking on and find a couple of broads that this means nothing to or that desperately need some money. Hiring girls is a lot easier than I thought it would be. Surprisingly, very few of the girls who make these movies are hookers. They are almost all straight girls and make these movies because they need a few extra dollars. They may fuck to get the job, but they're not out-and-out prostitutes. In fact, some of them are married and have families. Occasionally a woman may be forced to "star" in a film. She may have borrowed from a guy, or bet with a guy, and had trouble paying him back, so he would suggest she work in his film.

The plot is pretty standard: Boy meets girl, boy goes to bed with girl. Or with two girls, or a broad goes to bed with two guys, or just two guys go to bed, or just two girls, or some combination thereof. For suspense maybe they gotta find a bed. There really is no plot in an underground flick, just in and out, in and out. Every once in a while we throw in a little sadomasochism, whips and leather and beatings and that stuff.

Technically these films have been improving over the years. When I first started in pornography, films were made in black and white, poorly lighted, grainy and badly filmed. The camera just focused on one scene and never moved. Today a lot of these films are made by competent professionals, using good equipment in rented lofts. They are well lighted, sometimes use sound and are often in color. They end-cut from scene to scene and fade in and out, just like what you see in the movies. Only the sex is still the same as it used to be.

I made my film in a loft on Greene Street in downtown Manhattan. We rented the whole fifth floor for the weekend, even though we knew we'd only be there one day. The first thing I did was hire my technical people: a cameraman-director, two electricians to control the wiring and lighting, a "writer" to outline the action, and a sound man for the audio. Then I went out to hire my actresses. As I said, it was easier than I thought. I called a friend who operates a legitimate model agency and told him I was looking for broads to use in a movie I was making. "Go no further, my friend, here is a list of broads who haven't eaten in a week," he said. I called four of them and not one of them said no. The guys were even easier to find. They're getting paid to fuck—there are worse jobs.

Everyone showed up at 9:30 Saturday morning. I locked the building carefully. When you're making a stag film you don't want anybody coming who's not supposed to. There wasn't one person in the world who was going to get through those steel doors. By four that afternoon we had finished shooting. The day's total was six complete, totally different motion pictures. Shooting films like these is easy because you don't have to worry about rehearsals. Everything came naturally, so to speak. I used seven men and four women. If you're going to have more balling than blowing, you need more men than women. The girls can go all day, but you have to have a steady supply of hardons. The thing I had to do all day was keep those hardons coming. What I did was set up chairs on the side of the room, and when an actor wasn't performing he sat there and watched the action. None of the men had any trouble getting it up the first time. The second time seemed a little more difficult, and the third time we started having our problems. By then I was carefully rotating them, and then, as one of the men sitting on the side felt himself getting aroused he would raise his hand and I would rush him into the scene.

Finally, when nobody could get it going, we concentrated on letting the girls really get into one another. The girls seemed to love every minute of it, but those poor guys had to be dead when they left. It's not easy to put in a whole day in bed, and then have to go home and go to bed.

Technically, my films were pretty decent. The only audio we used was to further what I jokingly referred to as the plot: The phone would ring, the doorbell would chime, occasional dialogue and sexual feelings, you know, grunts and groans.

After we finished, our actors and actresses just got dressed and left. I don't remember anyone taking anyone else's phone number. One girl wanted to leave a little early because she had a date that evening. These people were really professionals. Now I'm a professional too, but the way this was done really threw me. Most of these girls were 18, 19, 20 years old. They either love sex or they're broke and most of them are aspiring actresses. That was quite a day, six aspiring actresses and one perspiring producer.

Some of the people who perform in these pornos do eventually go on to bigger things. Two of the biggest sex goddesses in Hollywood started this way, and one of the most famous old-time sex stars once made a fabulous sex movie with a horse, which made it difficult for her to go on to anything bigger! You can still buy nude photos of a lot of your big stars taken right from porno movie prints.

Television police shows would like you to believe that there is a lot of blackmail going on in this area, that agents are running all over trying to buy up every copy of early nude photographs of their now-famous clients. But I've never heard of or seen any of it. These things never hurt a girl, or a guy, once they've made it in legitimate films.

The most recent advance in the industry has been the introduction of massage parlors on a widespread scale. I would say at least 100 have opened in New York alone since the middle of 1971, and the mob is at least partners in the great majority of them. These massage parlors follow in the finest tradition of "body painting studios" and "portrait studios with live models." The parlor operation is beautiful: A man goes into one of these places and pays anywhere from $7.50 to $25.00 for a 15-minute massage. He picks the girl he wants and she takes him to a private room or booth. These girls are usually hookers, but they never proposition a customer. If he wants more than the massage he has to bring up the subject and specifically ask for it. Only after he starts the conversation will the girl negotiate with him and set a price for whatever he wants. The wonderful thing about this is that once he asks for it the girl has nothing to worry about. Even if he is an undercover cop, this is considered entrapment and any case will be thrown out of court.

Massage parlors come in all possible variations. There are some in the Times Square area that are nothing more than old offices divided up with wooden paneling and "furnished" with mattresses on the floor. There are others that are complete with swimming pool, water beds, closed-circuit television, scantily clad "hostesses" serving drinks, and private "massage" rooms with film projection equipment.

In New York this industry was created by the state legislature when they changed the state law and opened the field of massage to nonprofessionals. For the mob, which stays away from regular prostitution houses in most cases, this was an open invitation. A few independents opened up first and did very well. Once the organization saw this was a profit-making business they moved in.

When the state gets around to closing the porno movie places and massage parlors, the mob will go into the "key" club business. "Key clubs" are private, operate in hotels, apartments and brownstones, and offer the customer just about anything his heart or prick desires. There are gay clubs, straight clubs, clubs for people who like group sex, clubs for people who like weird sex, clubs for people who just want to get a drink after the bars close—you name what you want and somebody will open a private club for you. Most members join these clubs through the recommendation of a friend who is already a member. There is an initiation fee of usually between $100 and $250, which supposedly covers the first year, but many of these clubs are put out of business before the year is up. There are, however, no refunds.

CHAPTER *7*

BETTORS, BOOKIES AND BOOKMAKING

ambling is really the world's oldest profession: Whatever else the first hooker in history was laying, she was also laying odds she wouldn't get caught. Gambling is something man has always done and always will do. It is part of human nature, and no man-made laws are going to change the fact that most people are willing to bet on anything, anytime, with anyone.

Bookmaking, the business of providing a place for those people who want to gamble to put their money down, is the grand old crime of the organization. Other businesses have come and gone, but bookmaking has remained a simple, relatively safe, always exciting, challenging and profitable business.

In my career I have known at least 15 books who have become millionaires . . . and I've only heard of one honest bookmaker who died in the line of duty. In this business it's the slow-paying customers who disappear, the bookies live forever. Except one.

I was working as a runner for a New York operation in the early 1960s. A man who had been betting with me for over two years dropped a small bundle on the World Series and we made arrangements to meet in a coffee shop on 78th Street and First Avenue. He was in the middle of his second cup when I got there. I sat down, and he handed me $1500. I started to get up to leave, but he said, "Wait." So I sat down. I could see he had something on his mind. Finally he blurted it out. "I've heard you do hits. I have a job I want done."

As I said, I knew this guy for two years and I knew he was a stand-up guy. I might have considered doing the job for him, but I was not about to admit that I was a hit man. I told him he had probably heard a vicious rumor that had been going around about me. "I don't do hits," I said. "But I have a close friend who does."

He understood. "How much would your close friend charge?"

"The going-away price is twenty thousand dollars."

He almost choked on his coffee. "You're crazy," he said. "I can see two thousand dollars or three thousand dollars. But twenty thousand dollars?"

I didn't care either way. I said, "Listen, pal, it's an old story. You get what you pay for. I'm sure you can find some addict for two thousand dollars, but my friend won't even pick up a gun for less than twenty thousand dollars." I knew we weren't going to do business, so just out of curiosity I asked him who he wanted to hit.

"My grocery clerk."

I laughed. "You must really hate this guy."

"Yeah," he laughed right back, "he overcharged me on a jar of pickles."

Then I proceeded to forget about his offer. About three weeks later a bookie was killed and his body washed up on the shore. I knew it wasn't a professional job from the details in the newspaper, but I never made the connection between my customer and this book. One afternoon a month or so later I picked up the *Daily News* and there was my customer's picture spread right across the front page. He had done the job himself! He went to trial and was convicted. There is only one fact in the whole case which really sticks out in my mind. He killed an honest bookmaker because he was too deeply in debt to him. He owed him exactly $20,000.

One other bookmaker I know of disappeared about four years ago. His name was Gil Beckley and he was one of the biggest books in the United States. I don't include him with the guy who was murdered because that guy was straight. I have been led to believe that Mr. Beckley was about to make a deal with the federal government and instead went for a lonely, late-night swim. He must have gotten lost, because no one has seen him since.

Today booking, like pornography, is mainly a geographical crime. It is legal in many countries and in parts of some states. In New York State, for example, it's legal to bet the horses if you place your bet with the state, but it's illegal to bet with a bookie. This is ridiculous. It seems to me that the only criminal thing about betting on horses in New York is that the state is depriving the people of the right to bet with the bookie of their choice.

Bookmaking is a service industry. The organization does not force anybody to gamble: We simply provide the service for those people who want to. We tell people we're available if they want to bet, just like Macy's and Gimbels are available to anybody who wants to walk in and buy merchandise. Of course, in order to provide this service we have to deal with the problems of graft and corruption, but these could be eliminated—or at least sharply reduced—if the government would take its head out of its ass and give the people what they want.

There is no doubt gambling is what the people want. Look at Las Vegas, the Bahamas, London, Monte Carlo; everywhere you have legalized gambling you have a constant stream of customers coming and going and spending. Look at New York. When the state opened its Off Track Betting operation the only problem they had was trying to keep the computers running fast enough to record all the action.

I've been partners in a few offices and worked as a runner in some others, and believe me, I know that people want to gamble. The last office I worked in, for example, you would classify as medium-sized. We had three phones and betweeen 20 and 25 runners on the street. On a typical Sunday during the football season we would handle seven or eight million dollars' worth of action. Multiply that by maybe 50 offices in the New York metropolitan area alone and you come up with a respectable figure. Overall, throughout the whole country, I guarantee you there is more than two *billion* dollars bet every football Sunday. And it's not just football. On an average day during the baseball season you may get $30 or 40 million in the New York area alone. I would not even care to guess what the handle on basketball and the horses is, but it's tremendous. That's why so many bookmakers do so well, and so few ever go out of business.

Not that they win all the time. One Monday during football season I bumped into this guy Ruby, who is one of the biggest bookies in the country. He was really down in the dumps, and I was not about to make his life easier. The last time we were together we had made some silly bet and he lost a shirt to me. He hadn't come across with the shirt yet. Instead of saying hello I asked him, "Where's my shirt?"

He screamed, "Fuck your shirt. I lost two hundred thousand dollars yesterday and you're shitting about some shirt?"

"Okay, okay, I'll settle for yours." I started unbuttoning his shirt. He promised to pay off. And he did.

Opening a bookmaking office is neither an expensive or complicated proposition. All you need is permission from the boss who controls the area, contacts in the police department and eventually a regular contract, a place to lay off your action, an office, telephones, clerks, a place to get a good daily line, runners, customers and, occasionally, collectors.

If an area is not too saturated with offices and you seem to have the ability to run a good shop, it's not too difficult to get permission to operate. Chances are you'll have to take the boss who controls the area in as your partner, but in return he'll make sure you have the proper insurance coverage.

A lot of one-man operators think they can do without this permission and protection. They open up one phone and go to work handling just a few customers. Chances are they are going to be shut down within a few weeks because some guy who is operating a larger office and paying protection is going to find out about him and pick up the telephone and call his police contact. Goodbye, independent, no violence required.

It is a fact of life that as long as you have illegal gambling you have to have payoffs in order to keep going. The politician at the top can be anyone from a councilman to a state assemblyman to even the mayor of New York. When Bill O'Dwyer was the mayor, for example, he made more money from gambling than any bookmaker or bettor, but he made sure all the bookmakers were protected. Whoever the top man is, his influence has to be strong enough to reach into every level of the police department. Most of the time the local bookie never finds out how many people are sharing his payments. The only individual he actually deals with is the cop who makes the collections. Hundreds, thousands of cops are on the pad and they do their job, they keep bookmaking safe for the bookmaker.

The price usually depends on the number of telephones in operation or the number of runners on the street. Some offices only take bets over the phones and their runners don't carry any paperwork that could implicate them. So they pay by the phone. One place I know on Long Island, for example, had three phones and they were paying $2500 per phone per week, so you know the police and politicians were making money there. Other operations actually have their runners take business on the street and they pay per runner. Either way, every operation is going to be paying off.

Besides, cops are just like everybody else. They bet like it's legal.

One thing every bookmaker must have is a place where he can cover his action, lay off his bets. One problem with bettors is that they let sentimentality interfere with good common sense. In New York, for example, people bet mostly on the Yankees and the Mets and the Knicks and Rangers and the Giants and the Jets. When these teams are winning, New York bookies have a problem, which is why they need a place to spread the action around. People in Detroit bet Detroit, in Chicago they bet Chicago, and so on. So what happens when New York is playing Detroit is the New York books and the Detroit books will get together and look to get in the middle, so that each of them is holding as much Detroit action as New York action. That way the worst a book can do is make the service charge, which is known as the vig, or break even. The man who ran the national clearinghouse for laying off was Meyer Lansky. He received action from bookies all over the country and helped them cover both sides. If he didn't want to handle your action you would have to go shopping from city to city to make your deals, and there just isn't time for that. So Meyer became everybody's partner.

Meyer Lansky may be the smartest man in the history of organized crime. He has a mind that makes a computer look like a second grader, and it has brought him riches and power. Even today, with the government hounding him because of a tax problem and some missing gambling money, he is probably the most powerful mobster in the world. Nobody, but nobody, defies Uncle Meyer, and anyone who thinks he can has a very short life ahead of him. Bugsy Siegel tried and Bugsy Siegel died. I can't prove Meyer had it done, I don't even want to. But long ago Meyer learned how to eliminate every problem, be it mathematical or human.

I worked for him on and off from 1962 through 1970. I traveled all over the country collecting his share of the proceeds from various gambling enterprises. I was what you would call a coordinator. I made sure things were running smoothly and that money that was supposed to be there was there. I also did a little collecting from losing customers who were reluctant to pay.

Meyer made his fortune in the gambling industry. Not only does he finance a giant lay-off operation, he also supplied protection and equipment to individuals interested in starting their own businesses. He literally took a place in the desert and made an oasis out of it—it's called Las Vegas. I was with him down in Miami Beach one Friday and he made me a small wager that he could predict within five percent the number of rooms that would be filled—*hotel by hotel*—in Vegas for the coming weekend. And to make it more interesting he also said he could figure within $20,000 the total amount that would be bet in Vegas during the weekend. I took the bet. Meyer made one phone call—he called a friend in Vegas to find out what the weather forecast for the weekend was—and then wrote his estimates down. We checked the following Tuesday; he won easily.

Besides creating Vegas, Meyer Lansky also saved the economy of several countries, the Bahamas for instance, by putting honest gambling in. No one has ever been cheated in an establishment run by Meyer Lansky. Actually he has no reason to cheat; in the end everyone beats themselves anyway.

I first met him in 1962. A friend of mine in New York had informed him that I used to work for Dragna. Meyer asked me to come down to

Miami. The first time I saw him was in a place called the Colonial Club. He was wearing a gray-checked sport jacket, a light-blue sports shirt open at the collar and a pair of dark blue slacks. Physically Meyer is a small man, about five foot four, and he speaks in a New York accent with just a trace of Russian. I recognize this combination because my father used to talk in the same way. I was introduced to him, and he said, "I understand you're a heavyweight." That's a man who has killed people.

I told him that I had done some work from time to time.

He offered me a job doing whatever he thought necessary. The starting salary was $2000 a week plus expenses, plus extra compensation for any heavy work that I did. I worked for him until the day he left for Israel in 1970.

I got to know Meyer fairly well during those eight years. I never ceased being amazed by his mind, by his ability to make important decisions very quickly—and almost always make the right one. I would guess that today Meyer must be worth close to a billion dollars.

Although he isn't known for his sense of humor he does have a kind of wit. I remember sitting with him once watching a football game, and one team was destroying the other. "Don't worry, kid," he said. "As soon as they get their new running backs in they're going to be great."

I asked him who the new backs were. He paused and smiled. "Smith and Wesson," he finally said.

I laughed. I thought it was funny.

Once you have your police and political contracts and a place to lay off some of your action, you have to get set up. The days of operating out of the back of a small candy store are long gone. Most operations are too big and use too much mechanical equipment for that.

The majority of small bookmaking operations are set up in apartments or office buildings. Usually the man who's going to run the operation will rent a place or find some housewife or family with an extra room that either owes him money or wants to make some. If he "moves in" with a family he'll pay them as much as $100 a week, take care of their phone bill and come and go as he wants. He won't bother these "landlords" in any way and for a few dollars a month he's got himself a quiet, well-hidden base of operations.

If he wants to be extra careful he'll set up a backstrap phone system. This is simply a matter of running an extension off the phone installed by the phone company and putting it in another apartment or building. He has to find two places, one for the original phone and one for the extension.

In the old days everyone knew where the local neighborhood office was and could walk in off the street and make his bet. The results would be posted on a big blackboard in front of a cigar-smoke-filled room, and there was always a mess of people moving in and out. Those operations were the real grandfather of Off Track Betting, but they had to close down when Congress passed a law that said all gamblers had to buy a tax stamp, a law that was eventually ruled unconstitutional (ha! ha!) because it forced the bookies to incriminate themselves.

The biggest bookmaking operation I ever saw was located at 179th and Oak Street in the Bronx during the early 1960s. They had taken two stores and made one big room out of them. It was just like a social club, curtains on the windows and an old dilapidated front door. But inside ticker tapes gave up-to-the-minute results, and they served coffee. You could just walk in there and meet your friends, place a bet and relax. They must have had 20 phones going, besides their street trade, and I wouldn't want to owe the taxes they didn't pay. It was no secret that they were there, but they paid their police bills so they were never bothered. The only time the cops came near the place was when they wanted to bet.

Phones are the key to any operation. Obviously the more phones you have, the more work you can handle. The size of an office is measured in terms of the number of working phones, an average office having two or three. There are a number of different ways to set these phones up, depending on how safe you feel you have to be.

If you are totally secure and your contacts are solid you can simply use the actual phones installed by the phone company. When you first move in you tell them you are setting up a business and need phones with consecutive numbers, which they will supply. The only danger with this system is if the police decide they want you, they can easily find you by tracing your number.

When I operated I would always use a backstrap. Instead of renting one place I would get two. If they were apartments I would get them on separate floors, but located in exactly the same part of the building. In others words, I would have the north corner apartment on the eighth floor and the north corner apartment on the fourth floor. I would usually rent one of them myself and have someone else rent the other one for me. Then I would call the phone company and have them install phones in the eighth-floor apartment only. Once they left I would go to work.

I would bust right through the wall and drop a line down into the fourth-floor apartment, open the wall there, connect the lines and put my extension in. Messing around with electronics is my only real hobby, so I had no problem doing this work. Then I would close up the walls in both apartments, so there would be no way of tracing the extensions that were connected to the first phone. After it was set up, if the law was ever to get wind that I was operating and they wanted to make trouble, they would go to the eighth floor and all they would find is an empty apartment and some telephones. They would have no idea where the phones led to because the wall would be all sealed up. They would hear the phone ringing, pick it up and be able to hear me speaking, and they wouldn't be able to do a damn thing about it. By the time they found the extensions I'd be long gone.

You don't need two apartments to do this; you can actually run a wire from almost anywhere to almost anywhere. I set up a backstrap on Long Island once that ran a total of three blocks. I went through the basement of one house, through a 30-foot sewer duct, and finally up a telephone pole and into another house three blocks away. I stank like hell after going through that sewer, but we ended up with an almost undetectable line.

A second system that is often used, and is easier to set up than a backstrap, is a call-back system. A call-back system means using a third telephone as a middle phone. When a customer calls the number he'll either get a woman at some home phone or an answering service. The customer will say, "This is Mr. Clark for Mr. Star." Generally it's a woman who operates this type of system, either to make some extra bread or because she's in hock. She'll reply, "I'm sorry, Mr. Star isn't at home right now. May I have your phone number and he'll call you back shortly?"

She may receive eight or ten calls like this, and then every ten or fifteen minutes the bookie will call her and say, "This is Mr. Star," or another code name he may use. She will relay all the names and numbers she has, and the clerks in the office will start calling back. They'll call the bettor's number and say, "This is Mr. Star, did someone at this number call me?" The clerks won't ask for the man who called by name, because that would be an open invitation for whoever answered the phone to do anything he wants. The clerk won't ask, "Is this Mr. Clark?" He'll simply say, "This is Mr. Star," and if the man on the other end doesn't give the proper identification the clerk will simply say, "Thank you very much, I'm sorry, I have the wrong number," and hang up.

A call-back system makes it very difficult to trace the office. The only one who could possibly be traced is the girl who is operating the phone, and all she's doing is operating an answering service. The office calls her, she doesn't call in—in fact, she doesn't even know the number of the office—so the law can't get anything from her. The disadvantages of the system are obvious—it takes too much time and there is always the possibility of mistakes being made and bets being lost. Anytime you have to rely on someone outside the organization, like an answering service, you're looking for trouble.

In most offices all bets are recorded on paper and on tape, a method which eliminates a lot of false claims and helps iron out problems. A cassette tape recorder is just hooked right into the phone and records every word. It's a simple mechanical hookup. After the customer calls and makes his bet the clerk will say, "This bet was made at 3:45 P.M. on Thursday, April 16." Now if there is a discrepancy between the office and the customer regarding the bet, the tape will provide the answer. It's usually a foolproof way to settle a beef, but a tape almost got me thrown in jail once.

In this case a guy got hurt needlessly because of the stupidity of a clerk. I know, because I'm the guy who hurt him. I was working for a decent-sized organization and I had a customer whose code name was "Flowers."

It was a good name because he was a florist. He had made a parlay bet that involved the Detroit Tigers and the Oakland Athletics, as well as something like seven other games. He bet Oakland, and the clerk, unfortunately wrote down Detroit. This was the last game of an eight-game parlay, and Flowers won the whole thing. Our records, though, had him losing the last game, which means he lost the whole bet. When I came to collect instead of pay he went nuts, and when I look back on it now, I can understand why. But before he had a chance to really get going I just said, "Wait a minute, let's check with the office."

I called, and the guy who was running the place, a guy named Alex the Beard, started screaming, "He's wrong, he's wrong," like a maniac. I wasn't thinking, mainly because there was all this yelling going on, and I neglected to tell him to check the tape. Meanwhile Flowers is starting to get nasty and abusive, and I wound up picking him up and throwing him through the glass doors of the refrigerator on top of all those pretty flowers. Then I started to work him over pretty good. To make a long story shorter, the cops came in and a cop grabbed me. I didn't know who was grabbing me and I turned around and punched him in the face. The final toll was almost $6000, $1000 going to the cop to keep him from bringing me in, and the rest to cover this guy's medical expenses and repair his shop.

Finally it struck me that I ought to hear the tape. The operation kept it way the hell out on Long Island, far, far away from the office just in case they ever got bothered. I grabbed Alex the Beard and said, "Come on, let's go play the tape!" and it turned out Flowers was right. I blew my fucking top. I grabbed the Beard by the throat and called him every name under the sun. "You are gonna pay that man every dime he's got coming, plus you are gonna pay all his medical expenses and any payoff money it cost me, or so help me I'll break every bone in your body, wait until you come out of the hospital and then I'll kill you!" I was pissed! Then I went to the hospital and apologized to Flowers.

During the betting day, customers will call the office directly to place their bets, or call the system and have the clerk return their call. The clerk is the man who answers the telephone and handles incoming bets and figures out the finances of the office. After the action for the day is over the clerk will figure out who won how much and who lost how much. When a runner calls, the clerk will read him the list of customers and give him their final totals for the day. Then the runner either collects or pays off. For some reason the only people I have ever had any trouble with in bookmaking are the clerks. Generally these are quiet guys who keep mostly to themselves and make a good living. But sometimes they open their mouths and give me grief.

Once in 1966 I had been working for a New York office for about a month. I had maybe 60 customers at that time and none of them ever bet more than $20 on a given day. This one clerk opened his mouth and started spouting off. "What kind of shit are you giving me?" he asked.

I told him, "Listen, these are my customers and they will do their betting as they see fit. Now wait until the end of the week until you open your big mouth."

The boss of the operation got wind of the argument and said to me, "I didn't realize your action was so small; maybe the clerk is right."

"Before you judge it," I told him, "wait until the end of the week. Then you tell me if we're doin' good or we're doin' bad." Sure enough, at the end of the week we win $1800, $900 for the office and $900 for me. None of my customers were big bettors, they never bet more than $20 a day, but every single one of them was on the phone every single day. I stayed with that office nine months and I think I was the only consistent winner.

As a runner, I always preferred to have a lot of small bettors rather than a few big ones. On the surface that doesn't make sense, but the heavyweights can kill you, because if they are half smart and get lucky they can do a death-and-destruction job that might take a year to recover from. I used to work with a runner everybody called Skinny because he weighed about 265 pounds. He was not at all particular about the action he took; whatever anybody wanted to bet he would take. One Sunday he had a guy bet him seven football games at $1000 per, plus all kinds of parlays and round robins. The guy won six of the games and most of his other bets—in all a total of $140,000. It took Skinny almost eight months to get even with the office so he could start earning again. All he got every week was what he needed to live on. At the end of the eight months he had lost so much weight they started calling him Fats. When you have small bettors you can't get hurt that badly on one bad Sunday.

Years ago the clerks had a much easier job because betting was simple: The customer just tried to pick the winner and played the odds. But to encourage more gambling (nobody wants to bet on his favorite team if that team doesn't have a chance) and to offset the chance that the event might be fixed, the "line" was invented. Today most bets are made according to the line, or the point spread. This is the number of points in football and basketball, runs in baseball or goals in hockey that one team is favored over another. The line is actually the betting handicap given to the underdog. If you bet the favorite, in order for you to win, the favorite has to win by more points than the line. You have to "beat the spread." If you bet the underdog to win, the underdog, with the addition of the spread, must score more points than the favorite. If, for example, the spread is Dallas Cowboys by ten points over the New York Giants, the Cowboys must win by more than ten points for those people who bet on them to win. Anything under that and the guy who bet the Giants is a winner. If the Cowboys win by exactly ten, it's a tie (also called a push) as far as both bookies and bettors are concerned, and no money changes hands. To eliminate ties, a lot of spreads include half-points: If the Cowboys are a 10 1/2-point favorite over the Giants there is no possibility of a push.

The service charge (the vig) guarantees the office will be able to cover its expenses. It's ten percent of the bet, and you pay it only when you lose. So if you bet $100 and win, you only win the full $100. If you bet $100 and lose, it costs you $110. It's because of the vig that most books try to get an even amount of action on both teams. If $100 was bet on the Giants and $100 was bet on the Cowboys, the office ends up with $10 profit no matter who wins, because the winner is going to receive $100 and the loser is going to owe $110.

Betting on baseball, which a whole lot of people do, is a little more complicated. There is some betting by the line (the number of runs), but since most baseball teams are reasonably matched most betting is done by odds. In betting by odds, five is the key figure; everything is based on five. If you call and tell your bookie you want to bet the Yankees ten times, that's ten times five dollars, or a $50 bet. The odds are also based on five dollars. For example, if the Yankees are playing the Cleveland Indians the odds might read something like "Yankees 8 to 9." The favorite (the Yankees) is always mentioned first, but the points given to the underdog (Cleveland 8) are the first points listed. So by reading these odds you can tell that the Yankees are favored, the 8 refers to Cleveland, the underdog (you win eight dollars for every five dollars you put up), and the 9 refers to the Yankees (you win five dollars for every nine dollars you put up).

Here's another example. You call the office and get the price on a Boston Red Sox–Milwaukee Brewers game. Say the Red Sox are a 9 to 11 favorite. You like Boston so you tell your man to give you Boston 20 times. If they win you win $100, but if they lose you have to pay out $11 for every five you bet, or $220. If a guy bet the Brewers the same 20 times, if he lost he would lose $100, but if he won he would win $180, or nine times 20.

Most people usually bet the favorite in baseball, so the book is constantly rooting for the underdog. But in order for a bookie to get really hurt, the favorite has to win considerably more times than lose. Take Tom Seaver, the New York Mets pitcher, for example. There are some people who bet on him every single time he pitches. Whenever he pitches he's the favorite. When the Mets are at home he's usually 9 to 5, on the road he's as much as 8 1/2 to 5 (put up nine to win five). But I've never known him to go in as a shortie. Some wise guys think they can spend the winter in Florida by betting Seaver, because the guy is going to win more often than he's going to lose. But for the guy to actually win money on Seaver, he's got to win something like ten games for every four he loses.

I'll explain. Say the odds are 9 to 11 and you bet Seaver ten times. That means if you win you win $50 (five dollars times ten), but if you lose you lose $110 ($11 times ten). So if you go with Seaver and he wins ten games your total winnings will be $500—but if he loses four games you've lost $440, and that $60 difference won't pay for one night in Miami. You've got to go quite a ways in order to stay even.

Let's look at the 1972 season. Seaver won 21 games, lost 12 and started two games in which he didn't get a decision. Assume he won one of those and lost the other, that brings the Mets record in games he started to 22 wins and 13 losses. For argument's sake, let's say he went off at 9 to 11 each time. If you had bet on him ten times every game he started you would have won a total of $1100 and lost $1430, a loss for the year of $330. Which is why it doesn't pay to always bet on the local hero.

Both the lines and odds are used to stimulate business. If the play on the favorite is heavy, for example, a smart book might lengthen the spread or give better odds on the underdog to get people to go that way. On the other hand, if everybody's betting the underdog he might close it down a little to discourage any more betting that way. The lines themselves comes from oddsmakers, people who do absolutely nothing but figure spreads and odds. A guy gets to be an oddsmaker after he has spent considerable time as a bookie and has shown an ability to figure points and spreads. A lot of bookies subscribe to at least three different oddsmakers. The cost is about $75 per week for the service, which is how oddsmakers stay alive, and usually there won't be more than a point difference on any of the sheets, which is how bookies stay alive. The final decision on what line to quote to customers is the bookie's own decision.

The best-known calculator, or oddsmaker, is Jimmy the Greek Snyder. Now most people in the country have heard of Jimmy the Greek, but inside the organization his lines are not all that well respected. I think the best guy in the country is a guy in New York, a guy I once worked for when he was a bookie, by the name of Sholem. He is a true sports expert and a great researcher. He does his work by considering speed, accuracy, endurance, injuries, mood, weather conditions, and then he matches player by player and comes up with very accurate lines.

The customer can find out what the odds and the lines are in different ways. He can pick up his phone and contact the office he bets with and have the clerk quote him the price. Or, even easier, he can just pick up the local newspaper, which usually quotes the lines. This is one of the greatest hypocrisies going: Betting is illegal, yet newspapers always print the spreads. Who reads them? I'll give you one guess.

A bookie will take a bet on almost anything that there are odds on, from horse racing to elections. But when something unexpected happens the bookie will usually protect himself by putting a limit on the top bet, usually about $100. For example, a few years ago Fran Tarkenton had a dispute with the New York Giants when he was their quarterback, and walked out on them the day of a game against Houston. The order went out: No more than $100 would be accepted on the game. The same thing happened when the Knicks were in the championship against the Los Angeles Lakers. Willis Reed got hurt and the lid was put on. This is done by the books for their own protection.

Every bookmaking operation of any size has runners working for it. Your runner is your field representative. He collects debts, makes payoffs, finds new customers, encourages people to bet and, on a few occasions, will actually take a bet himself. People tend to say the word "runner" like it's a nasty word, but a good runner can make more money that the president of a big corporation. His salary depends completely on the number of customers he has. I know gentlemen who have made over $100,000 a year as runners. Real hustling gentlemen they are.

Your bigger offices will have at least 20 or 30 runners on the street, and each runner will have between 20 and 50 customers calling in. This tends to lead to some very busy telephones. The office holds a master list for each runner, and on that list is every one of his customers, how much he owes and how much credit he has. The runners have code names: Blue, Orange, 441. I had more names than Carter had pills when I was running. I was known as Apples, Oranges, 44, 56. I was known as Oldsmobile; I graduated to Cadillac. Now say you were one of my customers, you would call in and say, "So and so for Apples." The clerk would check the list of the runner to make sure you (the bettor) still had credit available for the week, and if you were okay he would take your bet. Every bet does not have to go through the runner, but the clerk has to protect the runner by making sure no customer bets more than his limit. If a customer does want to go over the top the clerk must contact the runner and get his okay. If the runner doesn't give his permission the clerk cannot accept the bet, and no one, not even the boss, can go over a runner's head if he refuses to extend more credit to one of his customers.

In actuality the runner is operating his own small business. He can work with the office in one of two ways: either on what is called a "half-sheet" or on a straight 50-50 proposition, depending on what he thinks is better for him.

A "sheet" is a list of customers. A half-sheet means that the runner earns 50 percent of whatever his profits for the week are, and in return is responsible for 50 percent of the losses. If he ends up ahead he has what is called a black sheet. If his customers end up ahead he has a red sheet. The advantage of working a half-sheet is you never have to put any of your own money up. If you have a red sheet for the week, the office covers the total losses and takes it out of your earnings the following week. For example, if I earned $6000 for the week I have a black figure of $6000. I get $3000 and the office gets $3000. If I have a red sheet, a $6000 loss, the office puts up the whole $6000, but then I am $6000 in the hole—the entire amount of the loss—the following week. I cannot earn any money until that $6000 is returned. In actuality I'm splitting my profits and am responsible for the full loss, which is how the office makes money. It may not sound like a great deal for a runner, but assuming I have a losing week, where else am I going to get interest-free money to pay my customers?

The second way of operating is covering your own end. You simply work out a deal with the office: Whatever we win, they win half, whatever we lose they're responsible for half. That means I don't have a red or black figure, everything is just canceled out. The advantage to me is that I don't have to pay the office back. If I lose $1000 I put up $500 and they put up $500 and we're clear. I don't have to wait until I win $1000 myself before I can earn again.

When I first worked as a runner, I was working for this guy Sholem (who became an oddsmaker) on a basis which was called five hot and cold, which nobody will give you anymore. That meant I earned five percent of the money I took in on horses—strictly on horses—five percent, win, lose or draw. So if I brought in $1000 in horse action I got $50 whether the office won $10,000 or lost $10,000. It was like getting a weekly salary. Today, when I work, I prefer to work on a half-sheet. That way I never have to take any money out of my pocket.

Every runner decides what's best for him, and that's the way he works. His decision is based on how many customers he has, how well he knows their betting habits, and what his own financial condition is. A runner is responsible for settling all his accounts. He has got to be tough enough to collect whatever is owed the office, and responsible enough to make sure every one of his customers gets every cent coming to them.

One thing about gambling with a mob bookie, we are very legitimate people when it comes to paying our debts or collecting our money. If you have money coming to you, fine, you'll get it, you're entitled to it, no question about that. I knew one guy who won $17,000 from a bookmaker and was petrified. "I wonder if I'm going to get paid? I've heard all these stories. . . ." Again, we have to go back to the bullshit from television and movies. I told him, "Believe me, pal, you will not only get paid, you will get an escort to the nearest bank if you want it." Sure enough, he met his runner at the appointed place on a Tuesday, which is generally settling-up day if you work on a weekly basis, was paid his money, and then asked if he wanted someone to go with him to the bank. The guy couldn't believe it. But if we weren't honorable men how long could we stay in business? The word would get around and no one would play with us.

If you feel you've been gypped you can call in to the office and make a claim and be sure it will be checked out. As I said, every bet is recorded on sheets and most of your larger operations use tapes.

I'll give you an example of getting paid under any circumstances. I bet a horse one day up in the Bronx and I had $100 to win on this animal. It won and paid $62. For the nonbettors, this is $62 for every $2 bet, which meant a nice payday of $3100 for me. But when I went to get paid the runner had disappeared, which meant my payday was now in jeopardy. I investigated and found out he was working for a guy by the name of Black Bart. So I went over to this particular restaurant where he hung out, identified myself and told him that one of his boys owed me $3100. He told me to meet him at six o'clock that night and the issue would be settled; he just wanted to check the office and find out (1) if the bet had ever gone into the office, and (2) what happened to the runner. As it turned out the bet had indeed gone into the office and the runner had taken a hike with my payoff. When I met him at six Bart said, "My apologies for the delay," and gave me my money. About six months later this runner was found stuffed into the trunk of an abandoned Edsel. The final insult.

There is only one way I know to get out of paying a customer, and that's to die. Even then, though, the office will pay off. But if an independent dies then the customer is in trouble because no one has an obligation to him. All his debts die with him. Who's gonna pay out or collect?

There is a wonderful mob joke about precisely this situation. A small independent bookie had been making a great living for 25 years. Then one day he was totally destroyed, he lost a fortune, all his savings plus more than he could borrow. So he decided he would fake his own death and then skip. He holds his own funeral and all his customers come, just to make sure he's dead. They curse him out and they spit on him and he doesn't move. Then they leave, all except this one little Italian butcher. He waits until every other person is gone and then he stands over the coffin, looks down at the bookmaker and says, "I'va been bettin' with you for twenty years and I'ma never win. Yesterday I finally win and then you die. So, 'causea that, I'ma gonna cut your heart out!" With that the bookmaker opens his eyes, sits up and says, "You, I pay!"

Just as any office will pay off anytime it loses, every customer is expected to pay when he hits the hole. Runners get to know their customers, they become very friendly, and so a runner doesn't like to lean on a man unless he is forced to. There's no reason to get violent.

Every now and then though you get a guy who gives you a song and dance—and no money week after week. Usually, the runner, with maybe a little local muscle, can handle it. But sometimes a runner is just not strong enough and outside muscle has to be called in. I was working in Cincinnati once when I got word that Meyer Lansky wanted to see me down in Florida. I hopped on the next plane and flew down there. Meyer met me at the airport in his big chauffeur-driven limousine, which was being driven by his bodyguard, chauffeur and what-have-you, Phil the Shtick. I got in the car and asked Meyer what the problem was. I could see he was burning. "I got this guy," he tells me, "and he won eighteen thousand dollars and he got paid. Now he loses thirty thousand dollars and he ain't come up with the money in six months."

"Wait a minute," I said. "You got half a dozen guys down here, what do you need me for?"

"Because this is a special job and I want you to handle it. My man went over to see him last week and this guy says to him, 'I'm gonna write a letter to the attorney general. If he says I should pay you, I'll give you the money.'" Meyer was getting more upset as he told the story. "Go collect it," he told me, "or I want to read about it." That is a direct quote.

I went over to the guy's place that same morning and knocked on the door and when he opened it I smacked him across the top of his head with a gun butt. I said, "This is it, fuck. It is now ten o'clock in the morning. I'm gonna be back here at two o'clock this afternoon and I want thirty thousand dollars. Otherwise make me up a list of your six closest friends to act as pallbearers." He was sprawled across this very pretty couch with gold thread running through it, fingering the dent in his head, and to make sure he understood what I had in mind I put one bullet in the couch to his left and another one to his right. When I got back that afternoon he paid me that money so fast I thought I was going to catch cold from the breeze. You don't actually have to use violence, you just have to remind people it's there.

One way or the other the bookmaker is going to settle every debt. Many times this leads to an involvement in legitimate businesses. A guy gets in the hole to his bookie, he goes down the drain and he's got to bail himself out. Say the guy owns a bar. So he takes in a new partner, the bookmaker. Only the guy's name is on the liquor license but he is paying the office a percentage of his profits every week. A large bookmaker can end up owning pieces of dozens of businesses, and I do mean dozens. A well-known restaurateur in New York lost half his place in one afternoon. He went for five races and the football games, and lost every one. He had to use the restaurant to pay off.

There are two types of gamblers: your regular run-of-the-mill win-some, lose-some gambler and then there's your degenerate gambler. The degenerate gambler is the worst kind, because he is in hock to every shylock in town, he borrows everywhere, he works nine jobs just to try to stay even. He doesn't care about his family, about anything but getting his bet down. He just doesn't know when to stop. I see these guys, they'll bet on anything, on a cockroach race, on how fast your nails grow, anything.

I don't like to have customers like this because I know eventually they're gonna have problems paying me back. So when I meet a new customer I'm like Dun and Bradstreet. I ask them what they do for a living, what kind of money they have, where they live, who they associate with, who recommended them to me, how much betting they will be doing, everything. I may or may not do a little outside checking. If one of my old customers brings him in I usually accept his word that this guy is good. But I don't like to go chasing my money so I take these early precautions.

There really is no such thing as a typical gambler. Some are very smart, some are very stupid. As a bookie I obviously prefer the stupid ones. One guy I once had had an unbeatable system. He would bet round robins and always take 30 to 1 shots. He was convinced he couldn't lose. Instead he lost convincingly. He will not make up the money he lost until approximately 1993. He had three chances: Chinaman's, slim, and no.

The opposite is a guy I know called Tony "Pickem," a professional gambler. This is the way he makes his living, this is what he works at. He subscribes to the local newspapers of every college and pro football team he bets on. (I would hate to be his mailman.) He reads these papers carefully and he looks for little injuries, or a guy being disciplined or someone having trouble with his wife. Knowing this information gives him a considerable edge. I'll give you an example. The Vanderbilt University basketball team was playing some smaller school and he asked me who I liked. I said, "Vandy is a fourteen-point favorite and they're better than that. I guess I like them."

"No you don't," Tony says, "take the other side." He said he read that Vandy's star received a minor twist of his ankle during the week, and even if he played he would be both taped and sore. Sure enough, Vandy won but didn't cover the spread. This guy looks for these things and when he finds them he pounces, which is why he is a winning gambler.

Tony and Mrs. Pickem have three phones in their house. One is for social calls and the other two are strictly for business. On one of them he calls the bookies and on the other one they call him. If a customer is big enough, as Tony is, bookies will call in and let him know what their lines are or if they've changed since he called. The ones he don't hear from he calls. After he has spoken to or heard from maybe a dozen different people he'll sit down with his pad and pencil and do some comparison shopping. He may have four different lines on the same game. Finally he'll get down as much as he wants where he wants. But that's only for starters. He watches the prices shift as bookies try to even up their action. If a really good price pops up he may bet some more.

On a Sunday afternoon this guy is like a living cartoon. He's got two television sets in front of him and a shortwave radio on the floor next to him. He's got one phone to his left and the other to his right. He'll settle into this big, ugly red chair they have and he won't leave until the last game is over. As the afternoon progresses he'll be figuring, charting, playing with the radio, calling and getting calls and getting down on the West Coast games. If he sees a good halftime bet—in which you only bet on the second half—he'll take it.

I've seen him bet more than $100,000 in a single afternoon. It's really not that much of a gamble because he's too good and too careful. Even if he loses more games than he wins, which is rare, he isn't going to lose that much. I did see him come up $30,000 short one particularly devastating afternoon. He looked at me and tried to smile, but he couldn't make it. "Let me tell you something, kid," he said. "A lot of people will tell you gambling is fun. They're wrong, it's a tough job. Winning is fun!"

The only problem Tony has is with his wife, who doesn't like him hanging around the house all day. She makes him take long walks with their mutt.

There are a lot more losers than winners. One time while I was running I had about 14 guys who owed me money and were paying me every week. They couldn't bet with me because they had gone to the limit of their credit, but they had to pay me every week, including the interest of course. None of them was paying more than $100 a week, but this was a nice little income. All I had to do was give the office its half, which I did, and no one had any complaints.

A good runner or bookmaker is like a family friend. He gets to know his customers, and his customers get to know him. Professional bookmakers, your people who run the big operations, really value their regular customers. They'll supply them with women, liquor, even junk if that's what it takes to keep them happy and betting. This personal touch is one of the major reasons people will continue to prefer us to any sort of state-run gambling operation—that and the fact that if they win with us, they don't have to declare it on their tax forms.

No one in the world should have trouble finding a bookmaker. Go to a place where they sell racing or sporting papers, or go to a racetrack and talk to a couple of people, or check into a hotel in any major city and ask the bell captain. I can go into any major city in the country and get a bet down within 24 hours. In some operations new bettors have to put up a cash deposit, $500 or $1000, just to make sure they will be available if they should lose. A legitimate guy won't object to that. No bookie is going to run away with your money. Chances are he's been in business at that same spot longer than you've been betting. But you can usually avoid putting up the deposit if you get a regular customer to introduce you to his office.

The laws against bookmaking are funny, because both the office and the customer can be guilty—or innocent. To this day you can transmit race results over an open telephone or radio, but you cannot make a bet across interstate lines. In other words, if I live in New Jersey and I call my bookmaker in New York to place my bet, I, not the bookmaker, am violating the interstate gambling law. The bookie has no way of knowing where the call is coming from. The federal law prohibits you, the customer, from making the interstate bet. There are no federal laws against bookmaking.

On the other hand, there are no state laws against making a bet—the state laws are against booking it.

And, finally, there are both federal and state laws about income-tax evasion, which an individual does if he wins money from a bookie and doesn't declare it.

The penalties for gambling vary depending where you are. In some areas it's a felony, in others it's only a misdemeanor. In New York City, for example, you can get up to four years on a bookmaking felony, but much less on a misdemeanor. The difference between the two is the amount of cash they catch you with. As a rule, few people go to jail for gambling. The penalty is almost always a fine, and if there is one thing a successful bookmaker has, it's money.

A business that is associated with bookmaking, but may or may not be part of the local office, is your football betting cards. These are the cardboard lists of maybe 15 or 16 pro games being played and the spreads. The customer has to pick a minimum of three games, but the more teams he bets the higher the payoff. If you get every game on the card right you win $5000, but I have never known anyone to win that apple. I used to run these cards, and listen, if I had my druthers I would take numbers and these cards and that would be it. I would make a good living.

There is absolutely no way to figure out how much is bet on these cards, but it has got to be substantial. Go to any big office in New York City and you can pass out 30 or so cards. All you have to do is deliver them and pick them up. We figured it out one day. The average bet on these things is between two dollars and three dollars. So if you've got 30 guys playing you've got maybe $75 coming out of one office. Am I making money or not?

In 1971 I worked as a controller for a guy printing and distributing these things. I was getting 50 percent of whatever I took in and my runners were getting 25 percent. I was dumping 5000 tickets a week. I had one runner, for example, a guy who drove a cab who used to give me $300 a week business of which he kept $75. This is a nice salary boost.

The government has got to get into the gambling business eventually. Off Track Betting in New York is only the beginning. If anything, OTB has helped bookmakers because it is such a badly run outfit. What do you expect? Has Howie "the Horse" Samuels any experience in that line of work? OTB has created new customers who, once they get smart, realize they can do better with a bookie than with the state. No income tax. Yet, as badly run as it is, OTB still makes money for the city of New

York. Of course, the money it pulls in compared to what is available is ridiculously small.

What hurts OTB is that it is pretty well limited to New York tracks and can't handle out-of-state action. A gambler wants to bet where he thinks he can win, not at only a small number of tracks. Eventually OTB will have to be expanded to take bets on other sports because taxes are driving your middle-class people (the bettors) out of the cities and gambling revenue is the only answer.

If the cities were smart though, they would forget about our pasts and let guys like me run these organizations. They would have to pay us a good wage, but they would be making so much money as a result of our experience they could afford it. I personally would like to work for the city. Listen, I love gambling, I love the game, and I would love it just as much if it were legal.

Well, almost as much.

CHAPTER *8*

HORSES AND
OTHER ATHLETES

made my very first real bet on a hot day in August 1946. Bookmakers should set that day aside and celebrate it as a holiday. A friend of mine who we called Ears, because his stuck way out of his head, had a tip on a horse named Sister Union. I bet the monumental sum of $50, which was good money to me in those days, and then I held my breath until I heard the results. Unfortunately, Sister Union won and paid $13 and change.

I say unfortunately because that's what got me hooked on gambling. That was the easiest money I ever made. I couldn't wait until the next race. I sat up all night with the *Morning Telegraph* trying to figure out which horses to bet on. Gradually I went from horse racing to football, basketball, baseball, dog racing, jai alai, cockfights and just about everything else you can think of.

But I always came back to the sport of kings—horse racing. At one point this was the biggest betting sport, and the crookedest. Today football attracts more action, but horse racing is still the crookedest. It is considered difficult to fix a horse race, at least the flats, but somehow people still do it. I don't even consider the trotters racing. Anyone who bets on the trotters is throwing his money away. It's like betting on a wrestling match.

The first time I realized horses can be set up was in 1952 when I was picking up horse action for a bookmaker in New York. All of a sudden my two-dollar bettors were betting me $10 and $20, and my $20 bettors were giving me $100s, and it was all going on one horse. We will call the horse Statue of Liberty, which was not its name, but it was running in the eighth race at Washington Park. My very worst fears were confirmed when I looked at the scratch sheet and saw this nag was going off at 30 to 1. I called the boss and I said, "I don't want to hurt your feelings, but I think you'd better buy some plane tickets. If this horse comes in you're gonna be leaving town." I tell him the story and he tells me to hold on.

He went to another phone and then he comes back to me and says, "Take all the action you can get on this animal." I said okay and, eventually, I wound up with about $30,000 on this one race. I didn't care personally because I was getting five percent win or lose. That night I bought the racing paper and very cautiously checked the results. I wanted to know if my office was still in business. I don't see Statue of Liberty on top, or in the second slot, or even in the third slot. I read down and the horse is at the bottom. Finally I get to the synopsis and it says, "Statue of Liberty—tail caught in gate." I laughed so hard I cried. They had gotten to one of the gatekeepers and when he locked the horse in the gate he simply grabbed part of his tail and stuck it in. So when the gate opens half his tail gets pulled out and you've got one hurting animal and he just doesn't want to perform.

There are a lot of ways to beat a good horse. I've seen grooms kick horses in the foot just before a race began. That makes the horse limp a while. I read recently some guy had come up with a new idea. He was going to use a laser beam to sting horses as they were running and make them break stride. The best way, though, is to get to someone that talks. Unless you're dealing with Mister Ed, that means the jockey or the trainer. Jockeys bet, but very, very few of them do business. Same with trainers. They're just dealing with too much money. I remember one horse who won at Monmouth Park. The jock was caught using an electric buzzer on his whip, or in his hand or something. They immediately disqualified the horse. The jockey, a Panamanian, was suspended from racing in the United States. I mean, the jocks could certainly get together and fix a race if they wanted, but chances of eight or nine guys being able to keep it quiet would be small, and these guys have too much money to lose.

Take a jock, even if he never wins a race he runs six, seven, eight, nine times a day at $20 a shot, which is at least $120 for the day just for getting up on the horse. If he wins he gets a percentage of the purse; if he comes in second, he gets $75 and third he gets $50. So no matter what happens it's payday. And if a jock ever gets in a stakes race he can get ten percent of the purse, which ain't chopped liver.

All of which means you have to get to the horses if you're going to do business. Either you have to speed one horse up or slow all the rest down. There was a New York State hearing in 1972 at which this guy started singing that he fixed horses by slowing them down. I have a very strong tendency to disbelieve him on the basis of numbers. In an average race you have something like eight or nine horses, and that means you'd have to put the needle into at least six animals and that is not a very easy thing to do. There is a lot more than just one little old man sitting by a gate to keep you out. The security setup at tracks is pretty good; the flats in particular are well policed because the state wants it that way. The state makes a lot of money from these places and a scandal has got to cost them—it has got to cut down attendance and betting. Every once in a while someone will slip by, but the man who wants to set something up has to travel to a place like Caliente, Mexico, for instance.

In 1956 I was living in southern California. A friend of mine calls at eight in the morning and asks me what I was doing and I tell him I was sleeping. "Let's go to Caliente," he said. I told him he was out of his mind. "Come on," he pushed, "I promise you'll have a good time." He talked me into it. We drove down and sat on the veranda and had breakfast and started playing cards . . . through the first race, the second race, the third race, the fourth race, the fifth race.

Finally I asked, "What the fuck did we have to come all the way down here to play gin for?"

He says mysteriously, "I'll tell you when." Just before the sixth race he says to me, "Here we go. Now bet this horse but don't bet more than one hundred dollars because I don't want to bring the price down."

I looked at the racing form and I couldn't believe it. This horse never even showed in a race. This horse was lucky to be breathing, much less winning a race. "You want me to put my hard-earned money on this pig? You're outta your fuckin' head."

He never blinked an eye. "I'll tell you what, kid, you bet the horse, if he loses I'll give you your money back." It's a free bet, you've gotta go. So I bet the $100 on the horse to win. This animal takes off out of the gate like Man o' War and wins by 28 lengths or something. I'm looking and I can't believe it. The horse paid 90 some-odd dollars.

He calls me up about two weeks later and asks, "What are you doing?" I didn't even hesitate. "Anything you want." Same procedure, down to Caliente, playing cards, seventh race, the horse wins by half a mile and pays $70 and change. About every two weeks for six months we went down there. Each time we only bet one race. Finally, we were driving back one day and he says, "By the way, kid, we can't go back there no more." I asked him why. "Too many horses are dying," he answered.

"Okay," I said, "now that it's over, tell me how you did it."

"Very easy," he said, "we were getting the horses stoned before the race. We were blowing marijuana up their noses just before they went to the post." This was done by the groom or maybe even the jockey, but I don't really understand how it worked. I guess after two joints the horse is flying. Unfortunately, some of the animals overextended themselves and had heart attacks or whatever horses have when they drop.

Anyway, I thought that was the end of that. Time passes and I move back to New York. One day the phone rings and it's him, he's calling me from the airport. "Hey, kid," he said, "feel like playing some cards at Belmont?" Off we went to Belmont Park.

We're sitting there playing cards and it's raining and I'm drinking coffee and overall I'm pretty miserable. Finally the race comes up and he looks at me and says, "The horse is Joanne" [or whatever the name was]. We went flying up to the $100 window. The favorite in the race got all the action and Joanne went off at something like 45 to 1. I bet the horse $400

127

win, $800 place. She goes out of the gate, leads wire to wire, and wins by three lengths, one-fifth of a second off the track record for a mile-and-an-eighth, and pays $57.80 and $28.00 plus to place.

Right after the race my friend went to Europe. He told me some letters would be arriving for him and gave me an address in Europe to forward them to. Turns out he had been down with just about every bookmaker in the East. I was getting six or seven envelopes a day, and there must have been a good price in each one. Now had the bookies known about this, they probably would have been interested in my friend's forwarding address, but I don't think they ever found out what happened. Incidentally, Joanne never won another race that I heard of.

There is one racket where you don't even have to touch the horse—all you have to do is exchange him. This is a racket that used to be very popular but was almost extinguished when the various racing associations began tattooing serial numbers on horses' lips. The way it works is you get a class horse, maybe a $10,000 animal, and you slip him in under another horse's name in a race against $4000 animals. Obviously the $10,000 animal is going to win every time; it is like putting Johnny Bench in the Little League.

Betting with bookmakers on horses is different than betting on football, basketball or baseball games, because you have an option—you can legally bet on horses if you want to go to the track or bet at state-run places, like OTB offices. In New York City the bookies have competition so they have to handle the action a little differently. To avoid a really big hit, which would cut deeply into business, they set limits. They will pay off at 30 to 1 up to the first $10 a man bets, 20 to 1 on the next $20 and 15 to 1 on the next $20. They will let you know their limit is 30 to 1, and even if the horse pays $10,000 at the track the limit is still 30 to 1. On parlays, which means betting on a few races with the winnings on one race being rebet on the following race—a snowball effect—they might pay 50 to 1, and even more on the exotic type of betting known as round robins. A round robin is three parlays in one. You bet on three horses in three different races and two of them must win for you to win your bet. There are numerous ways of betting, ways which OTB doesn't give you, which is another reason bettors will stay with their bookies.

Not everybody, of course. When I was booking, this guy calls up and asks what I pay for exactas, which means picking the exact order of finish in a race. I told him I didn't pay more than 50 to 1 on anything. He said, "Sorry, not enough, what do I need you for?" I could care less.

He found out what he needed me for a week later. He calls one night and says he hit the exacta at Yonkers and it paid $700 and change and he asked me if I could cash his five tickets for him. I told him to beat it. I could have arranged it with no trouble but I didn't want to bother because this guy was a smartass. If he had been a nice guy about it, I gladly would have done this deed for him. Now here he's holding five tickets worth more than $4200. Legitimately he makes about $15,000 a year and this new money is going to upset his entire tax structure—that $4200 has got to cost him $2000 in taxes. If he had bet with me he would have done much better and wouldn't have had to worry about taxes at all.

The organization refers to the tracks as churches. We refer to Aqueduct for example, as Chapter Aqueduct, Psalms one through nine. Because if you ever go to a racetrack, you will see praying like you have never seen before in your life, nine times a day.

The organization makes a great deal of money at the track, most of it by helping out the poor horseplayer. One of Gil Beckley's rackets was to have his runners working right at the track. They took the action of the customers, which was great for the customers because this way they can have their day at the races and still avoid taxes. But there is even more to it than that. If any of his bettors lost, Beckley returned them five percent of their bet and, if they won, he paid off at ten percent higher than the track. He generally had two or three working men at the tracks. The customer comes over, makes his bet verbally, and no money changes hands until after the race is over. This still goes on at a lot of tracks. The tracks know these people are operating there but can't catch them.

One of the very best rackets going, which is literally foolproof, is cashing tickets for winning bettors. People who do this are known as ten-percenters. What they do is have feelers out and if a guy wins more than $600, and wants to avoid paying taxes, they buy his ticket from him for cash, at 90 percent of its total value. The ten-percenters have phony identification and sometimes the cooperation of track security people. The security people are important because they would eventually realize that the same people are cashing winning tickets—even with different identification—after nearly every race. This is a very profitable little business. Say a ticket paid $5000. The bettor would be paid $4500 clear, the mob man goes to the window and collects the total amount. A quick $500 profit and everybody's happy.

Then there is the tout. He'll hit nine different people for the same race and give each one of them a different horse. Everybody wants to believe something crooked is going on so they listen to this guy and believe him. After the race the tout goes to the guy he gave the winner to and reminds him about the "tip." Unless the favorite wins he usually earns himself a tip. Few touts retire on what they make, but it's a living.

Me? I just like to bet. No rackets at the track, just out-and-out betting. I like the atmosphere of the track, I like the people and I like the excitement. I don't like losing, which, unfortunately, is what I do too often. When I go to the track I usually never bet more than three or four races the whole day. I've learned that you can beat one race, but you can't beat the races. I've seen guys hit six races in a day and I tell them, "Come and see me next week," and they invariably lose it all back.

The main thing I look for when I bet a horse is what kind of company he's been keeping. I like to know what kind of race he's been running in and what price he's paid. Now you take a horse that ran in a $20,000 claiming race and they write down, "Tired," meaning he was fading as the race ended. Now he's been dropped down a few classes, maybe five or six thousand dollars. This horse is going to be a very tough animal to beat. Our Johnny Bench in the Little League again—older, slower but still Johnny Bench.

I also look for a maiden (hasn't won) dropping down into a lower category. He has been running against tough horses, and even though he was beaten by 12 lengths in his last race he may still be a good animal. People don't see this, all they see is that 12 lengths, they don't even notice he's dropping down in class.

I caught an animal like this at Bay Meadows in San Francisco. I wasn't planning to go out to the track this particular day but I got a phone call in the morning from a friend in Los Angeles. He said he had a horse in the second race who really looked good. There was no fix or anything, the horse was just dropping down a class, but for some reason the odds on him were big. He asked me to spread some action around at the books and then go to the track. He told me to be careful not to bet too much because he didn't want to draw attention to this animal.

I placed about $4000 and went to the track. The horse was running in the second race, so I looked for a horse in the first race to hook him up with so I could go for the daily double. I finally found a long shot I liked and bet him $200 to win and $40 on the double. The horse in the first race wins and pays $59.

Then the toteboard began flashing the possible daily-double combinations. If my friend's horse wins in the second race, according to the board, the combination I had would pay $4900 for every $2 ticket. And I'm holding four $10 tickets—at $98,000. The second race starts and this horse comes out of the gate like a shot and wins going away. I'm just starting to go sky-high when the "Inquiry" sign lights up.

My horse was disqualified for crossing in front of another horse coming out of the gate.

I wrecked Bay Meadows. I threw punches, chairs, anything I could get my hands on. It took nine security people to calm me down. They kept asking me what was wrong and I was so mad I could hardly talk. I just kept waving my four ten-dollar tickets. They understood.

Everybody in this country loves to bet. Even my wife bets. Like most housewives she is a conservative bettor. I take her out to the track with me and I give her $50. First thing she does is put $30 in her pocket. Then she bets two dollars a race on horses that have the same first name as a good friend, or are wearing her favorite colors.

She also gambles at home. She plays cards with her girl friends, or bingo, or Mah-Jongg. They play for what they call three-dollar-pie. That means if you blow three dollars, you can't lose any more money. You play for nothing. You can win, but you can't lose.

My one real dream in life is that Aqueduct will adopt my wife's three-dollar-pie system.

I would have to guess that in the last 27 years I've gambled away close to three million dollars, which comes to a little over 100 grand every year. I don't consider myself a degenerate gambler because I've never bet a penny I didn't have in my pocket. If I don't have money I don't bet. If you start betting on hope you're gonna end up in the hole.

I also make it a point never to take a hit to raise money so I can go gamble. When you get to the point where you are desperate for money you should get out of the heavy part of the business. Because this is when you start pressing, and when you start pressing you make mistakes and when you make mistakes you're dead. I never spend money before I have it and I never plan what I'm going to do with money that I'm going to make. I make it first. Then I give my wife her share, and somehow the rest disappears.

As any gambler will tell you, gambling is known as the if game: If only he had run faster; if only he had caught that pass; if only he hadn't swung at that bad pitch. There's only one answer to silly chatter like that: If only the queen had balls she'd be the king.

The "if" is what makes gambling a gamble: no ifs, no bets. Take the if out of a bet and you can determine who the winner will be, which is exactly what some sharp gamblers try to do. I've heard people say that bookies don't want anything to do with a fixed sports event. This is the biggest crock of shit I've ever heard. A gambler will do everything in his power to influence an event because he knows he can make a ton of money. Now, by "fix" I don't mean getting one team or one player to throw the game to the other side. I mean being able to "fix" the scores. The bookmaker doesn't give a crap who actually wins or loses; it's the points that interest him. As far as he's concerned, if the Los Angeles Rams are a ten-point favorite over the New York Giants and they only win by four, they've lost.

All a bookmaker needs is the edge and he'll work it to death. And that edge can be anything. By the end of the 1972 football season the New York Jets had been eliminated from any possible playoff spot. Their final game was against the Cleveland Browns, who were in contention for the play-offs. All week long the Jets were announcing that quarterback Joe Namath was a questionable starter, and that the final decision on whether he would play or not would be made right at gametime. Obviously if Namath were to play, the Jets would stand a better chance against Cleveland.

The Browns were a three-point favorite all week. The morning of the game, however, the spread was increased to six. As anyone could have pre-dicted, just before gametime Namath threw a few practice passes and the Jets announced he would not play. The bookmakers had obviously received the information from someone long before the decision was "officially" announced. The edge.

Bookmakers have been known to try to influence results by sending women up to a guy's rooms, by supplying liquor, even by making noise in the room below where some quarterback or pitcher is sleeping. How much is it worth to know the starting quarterback didn't sleep too well the night before the game?

I know of one quarterback, a guy who has a reputation of being a clean liver, a good family man, church, the whole thing, I know at least three girls he met through bookmakers who wanted to know what his story was. He never even knew he was being set up, but these gamblers wanted to know how he felt and how he thought his own team was going to do. And he thought the girls loved him for his body.

Of course, as I found out the hard way, the edge doesn't always work out. I was in Los Angeles one Saturday night with some people. We were just cruising around and we finally decided to stop at this small, out-of-the-way bar. We walked in, and sitting right there at the bar was the man who was supposed to start as quarterback against the Rams the next day. I say sitting but it was more like leaning. I mean he was drunk. He was so blotto that the people he was with literally had to pick him up and push him into a car.

This was the closest thing to a religious experience I ever had. "Thank you, Lord," I said to myself, "for bringing me to this joint."

The next morning I got on the phone and I started betting. By the time I was through I was down for about $15,000. I figured there was no way I could lose, there was no way this quarterback could perform. Unfortunately, nobody ever bothered to tell me that this guy couldn't play *unless* he was drunk. Sober he was a bum. With a hangover he was a superstar. He drank his way into the Hall of Fame. He wobbled out on the field and ran the Rams out of the ballpark. I handed the bookie my 15 Gs and tried to figure out what I'd learned.

If I don't have any edge I'm just a very ordinary gambler. What I do have is confidence in myself, which is a real problem. Too much confidence and no special information usually means you're gonna lose a lot of money. The worst betting day of my life came one football Sunday in 1964. I bet $15,000 each on four different football games. I considered them locks. I was wrong all four times. With the vig I went for $16,500 on each game, which is enough to make a man dislike football. For a couple of days.

No legitimate bookmaker will go out of his way to really jeopardize a man, but they may try to wear him down a little. I don't care how good an athlete's condition is, broads and booze and no sleep have got to wear him down. Two former New York Giant running backs come to mind. They both could have been great, but they got into the New York good life and that was it. One of them was the biggest whoremaster I've ever heard of. If you introduced him to a broad, 15 minutes later he was looking to get her in the kipper. I used to meet broads who would tell me how quick he was, and a couple of these broads I know for a fact were supplied by gamblers. Both of these guys are out of football now.

The only team I know which really never had a chance to move around was Green Bay when Lombardi was there. First of all, Green Bay, Wisconsin, is not New York and there just isn't that much opportunity, and secondly, Lombardi watched these guys like a hawk. The only guy he had trouble with was Paul Hornung and he was very, very hurt when Hornung got nailed for gambling. Hornung and Alex Karras of the Detroit Lions both got caught betting on themselves. That was the last time anyone was even accused, which shows you how bad the National

Football League's security system is, because there are many professional football players that like to get down.

A few years ago a major magazine had a big exposé planned. They had a story naming four of the most famous quarterbacks and accusing them of gambling, not necessarily against their team, but playing the points. The magazine's lawyers wouldn't let them print it. But believe me when I tell you Hornung and Karras are not the only players who bet.

For example, let me introduce you to a now retired Hall of Fame quarterback. I was in Baltimore and the Colts were playing his team. I was going with his team because I figured there was absolutely no way they could lose, because in those days Baltimore was a very bad football team and his was a very great football team. His team was a six-point favorite and it was like taking candy from a baby with a machine gun. But the day before the game I was sitting with a friend of mine and he asked me who I liked. "The visitors," I said, naming this guy's team.

He says, "No you don't. You love Baltimore and six." I asked him if he was out of his fucking head. He looked at me and said, "I just bet ten thousand dollars for [our Hall of Famer] on Baltimore."

"You're right," I told him, "I think I'm in love with Baltimore."

It is really rare when a player bets against his own team, and when you get word you get down with everything you can beg, borrow and steal. Which I did. The next day this quarterback was as great as anyone you'll ever want to see between the 20-yard lines. But once he got inside the 20 he became incredibly bad. He would fumble, he would get intercepted, he would get dumped, something would happen and his team wouldn't score. In the end though, he moves them downfield and gets them within field-goal range, they kick a field goal and win by three, which means they lost on the spread. I won big and I assume the QB did too.

Now let me reemphasize one thing, almost 99 percent of the time these people are betting on games they're not playing in, or they're betting on themselves to win. This isn't a matter of throwing games. But when they make a bet it gives us an edge because we know they have inside information. They may know somebody is hurt, or somebody is slowed up, and this helps. We also know they're confident. For example, if one guy bets on himself six weeks in a row and then lays off, we've got to figure he thinks he's gonna get beat, so we go the other way. But either way they bet, it's valuable information for us.

Take the 1969 Super Bowl. I have a friend who is also a close friend of one of the Jets. One day he calls me from Miami and asks me what I'm doing and I told him I hadn't decided yet. The Baltimore Colts were 18-point favorites and this is a lot of points, even in Midget League football. "Believe me," he says, "take the eighteen points." He also told me to try to find someone who would take straight win-lose action on the game and give me good odds on the Jets. I couldn't get odds high enough to make that worthwhile but I did get down pretty heavy on the Jets with the points. Then, as the game started, I began to wonder what I was doing. I thought my friend was out of his mind. Then I realized he was there and must know how the players felt, not how the newspapers said they felt.

After the first quarter of the game I knew I was home. Me and at least two Jet players that I know of made a good dollar out of that game. I understand one of them bet so heavily he broke about ten bookmaking offices in Philadelphia and they had to go to a boss and borrow money to pay him. The other made as much money as he was originally signed for, although he proceeded to lose it that same winter betting on bad basketball tips.

Again, in 1971. The Wednesday before the Oakland Raiders were scheduled to play a very important game with the Baltimore Colts, I received a phone call from a bookie who owed me a favor and he advised me to go put my lungs on Baltimore. I hesitated because Oakland was a short favorite. I said, "You're kidding?"

"Look," he answered, "I have just wagered seven hundred fifty thousand dollars for Carroll Rosenbloom [the owner of the Colts] and [he named three players]." With this much money on the line I have got to figure these men know they are going to win and that they are going to play their hearts out. I got to figure they don't make a bet like this unless they figure they can walk away with it. Besides, Rosenbloom has been known to bet against the Colts when he thought it smart. I figure if he's going with them, so am I. I began making calls the morning of the game and I bet this team until I was blue in the face. Unfortunately, most of the world did, too, and the bookies were hurt very badly when the Colts won. I made approximately $40,000.

None of the athletes actually put the money down themselves; it would be kind of stupid of their part to let it be known that they were associating with a bookie. So they have someone, a friend, a relative, getting them down. That's why it is almost impossible to prove anything against anybody.

I say almost because there are always people like Denny McLain around. McLain was a great pitcher who started investing for his retirement. Unfortunately, he invested in a bookmaking ring. He was set up like a pigeon, and everybody knew exactly what was going on. I found out through a guy I know in Detroit. He was in New York on business and we were talking and McLain's name comes up. I said the guy seemed to be a flake. "You ain't got no idea what kind of flake he is," my man tells me.

"All right," I answered, "educate me."

He laughed. "This guy thinks he's a partner in a bookie outfit. They got an office going and he puts money into it. Every week they tell him they ain't winning, they losing, and every week he keeps coming up with fifteen hundred dollars, two thousand dollars, to cover his end. Once in a while they give him a piece of bread." He guaranteed me McLain went for a total of $40,000 or $50,000. McLain eventually got fired, but his so-called partners never got bothered.

Baseball probably has the best security system. When a kid comes into the major leagues they indoctrinate him pretty good. They tell him don't hang out, don't gamble, don't do this, don't do that. And the kids listen. But the late 1950s I knew of four pitchers that were doing business. They were actually trying to fix games—their teams would be favored and they would do their best to throw it. And, as pitchers, their best was usually good enough. As a matter of fact, so much evidence was put together by the DA's office they were going to get an indictment. But instead they went to the commissioner's office and a deal was made. At the end of the season the pitchers were traded and eventually eased out of baseball. They were happy to stay out of prison, and baseball was willing to go along to avoid the publicity. This was the last time I ever heard the slightest thing about baseball.

There is some action in basketball, both college and pro. It's easier to get to the college kids because a lot of them come from the ghettos and these big schools give them scholarships and teach them to cheat in class and give them money under the table. So when an outsider comes up and offers them a pot of gold to hold back a little, not to lose, but to fall under the spread, why not? The pro ballplayers pick it up pretty good too I'm told. I've never made any money on inside knowledge on basketball. I hear a lot of stories, but all secondhand. Who needs it?

For years boxing was the most controlled sport. It was almost totally mob-dominated. Frankie Carbo, who eventually went to jail, had an iron grip on that sport. I knew Frankie when I was a kid because I used to hang around with his crowd. I would see him on a Tuesday or Wednesday and he would tell me who was going to win the Friday-night fight at Madison Square Garden. He never gave me a loser.

Since there are no lines or points in boxing, only winners and losers, a man has to agree to throw the fight. Some people still do, and a lot of money changes hands, but nowhere near the amount that went around when boxing was still popular.

There isn't a tremendous amount of business done on boxing today because books have gotten too smart. The only real national interest in the sport is in the heavyweight championship, and any champion would be kind of difficult to do business with because he's got $2 million in his hand, so what are you going to do for him?

I gotta say I have my doubts about the Liston-Clay fights. In my opinion Sonny Liston could have killed Cassius Clay any time he wanted to. This guy was pure animal. You try to make me believe this guy, who could take on seven or eight guys in a street brawl and beat them all, could be so badly bothered by bursitis that he would quit? No way. I bet on Clay their first fight because I knew Liston had mob affiliations and also it was logical. Let me ask you this: What in the world did Liston have to gain by winning? If he won there wasn't another guy around for him to fight. If he lost he was guaranteed a return match and at least one more big payday. Now which way do you think my money was going?

I had decided to bet on Liston before the second fight, figuring he would win that one so they could have a third payday, but I kept hearing rumors that the Black Muslims had threatened to kill him if he won. I didn't know whether or not to believe this until I saw Liston the morning of the fight. I went right back to my room and began betting on Clay. Liston moved so slow, he seemed in a trance. I don't know. I could have been wrong. All I had was the rumors and what I saw. But I bet I wasn't and I won.

I booked the Clay-Frazier fight. Surprisingly—at least I was surprised—most of the money I got went for Clay. I took a big gamble because I'm sure this fight was straight; I held the Clay money and dumped the Frazier money. It was worth it.

Sometimes fighters get attached to the mob because that is the only way they can get fights when they're starting out. One of the most popular heavyweights in recent years, although he never made it to the championship, was controlled by the mob. It wasn't his fault. When he started fighting no one would help him until he went to someone in the mob who tied him up. This fighter retired from the ring a wealthy man. I'll never forget his last fight; the tenth round was one of the funniest things I have ever seen. We had all bet his opponent because we had the word. Unfortunately, his opponent was not really a good fighter, he couldn't actually break an egg. Our man made the mistake of hitting this guy in the tenth round, not too hard, but hard enough to make it look good. The guy's legs turned to rubber and he started to go down. In his best days our hero would have waltzed in and killed him, but this time he waltzed in and just kept on waltzing, clinching, holding him up. I could see his lips moving. I can imagine what he was saying, "Come on, babe, don't go down on me now!" He got $30,000 for the fight plus whatever he bet on his weak-kneed opponent, which must have been a goodly amount.

139

There is no doubt that any sport can be fixed. In boxing you have to get one of the fighters; in football you need the quarterback; baseball is tougher, the pitcher can't guarantee nothing because the manager can yank him, but you've got to have at least the pitcher to have a chance.

Up above I said "any sport." I got to admit I never heard anyone who tried to fix a Harvard-Yale track meet. It just shows you there are still new frontiers in this country.

CHAPTER *9*

BIG DEAL

ome people make their living by playing gin and poker. They are what you would call cardsharks. Unfortunately, I am what you would call a card tuna. If I had to depend on my cardplaying for a living I would be staying in an unheated tent outside Taos, New Mexico. All the money I've ever made from cards comes from running games. I learned a long time ago that the only thing that beats a full house is a nice apartment.

Running a card game is an easy way to make an income. Games are inexpensive to set up, easy to run and they bring in some big bucks. All you need is an apartment, the cooperation of the doorman if there is one, two or three or four tables, a couple of dealers for each table, girls to act as waitresses, some food and drink, permission of the local organization, the cards and the customers. You are then in business.

The apartment is easy to find. It can be any place at all, but if you plan on keeping the game running more than a night or two you'd better make sure the walls are thick or you are going to have neighbor problems. And neighbor problems mean police problems.

The doorman will cooperate because he understands people like to play cards, because he's probably a nice guy, and because I'm giving him $50 for the night.

The dealers work two to each table, a half hour on, a half hour off. I pay them $50 a night, but they also get a tip from each pot, and every one of them can take home as much as $300 if they hustle.

Every hour we take four dollars off each table for the girls, plus every time she brings something to a player he is expected to tip her. If a girl works from nine at night to six the next morning she could make as much as $150, which is better than most of the players do. The food is on the house when I run a game. How much can beer and sandwiches cost me?

The big nut is the organization. Even in a card game I'm beholden because they probably financed part of the operation and gave me the police contacts to make sure my players wouldn't be bothered. For this they get 50 percent of my earnings, which may sound like a lot. But you do well to treat the mob kindly. Let's say, for example, that you close the game down and six months later decide to get into something else. You can be pretty sure they'll be right there with the money. Or if you need a favor they're right there. The local organization usually has the necessary politicians under control. You don't have to waste your time shopping for contacts.

Your normal price for running the show is five percent of every pot. A good dealer might run between eight and ten pots per hour, and each pot is somewhere between $150 and $200. I'm making $7.50 per $150, or a minimum of $75 per hour per table, and I've probably got at least three tables going. So that's a total of $225 an hour. Round it off to $200, and the game should run at least ten hours, so I'm making at least $2000 for the evening, minus the abovementioned expenses, which still leaves me with a good night's pay.

Some people run their games another way. They don't take any money from the pot, they just charge $25 per man for two hours at the table. That way they make between $125 and $175 per table every two hours, depending on how many players you have. By this system the players do their own dealing, so there's a little saving there too. Either way, though, set fee or part of the pot, I'm making more than anyone in the place and I don't have to touch a card.

Of course, there are other ways to make money near the card table. One of them is to provide a loan service for those people whose money perishes before their enthusiasm. A guy may go bust and need $1000. The price is five percent per day. This is a high interest rate, but I didn't come to him and force him to take my money, did I? If he gets lucky he can pay me back that same night from his winnings—but even if he does he still owes me the first day's five percent.

Finding customers is easy, all you have to do is let the word out that you're running a game and they find you. I try to have seven men playing on each table. The games they play vary: high-low, spit in the ocean, baseball, seven-card stud, five-card draw or whatever they want. But the game is picked beforehand and no one is going to change it in the middle of the evening. Almost invariably the game is some sort of poker, although every once in a while you can get a game of gin. For some reason celebrities are really into gin rummy. And occasionally a table will play a Greek card or dice game called babaut.

Gin is played mostly in what we call goulash joints. In the old days, all you could get to eat in one of these places was goulash. They're a lot like social clubs. You got bookmakers, shylocks, fences and thieves all hanging around trying to pick up business. No one actually runs games in places like this; the players arrange to meet there and just pay for the deck and the time they're on the table. This is fine if you have a regular game with high-stakes players, but how many people do? For some reason the game they play in these places is gin rummy.

The only thing you have to guarantee when you run a game is that it is totally honest. Now I am never going to throw a sharpie in there because there is no percentage in it for me. Why do I have to cheat? I'm not going to make any more money. First of all, no matter how much a guy wins, I still get five percent of every pot. I don't have to go for more, so my players know they don't have to worry about me or my dealers. I try to make it a policy to keep card hustlers out of my games.

These are people who play a very professional game of gin or poker and are always looking for some sucker to make a run against. But even if a so-called shark gets into the game he may not win. Cards are 98 percent luck and 2 percent skill, even on this level. If you ain't got the cards, no matter how good a reader you are, there is very, very little you can do about winning. But I do my best to keep my games spotless. It keeps the amateurs happy.

There are only about a million ways you can get taken. A few years ago, for example, there was a big scandal involving a comedian and a singer whose names the lawyers won't let me mention plus some other important types. They were playing at the Los Angeles Friars' Club, and they were getting caught by people using peepholes in the ceiling to read the cards, and then transmitting the information to their accomplices.

One thing to watch for is a rigged deck. A good mechanic can rig a deck in 15 minutes. What he does is use his fingernails to dig very small marks in the cards that he can read. Then he's home free. There are also fixed decks, called "readers," which are introduced into the game by somebody looking to hustle people. By putting my own dealer in the game I'm guaranteeing the honesty of the cards. If the dealer feels anything in the deck he can throw it away. Just to be safe we change decks every four or five hands anyway.

Card games go one every single night of the week just about everywhere. And very few of them are one-night shots. I've seen gin games run for three days at a time, poker games run for weeks, with a continual stream of new players coming in with fresh money. I once had a game running on Sutton Place in New York that went on for two weeks. I was going crazy trying to find dealers because my dealers kept going to sleep. A normal evening, though, begins about nine o'clock, and by 10:30 there are four tables running and ready to go all night. I've usually got my players at the table and an additional group inside another room watching television, waiting for someone to fade so they can sit down.

If the government was smart it would license poker palaces, places where people could go and legitimately play for money. This income, which would be considerable, would be very beneficial to the noncard-playing public.

One thing tends to worry potential customers about playing in mob-run games. Every once in a while you read about some guys playing poker and some hoods come in and make them strip and take their money. Now, this happens once in a while, so you have to know who's running your game. This ain't never happened to a game of mine.

In fact, in my life I've only seen two games interrupted. I was playing in a game in Brooklyn and some guys came in to hold us up. I asked them, "You guys know whose game this is?" Actually it was a stupid question; if they had they would not have been there. They said they didn't, but they were desperate. A guy they work with had gotten thrown in the can and they were raising money for his defense fund. Now understand, these were not mob people, these were free-lancers, but it sounded reasonable and I suggested everyone chip in. After this the guy actually told me his name and said if I was ever in a jam he would be glad to help me out, too. What the fuck, if he was holding us up for himself I would have tried to kill him, but this was different.

As a rule you're crazy to try to hold up a card game because you're always going to find some idiot who's looking to protect his $50 or $60 and he's going to get killed and you're going to have a murder rap on your hands. It just isn't worth it.

The second game I was in which was interrupted was a personal thing. A guy was looking for another guy and he came into the social club with a gun. He says, "Look, I'm not looking for the rest of you. This guy owes me and I want my money." He took the guy outside, got his money, beat the guy up pretty decent and then left. He never bothered anyone else in the game.

Running a card game is different than craps. Craps is another money-maker, but instead of a nice apartment the game is usually held in a garage or hotel room and attracts a different clientele. I don't play the game personally because I don't like it. It's all luck. But I have worked protection in a few games. I once rode shotgun in a game in New Jersey. That means I stood right behind a wall with a nice big hole in it and watched everything that happened. I had a nice little sawed-off shotgun with me. If the wrong guy came in and tried to make a move, it was my job to welcome him. For this I was paid $100 a night.

At the end of the evening, if one customer won a lot of money, it was my job to make sure he got home safely. I'll never forget one Friday night in 1960, a game in the back of an Esso station in Bergen County, New Jersey. This game was run by people who were pals of Joey Adonis, who had been deported by then. One lucky customer won $80,000, and I drove him home to Scarsdale. I get him there and say, "Good-night and good luck." He panics.

"What do you mean good-night? You can't leave me here with all this money. Please, I'll get you anything you want, but don't leave." So me and my shotgun stayed with him the whole weekend. We had a great time, fine food, liquor, and he had a nice family. I don't know how he explained me to them. I refused to carry the shotgun around with me. What the fuck! Not in Scarsdale. That's in your Westchester County. Finally, Monday morning I took him to the bank and went home. I was paid $1000 for the weekend, from him, plus a bonus from the people running the game.

My editors tell me I have to end this chapter because I haven't killed anybody in at least 20 pages. So I'll end with one of my favorite card-playing jokes. It seems two mob guys were playing poker for big stakes and finally one of them calls. "Whattya got?" he asks.

His opponent slowly lays down his cards. "Four aces," he sneers.

The other guy shakes his head. "That's too bad," he says, "because I got you beat."

The man with four aces can't believe it. He opens his mouth and asks, "What in the hell beats four aces?"

The first guy puts his hand down to show him. "A pair of twos and a forty-five."

This chapter is now officially ended.

CHAPTER *10*

SOME OF OUR BEST
FRIENDS ARE IN
SHOW BIZ

t's only fair that Hollywood make money off the mob through movies like *The Godfather* and *The Valuchi Papers*, because the mob has been making money off Hollywood for years. Show business is dough business, if you'll excuse the expression, and where there is money to be made you can always find the organization there to claim a share.

We are in movies, nightclubs, records, radio and very occasionally television, but not like the general public thinks. We don't control these areas at all, but we have invested heavily and make a nice buck. We do it legally most of the time, just using friends of business "contacts" who either control a name performer, or have access to publicity channels, or own a nightclub or a record company. There are many, many entertainers and entertainment facilities that have mob money invested in them, from country and western singers to freaked-out rock-and-roll groups, from small New England clubs to the biggest Las Vegas hotels.

You really can't blame a performer for accepting mob help and making a deal. The mob has connections and distribution facilities in the record industry, the mob has important clubs, and the mob has money. And there are a lot of talented people around looking for a break. I know of singers with really good voices and great style but they can't get booked even by the police. They just don't know the right people.

There is one well-known young Italian singer that serves as a perfect example. The mob was pushing him, and he looked like he was on the verge of a big career. It was a standing joke among disc jockeys that they said whatever they wanted to about this singer. First the mob told them what they wanted to say, then they said it.

This lad was owned lock, stock and barrel by a guy named Buckle up in the Bronx, and he had kicked around for a long time with little success before he made his deal with Buckle. Again, there is nothing illegal involved here, but Buckle had the contacts to make this guy move. Unfortunately, this kid eventually forgot how important Buckle was to him and he decided to split. Up-and-coming young Italian singer was suddenly down-and-going old croaker.

Las Vegas is the perfect example of mob influence in the entertainment world. The organization built that city. You've got the Detroit mob in there, the Cleveland mob, the Philadelphia mob, the New York mob, the Chicago mob, and then you've got Meyer Lansky who controls all the mobs. Meyer was the man who first put gambling in there, just as he did in Curacao, in Aruba, in the Bahamas, in Puerto Rico.

And with gambling comes entertainment. So the mob built the Sahara, the Thunderbird, the Riviera, the Flamingo, and the best entertainers in the world started coming in and getting great salaries.

This was all before Howard Hughes appeared. The organization let him have some property because it was catching a lot of heat from the government for skimming off profits (taking money out before paying taxes). And wherever Hughes goes, he attracts attention, which is something the mob wanted less of. Hughes controls what he bought, but the mob controls just about everything else.

What we control we control completely. A few years ago, for example, there was a nice little trio working in New York. They were pretty good, never big star stuff, but talented enough to play the Las Vegas lounges and make some good money. My cousin caught their act one night and asked me if I would help them get some work in Vegas. So I called a friend, and he sent the assistant entertainment director of the Flamingo to New York to see me. We went up to City Island, to a place called Ginger's (which eventually burned down—I guess Ginger needed the money), and listened to the group. They did a great job, and he spoke to them and explained the way the hotel worked. "The first time you go in," he said, "you go in for union scale. After that, if we pick up your option, you will do very well."

The leader of this group was a temperamental fuck, and he blew his big break. "I don't work scale for nobody," he said. To this day that group has not worked Las Vegas. The best they can do is clubs in the Catskills and small spots around New York. If the big mouth has ever been to Las Vegas, it's as a tourist.

The mob can make someone known pretty easily. It's not that much trouble. They own a great many agents and managers and have working agreements with others. Assuming the performer has talent (because if a performer has no talent even the best connections can't get him booked into the A & P) the first move would be for the agent or manager to get the performer an act. The act itself should be written by reasonably expensive talent and be professional. The next step would be to get him booked into some small clubs to break the act in. Then the connection would use his influence to get bookings in clubs like the Copa in New York, the Chez Paris in Chicago, Bimbo's in Philadelphia. After the performer had gotten a few songs down really well, the manager would get a record cut and get hold of disc jockeys who owed the mob money or favors. This would guarantee the record a good play. There are enough favors owed, believe me, so no one has to make any threats.

If the record has any success at all the real maneuvering starts. You want to get your performer on television? Find out who's betting and who's beholden to the mob. Dean Martin, for example, is a gambler. If he was in hock to somebody—and I'm not saying he is—your boy might get on his TV show as a favor. The movies? Who do you think puts up money to make a lot of these independent pictures? Goodwill Industries? Forget it. Eventually, if the performer is any good, he'll start generating some momentum on his own. Flip Wilson's producers see him on Dean Martin and they want him for their show. Johnny Carson will use anybody. So finally you've got a solid performer on your hands who can make money for a long, long time.

Both the performer and his connection will make good money. Although the connection had to advance money for vocal training, getting an act written, costumes and whatever else, he can get even in a short time. Right at the beginning the performer signs a contract that "marries" him to his angel. The contract is usually pro-rated until you reach 50 percent. This means that, after expenses, the performer gets 50 percent and the agent and backer share the other 50 percent. If a backer has two or three acts that are making money, he can do quite well. And these don't have to be superstars. They can be decent acts most people have never heard of. If they can work 35, 40 weeks in clubs and Vegas lounges, they make great money. Occasionally the mob does get its hands on a legitimate superstar, and then the sky's the limit. (I'm not allowed to mention any of them by name or some big ugly lawyer's gonna get after us.)

It's not only performers who benefit from mob contacts. Nightclub owners can get performers when they need them, and people in other aspects of the business can make a buck or two. A man named Frank Military, for example, had a song he was trying to push by the name of "The Coloring Book." He had recorded three different versions by three different singers and wasn't getting anywhere. Frank wasn't starving, but he wasn't a millionaire either, so he went to an influential friend and said, "I've got a good song, can you help me move it?" This man gave him the names of six of the top DJs who owed him favors and said he would contact them and ask them to give the song a good play. He did this not because Frank was paying him, but because he happened to like Frank Military.

The irony of the story is that one of the versions he had was by Sandy Stewart, one by someone nobody has ever heard of, and one by a young singer on the way up named Barbra Streisand. When Frank had to pick the version he was going to try to sell he took the one on top of the pile—by Streisand. It was a guaranteed play. Everyone knows what happened to the song and the singer, although the mob had nothing to do with her success. I remember Frank shaking his head once and telling me, "If only I had known the lightning that was in that barrel."

At one time you only had three big record companies: Columbia, RCA and Decca. After that, nothing. And anybody who was good was just out of luck if they weren't with these people. So these out-of-luck people were more than willing to make deals with the mob to get backing and get a chance to see how good they really were. Mob men aren't stupid and they know where money can be made. They didn't just give the money away. They investigated the people they were helping, they made sure they had talent and they didn't interfere with the business. So today many of your record labels are mob-connected.

The mob could hardly lose money in this industry. When you are heavy with distributors and with disc jockeys you can ensure your records a fair play. When you own jukeboxes you can put any record you want in them. That makes a record company a solid investment.

Disc jockeys are probably the most important people in the industry. They can boost a bad record or kill a good one. You might be the best singer in the whole world, but unless you're lucky or connected you won't get through the front door of a record company. So you say fuck them, who needs them, and produce your own record. It's been done, people do it. Now who's gonna play it for you? What are you gonna do, stand on the street corner and play it with a loudspeaker? That's where being friendly with a disc jockey is still very important.

Payola still exists on radio, but in different ways than it used to be. In the old days it used to be out-and-out cash, so much money for so many plays, and a few gifts. After the scandal a few years ago people started being careful. No more gifts for DJs. But now the same gifts go to other members of the DJ's family. I had an argument with one of the biggest disc jockeys in New York about just this subject. He was talking on the radio and complaining about tipping taxi drivers in New York after the taxi rates had been raised. I happened to see him in a restaurant a few days later and I said, "You've got a lot of balls to complain about tipping cab-drivers. These guys are working men. You make a salary of one hundred thousand a year and you take tips."

He didn't know what to say, but he denied ever taking anything. "How many times," I asked him, "has a singer's manager taken you out for dinner and picked up the tab to get you to play their record? That's a tip. And how many times has a bottle of perfume been sent to your wife, or a toy to your kids, or theater tickets? These are tips. Tip shit, that's fucking out-and-out bribery." He just shut his mouth. He's no different from most other guys on the radio, people offer and they take. These favors are part of the business, because without plays from DJs no record stands a chance.

Probably the best-known story of the mob using its connections to help someone get ahead in the music industry involves Frank Sinatra. Sinatra was a skinny kid with floppy ears who originally had the backing of the New Jersey people, the Joey Adonis group. In the beginning of his career he was under contract to Harry James. James let him go and he joined Tommy Dorsey but James still held the contract that could have null-and-voided Dorsey's deal. But he didn't choose to do so. Eventually Sinatra wanted out of his deal with Dorsey, and a deal was made with the help of Frank Costello. Now I know all those stories, how Willie Moretti put a gun to Dorsey's head and bought the contract for one dollar and that crap, and that's all it is, a lot of crap. There were no threats made, no violence was involved at all. Dorsey was smart, he realized he had a million-dollar talent on his hands. An arrangement was made that for a number of years Dorsey would receive ten percent of Sinatra's earnings. So Sinatra was given a manager, and the combination of his talent and the mob's connections—everything was done legitimately—made him the most famous singer in the country.

At one point the mob virtually controlled the motion-picture industry. But the decline of Hollywood likewise meant the decline of mob influence in pictures. Today a great number of your movies are made on location by small independent companies formed to make only one or two movies. On occasion there will be mob money backing an independent, or somebody beholden to the mob through gambling or drugs will be in an important spot in one of the companies, but the real boom days when the mob had the final word are over.

The mob still has influence in what's left of Hollywood. Many of the unions that are necessary in production can be manipulated. You want to get into AGVA or Screen Actors Guild or the stagehands' union? Call

Joey, I'll get you in. If we want to cause a problem all that has to be done is to contact the proper union people and tell them to blow up a storm. We set up a picket line and it's all over—including the shooting. Years ago this would happen all the time, but then some people got nailed on a labor-extortion rap and so this doesn't happen too often anymore. But the threat is there, as the people who made *The Godfather* found out.

The mob really didn't have to do very much to let Al Ruddy, who produced *The Godfather,* know there were people watching him. The threat of what the mob was capable of doing was enough to make him agree to certain demands, including putting members of the Italian-American Civil Rights League in the movie as main characters, deleting all mention of the word "Mafia," and a number of other small changes.

The power of the mob in movies was shown to me by Frank Costello in the 1950s. Jack Dragna had sent me back to New York from California to speak to Costello about some business, and I met him in his apartment on Central Park West and 72nd Street. We discussed our business and walked into the living room. There were a number of people, and Frank drifted away into another conversation. But then someone went over to him and whispered in his ear and Costello nodded. About 20 minutes later a famous entertainer arrived to speak to Costello. This was a man the mob had helped early in his career. Once he reached stardom he forgot the people who helped him get there, and his career had subsequently suffered. There was a part in a movie he wanted very badly, and he knew Costello, who had great contacts in Hollywood, could get it for him.

The room went silent as this guy walked into the room. He went right over to Costello and, ignoring the people in the place, said, "I need your help. I need the part of [he mentioned the part and the movie]. It would put me back on top."

Costello wasn't very sympathetic. "Why do you come to see me? Why don't your agents submit you for the part?"

"Because you're a close friend of the people at the studio. You can get it for me."

I could see Costello was trying to put this guy down. "You know," he said, "you're a pain in the ass. We helped you once and you became a big star and then you started abusing people."

"Please, Frank, please help me," the star said. He was beginning to whine.

Costello paused. "Show me you want it."

This big-name entertainer got down on his hands and knees in front of Costello and begged. "I'll do anything. Don't turn away from me."

Actually this was not a big project for Costello. He had done the same thing for a number of other performers he liked for one reason or another. He finally agreed to help this guy. "Get up," he said, and he went to the telephone and made a call.

When he got the proper party on the line he explained the situation, then he asked the star how much money he wanted.

"Whatever they want to give me," was the answer.

Costello reported that into the phone, then said, "You're getting thirty-five thousand dollars." Finally he hung up. The star swore he would never forget the people who had helped him again and, before he left, he borrowed $5000 from Costello against the $35,000. Once he was gone Costello turned to me and said, "Let that be a lesson to you. You never get so big you can't be carved down."

One thing the mob gets out of its contacts in Hollywood is access to starlets. Every girl with a pretty face and tits wants to become a movie star. In most cases they end up as legalized whores. The majority of them have no talent; what they have is their bodies. So what happens is some mob guy gets a broad a bit part in some movie. Then he suggests she go to bed with some guy for the sake of "her career."

This is business. A lot of singers, for example, if they want to work, have to sleep with people. The funny thing is, it's not only the mob guy who does this, the legitimate guy does exactly the same thing. But you can depend on your mob guy to keep his word. Your so-called honest citizen will take some broad and bang her and not even put her to work. Whereas a mob guy, if he makes a deal with a girl, she'll go to work. It may not be the Persian Room, but it's work. This kind of deal is good for everyone; it keeps the girls working and happy and lets the man who sets the thing up make his connections a little tighter.

Nightclubs are wonderful investments for mob people. If you own a good club, your markup on food is 200 percent, your markup on booze is 600 percent (and some of it you're buying bootleg, which is even more profit for you), and as long as you've got customers you're making money. You may even have a cover charge if you've got a name performer. And that name performer is your only big overhead once you get the place going, because you've got to have somebody to bring people through the door. The mobs got into clubs right at the beginning. The best of the original clubs depended on bootlegged liquor. And who controlled the bootlegging? The mob. So when liquor became legal again, who do you think controlled the clubs?

There is rarely a hassle about getting good solid performers into mob clubs. The organization has the ability to supply drugs to any performer and, on the other hand, shut off most of the flow. One famous black singer who draws very, very well in clubs cannot exist without cocaine. She will literally do anything for her coke. I mean anything. She's ours.

I once went up to her apartment with her coke supplier. When he walked in she came running to the door wearing panties and nothing else. She didn't care who saw her, she just needed her coke. But he wasn't what you'd call a nice guy. Before he would give it to her he said, "Get down," and she went down on her knees and gave him a blow job. Then he gave her the coke.

Rock groups? We'll give them what they want to get them to perform, and what they usually want is money and drugs. We have both, therefore we have a lot of the groups.

Some performers who don't use our drugs do use our gambling facilities. And once they're on the losing end, they're ours. A lot of your big entertainers are big gamblers and they get in hock, and they often end up working in mob-owned places to pay their debts off. Any performer who is a big gambler is going to wind up deeply entangled with the mob in one way or another. He's going to have to work their places or he's going to be under their managerial contract.

One famous comedian made a joke of his huge debt. One night, about 2 A.M., I think it was in the Sahara, he came into the casino totally and completely bombed out of his mind. He took off all his clothes and threw himself on a crap table yelling, "Fade me."

The best of all possible worlds is controlling a big-name performer and owning a club to put him or her in. This way you're saving money on entertainment and making money on the customers that are drawn in. Or owning a big-name club and putting a young performer you control in as second or third act. The exposure has got to help their careers, and they might eventually make it as the headliner. Either way, you're going to be making money.

The influence of the mob doesn't really extend too deeply into television. I mean, maybe the producer of a show owes some money, or the star of the show owes some money, and then the organization can get young people on that show. But other than that, the most the mob does is invest in the production of new shows. A perfect example, which goes back a while, is "You'll Never Get Rich," the show in which Phil Silvers played Sergeant Bilko, which was a big hit on TV. Nat Hiken, the man who wrote that show, had to go to the mob for backing. Hiken was not the most popular man in the world. He had a great many difficulties with people in the entertainment business. He went to see some mob people in New York, and they put up the money for the show. Everybody did very well with that one.

I was once a television producer myself, involved in making commercials. I had a guy at one of the biggest advertising agencies in the world who bet with me enough to be almost $80,000 in the hole. This is a pack of money. I let him bet because I knew the man made big money and, go man go. Even if he can't pay me the entire amount, he can pay me so much per week. That's even better than a pension. He was paying me $250 each week, every week, and this went on for a while. Finally he calls me one day and says, "Look, the way we're going I'm going to be married to you for the next nine years. I've got an idea how I can get out and you can make a lot of money." So I told him to continue proceeding along this very interesting path. He asked. "How would you like to produce television commercials?"

I laughed. "I don't know the first fucking thing about commercials except most of them are ridiculous."

He wasn't laughing. "You don't have to. Let me show you how it works.

An advertising agency lets out, or asks for, bids regarding a commercial. The bids come from commercial production houses. As a rule we take the lowest bid, although sometimes we'll take a higher bid because we know the person's work. Now, I am in the position of awarding contracts. I'll let you know what the low bid is and you come in a few hundred dollars lower." So I was in the advertising business. Me, a Madison Avenue man.

My friend in the agency hooked me up with a producer-director, and we made a deal. I agreed to give him 30 percent of everything. We formed a production company, got incorporated, the whole thing. My agency bettor told us three places we could rent space and where to get the equipment we needed.

"When you are awarded the contract," he said, "we give you one-third down, when you go into production you get another third and when you finish you get the rest. The average bid on a contract runs between twenty-eight and fifty thousand, depending on the length and type of commercial. All I want you to do is knock ten percent off my bill for every commercial I give you."

We set up our "office" in my producer-director's apartment. All it cost me was half the price of printing up cards with the name of our production agency on them and an answering service. We didn't do any business except with this one agency because it wasn't necessary; within two weeks we had our first contract. Overall, I produced six commercials with this outfit. Produced? I collected the checks, which were very nice, thank you.

When we made the commercials we rented either Pelican Studios, which is on 109th Street and Madison Avenue, or we rented space at MPO on 44th and Second. So we had no problems.

We did one lipstick commercial, two hairsprays, two hosiery and one tire spot. The only time I ever opened my mouth was when we were interviewing models for the hairspray commercials. We did the actual interviewing in my partner's small office. I just sat in the back and watched these beautiful models parade in and out. Finally one broad came in and I mentally crossed her off the list because she just wasn't as good-looking as some of the others. She walked right up to my partner and asked, "Are you the guy who decides who gets to be in the commercials?"

He nodded.

"Okay," she said. "Look, in the last six months I've been laid, lied to and bullshitted a dozen times. I'll put it right on the line. I want this commercial and I'll ball anybody I have to to get it."

I laughed out loud. "You got it, sister, I like your style," I said. Neither of us ever touched her—which is unusual for me—but we used her in both hairspray shots. Actually the fact she looked a little worn and torn made the ad more real.

We were knocking the jock off the other major production houses, including MPO, VideoPrints and Pelican, and finally my partner was approached by someone from one of the major houses who wanted to buy us out. He told them they would have to speak to me. They made an appointment and I put on my gray flannel suit and went up there. I didn't fuck around. "How much do you want to give us?"

"Three hundred fifty thousand dollars."

I never blinked an eye. "Sold." I gave my partner one-third, I canceled the debt, and walked away with $235,000. The corporation was then dissolved. And you ask me why I love television.

As new areas of entertainment pop up you can be sure the mob will get involved. And, let me repeat, most of the time it will be on a completely legal basis. These rock festivals, for example, mob members backed a few of them until they realized no one was going to make any money. Performers were flaky, they didn't show up, other people ran off with the receipts. Worst of all, there was no place you could take a crap. The last one anyone got involved in was a disaster in upstate New York, which ended the enchantment with these things.

The only area the mob has no interest in is Broadway, except, of course, for original-cast albums if they can make a connection. It's just too big a risk because too many shows go under too quickly. Otherwise the entertainment world has been one of the most successful, and most enjoyable, areas me and the mob have been involved in.

Besides, my mother always wanted me to be in show business.

CHAPTER *11*
THE COST OF HIGHS

The end of World War II was the close of one era of mob history and the beginning of another. In the late 1940s the first real crackdown on the mob began, and you had all sorts of committees and district attorneys running around screaming bloody murder (which was true, along with assorted other crimes). On the inside, this pressure caused a clearing out of the few conservative Mustache Petes who had survived earlier uprisings. A lot of young talent gained power. The first thing they did was look for new areas to expand the family business into. The war had created a shortage of everything, prices were skyrocketing. Finally, inevitably, the mob went to pot . . . and hashish, cocaine, speed, pills, heroin and more lately psychedelic drugs.

The marriage between the organization and narcotics was made in heaven. Narcotics today is the king of the crime world. It is by far the most profitable area to work in, and by just as far the most dangerous. A lot of important people, including Vito Genovese, have gone to jail on drug raps. And I could not even begin to guess the number of people who have died because drugs are so profitable. I have good reason to believe that a job I did in Pittsburgh in 1966 had to do with drugs. The good reason is simply that the man who paid my salary was in the drug-importing business.

I was working for Meyer as well as doing some free-lance at the time. A member of the Pittsburgh organization came to New York to meet with me and offered me a $20,000 contract. He told me his people would take care of all the details and the entire job wouldn't take more than three days. I was in Pittsburgh 24 hours later.

This turned out to be a very easy hit. My target didn't drive, so he depended on taxicabs to get around. He also had a girlfriend who he visited almost every night. I was told he left her house between 2 and 3 A.M. to go back to his old lady. I clocked him two nights in a row, then I gave my employers the okay. On the third night they went out and glommed a cab for me. I drove it to a spot about two blocks away from his girlfriend's house and then waited.

He came out of her house right on time. I saw him before he saw me, so I put the lights on and was in motion even before he looked in my direction. He was half drunk anyway so I don't think he would have seen me even if I had been parked right in front of her house. Sure enough, he signaled me and I picked him up. I drove about three blocks, pulled over to the side of the road and then turned around and shot him four times. He never had a clue. After killing him I drove the cab a few more blocks, parked it on a side street and got out. Fingerprints? I wore gloves. I went to a bus stop about five blocks away, climbed on a bus and went downtown to my hotel. The next morning I was back in New York.

Narcotics is another market created by the government. At one point you could walk into any pharmacy and buy almost whatever you wanted. Then drugs were outlawed, but the people still wanted. By shutting off the legal supply the government didn't shut off the want. As I've said, any time you tell people they can't have something they want, you've created a new business for me. Thank you, Uncle Sam.

In the early 1960s, because the market was so dangerous, the mob was allegedly getting out of narcotics. That's a lot of shit, they never even dreamed of getting out. There is simply too much money involved. The profit margin in the drug trade is unbelievable. Most narcotics are cheap to produce and easy to smuggle into this country if you know what you're doing. Since the supply will never catch up with the demand, the street price has absolutely no relationship to what it costs to manufacture and ship the stuff. One kilo of unrefined heroin which may cost as little as $1500 in Europe is worth more than $100,000 in this country after it has been cut and distributed.

The government really doesn't hurt you too much. Every time they pass another drug law the mob just claps its hands because all the laws in the world aren't going to stop people from using drugs. All these laws do is drive amateurs out of business and send the prices higher. Laws don't deter people from using drugs, they just make it more difficult and more expensive for them to get the stuff. But they will get it, we personally guarantee that.

Have you ever seen a real junkie who does not have his stuff? He will do anything to get his next shot or his next snort. I went looking for a guy one time and I knew he was good friends with a junkie. Rather than knock my brains out searching for the guy I grabbed the junkie and locked him in a room. It didn't take long; he told me exactly where to find his best friend. I threw him a small bag of smack and told him to be my guest.

I would guess that 90 percent of all the petty thievery and muggings in your major cities are directly attributable to narcotics. A junkie is a desperate individual. He goes through a torture not to be believed and when he needs a fix he is uncontrollable. The average junkie has a habit that costs him between $60 and $100 every single day and has to steal to survive. This is a lot of money, and the only way most people can make that much is to steal or shoplift or mug people or make prostitutes of themselves. Lots of your young prostitutes are addicts.

Don't blame all of that on the organization. As far as I'm concerned, the mob never created an addict. These people do it to themselves. It begins with grass. They feel they have too many pressures and instead of taking a Valium or going to a gym or talking it over with a friend or taking some booze, they start smoking grass. Pretty soon grass does not give them the buzz they want, so they go to pills. When that wears out they start sniffing coke, or they start shooting up. They begin by doing what we call chipping, a little here, a little there, and the next thing they know, they're hooked. Every one of them said the same thing at the beginning: "It isn't going to happen to me." Listen, I'll tell you, it's gonna happen to you. You are going to fall in, and then we will own you. I estimate there are a minimum of 4 million hard-drug addicts and another 30 million regularly using grass in this country. And there are loads of people like me, sitting back and watching, just sitting and saying, "Come here, sucker, I got your piece of candy."

One addict I know was once a very successful advertising man. The pressures of his business got to him pretty good and he started blasting grass. Within a year and a half of being a constant grass user he was on heroin. Within another year and a half his career was destroyed and he had to go out in the streets and steal in order to survive. His habit cost him his job, his family and everything he owned. Now it costs him about $150 a day, which he gets by stealing and shoplifting.

In my opinion the people that become junkies are afraid to face the problems of life, and I don't care how old they are. When I was a kid we were destitute. If I ate meat once a week I was very fortunate. My diet consisted of cereal, potatoes and macaroni. And we didn't know the word "welfare"; my people were too proud. One way or the other we survived. I used to hustle Coke bottles on the street or I stole. I stole, but at least I felt like a man. I didn't look for an escape. I have a 17-year-old nephew that I had to straighten out. This kid has never had a hungry day in his life. He doesn't know what poor means, yet he got into pills and he was always high and giving his mother a real bad time. One night I had enough and I laid into him. I mean I beat this kid. I don't care what he does with his life, but he'd better stay away from drugs. If he doesn't, I'll play four-walled handball with him again.

I would not touch grass, cocaine, hash, heroin or anything else if you put a gun to my head and cocked the hammer. I would tell you to pull the trigger before I'd take any of that stuff. Because to mess with any of it is the beginning of a slow and painful death. I'd rather die quick.

That doesn't mean I have any qualms about dealing in narcotics. I'm out to make a dollar. This is bullshit, qualms. If I don't have any qualms about blowing a guy's brains out, why am I going to let narcotics bother me? In plain English, to me this is a business. I am here to turn a profit. I've heard people say, "I don't want that kind of money." Now you tell me when money knew who made it or who spent it. Like the Swiss bank people say, "Money has no smell." As far as I'm concerned narcotics is money. I'm in this particular business because drugs have made a lot of people very wealthy. That's why the drug trade is so well organized; that's why people kill other people to control pieces of it. Money.

Every narcotics deal begins in a laboratory someplace. It may be Marseilles, France, or Des Moines, Iowa, but that's where the stuff is either made from chemicals (your psychedelic drugs) or processed from plants. The plants themselves come from places like Turkey and Asia. Marseilles is still supposed to be the capital of the drug world, but because of heat from international police agencies most of the actual business is being carried on in South America. Right now the country of Colombia is the major distribution point in the world for hard drugs. Hong Kong is second because all the Chinese merchandise comes through there, and Europe is third. The reason Colombia leads is because its officials are the easiest to deal with. There is no way an individual can operate in this business unless he knows he can depend on the cooperation of certain people in specific positions. I would have to say that some very rich people are the heads of the police departments in a bunch of these South American countries.

A narcotics deal can involve any number of people, from a very few to a great many. You need someone to put up the money to pay the chemists for their handiwork, someone to bring it into the country, someone to cut it and package it, and someone to organize distribution to street pushers. Before the dope reaches the street customers, as many as eight or nine or more people may have bought and sold pieces of it, and it may have been cut 12 or more times.

One thing is certain, everybody involved will make money; the manufacturer, the banker, the smuggler, the middlemen and the street pushers. There are chemists in Marseilles, for example, who work only four or five weeks a year. In that time they can purify 400 kilos of heroin, each kilo weighing about 2.2 pounds. In Europe you can buy a kilo of unrefined

THE COST OF HIGHS

heroin, as I said, for about $1500. (Refined stuff will go for between $5000 and $6000 depending on who does it and how it's cut.) When you get it into the United States, if you're selling in bulk, you can probably get close to $18,000 per kilo. If you want to do better than that, and go through the expense and problems of cutting it yourself, you can be your own middleman. You can dilute it as much as 95 percent with milk sugar and quinine and still get the same $18,000 to $20,000 per kilo. But now you've got a whole lot more kilos to work with. The street pusher ends up selling bags filled with five or ten percent heroin and the rest filler, which is fine, because the human system was not made to take anything much stronger than that. If an "importer" hustles he can make more than $100,000 per kilo pure profit.

When I worked in narcotics in the 1950s and early '60s, I dealt strictly in marijuana and heroin, your so-called big twosome. But now everything is a money-maker: coke, hash, psychedelic drugs and even pills. When people think of narcotics they tend to think of heroin and pot, but there is almost as much money to be made in the little multicolored capsules. People use pills because they feel they help them get the maximum out of their bodies. The ultimate high. And once, twice or three times the pills will work, but in the long run they've got to hurt you. Have you ever seen someone coming down off pills? It's bad. It's like going cold turkey. They throw up, get the dry heaves, they sweat, they tremble. But these people don't learn, they keep buying them as fast as they can get them, and believe me, they can get them.

About two years ago, for example, I was offered one million pills of all kinds for a penny apiece, a total of $10,000. At that time these pills were selling for 50 cents each on the open market. I didn't want to bother with them because I was into something else. And under any circumstances I don't like to get involved as a drug distributor. But I could have made myself at least a quarter of a million dollars. All I had to do was go out and hire a few pushers and I was in business. I would have paid the pushers maybe 20 cents per pill at most, and still made a $290,000 profit. From stinking little pills.

Athletes are among pill-poppers. They use them for pain-killing,

164

energy and courage. I knew an offensive lineman who wouldn't go near a football field unless he was flying. Before every game he took a whole rainbow of pills—green ones, red ones, yellow ones. When he saw the game films on the following Mondays he would be amazed at the things he had done on the field. Even the ultrarespectable New York Yankees keep a good supply of pills on hand. They get their supply from a drugstore on Greenwich Avenue in the Village.

The worst part about professional athletes popping pills is that kids follow suit. A high school on Long Island, for example, had a minor scandal in 1972 when the coach was caught supplying pills to his team. Once kids get into them, they can get hooked.

Let us now delve into the wonderful world of marijuana. People smoke grass faster than we can grow it. If someone wants to really make money let them invent artificial marijuana, like they did artificial real grass. I can see it now, Astro-pot! There is great money in marijuana. We can buy a pound of it in South America or Mexico for five dollars and ship it to any distribution point in the United States for a few dollars more. I can sell it to a wholesaler for $100 per pound, minimum of 10 pounds, and he can turn around and get $25 or more per ounce. In case you've forgotten, there are 16 ounces in a pound, which figures out at $400 for each $5 investment.

Marijuana is the most popular of all drugs. The best market is kids in high school and on your college campuses. But running a close second is your middle-class, respectable citizen. You would be amazed at how many doctors, lawyers, college professors, performers, politicians, professional men and women smoke grass. I don't care, it's their funeral.

And your college campuses! I knew a kid at the University of Michigan who made himself $300,000 in one year by selling at $25 per ounce. He had a steady clientele he knew he could trust and a good supplier. He would do an average of 15 pounds per week, which adds up to $4500. This is a perfect example of a young man taking advantage of a college education. He was very, very lucky though; when an amateur sells that much he almost invariably gets knocked off. They usually make the mistake of selling something to the man with the fuzzy nuts. Or maybe they dig into somebody's territory and that somebody, rather than engaging in a bit of violence, calls his contact at the local police station and tips them off. Either way, the amateur goes. The cops would just as soon nail an amateur as a professional, they don't care at all. You can't really trust the cops on the drug scene, which is why when I dealt in narcotics all I wanted to get involved in was the smuggling. In and out. I didn't want to get caught holding the stuff.

I was living in California and working for Jack Dragna when I first got involved. Jack made a good portion of his income from drugs. One of my regular duties was to drive down to Mexico and bring a load back across the border. Since I was on salary this was part of my job and I didn't get paid anything extra for it. There is no set rate for smuggling drugs in; it depends mainly on who you're doing business with, how much you're bringing in and how much danger is involved. If I was going to do it today I would figure out what the boss was going to make per key and charge him ten percent of that figure. Smuggling was one of the easiest jobs I've ever had.

To this day I could drive a car into this country, any car you name, and bring in four kilos of pure heroin with me. I would be willing to let any customs agent in the world search that car and he wouldn't be able to find so much as a pinch. I would simply take a tire off its rim and tape the bags inside the tire. It's hollow, there's plenty of room, and I would use electrical tape to hold it on because it is extra strong. Then I would put the tire back on its rim, put the wheel back on the car and drive through customs.

The only way customs can possibly detect the bags is by fluoroscoping the wheel, which is a very slow and tedious process, and unless they're pretty sure you're carrying something they are just not going to bother. In all the trips I made I was only searched once, and they made a good search. They looked in the hood, in the gas tank, they even went so far as to take the wheel off the car, but they never pulled the tire off the rim. If they had done that they would have found four kilos of pure heroin.

The Mexican border is easy to crack. You usually can come right in through a checkpoint, especially on one of those Sundays when thousands of people go down for the bullfights and all of them try to come back at the same time. But if you're the nervous type there are a thousand ways you can come in without being checked. You've got miles and miles of woods and dry-bed areas and you can easily drive a jeep or truck across one of these empty spaces. There is almost no possibility you'll be spotted, much less caught.

Shipping drugs in from Europe or Asia isn't really that much more difficult. All you have to do is hide them in something you're shipping in, the best thing being a car. Amateurs make three mistakes: Frst, they try to carry it in on their body. No way you can hide it, and when they nail you with it on your person it's all over. If they find it in something you're bringing in, they still have to prove you put it there, or at least you knew it was there.

Second, amateurs are greedy. They try to bring in too much at one time. They try to make a million dollars in one shot and they're going to get caught. You are much better off bringing in a few kilos at a time rather than a large amount. For argument's sake, say you bring in eight kilos of heroin, which weighs about 17 1/2 pounds. That may not sound like much, but eight kilos of heroin, sold in the right place, will be worth maybe $160,000.

The big mistake they make, and often it is their last one, is thinking customs people are stupid. Believe me, the border boys have seen every possible way of smuggling drugs into this country and if you make the slightest mistake they will nail you. It's very easy to hide a few pounds of drugs in a car. You can hide it in the steering column, anywhere. But amateurs make one mistake here, they forget that whatever you put in you have to take out. If a car is supposed to weigh 2750 pounds it better weigh 2750 pounds when it arrives, because it is going to be weighed and if it weighs too much it is going to be torn apart. Just like they showed you in *The French Connection*.

Let's assume I wanted to smuggle something in from Europe. I would take the heavy metal fender or bumper off and replace it with lightweight aluminum, and no one would ever notice the difference. I might have the sponge taken out of the seats and put the heroin in there. I might even take some heavy parts out of the engine, parts that don't have anything to do with the running of the car, like the horn or the windshield-wiper apparatus, and who's gonna notice they're missing. But that car is going to weigh exactly what it is supposed to. A few years ago some idiots tried to smuggle gold coins in the spare tire which they locked in the trunk. It might have worked, except the spare tire weighed something like 600 pounds.

Bringing narcotics in across the Canadian border is almost as easy as the Mexican border. You drive up to the gate, the guard asks, "You American?" "Yeah." "Good-bye," and home free. If that doesn't appeal to you there are dozens of officially closed roads which cut across empty areas and lead directly to major roads. In the daytime it's not easy to spot anyone using these roads, at night it's impossible. With a four-wheel-drive car and some soft headlights, this trip is a cinch. One guy who had made the trip dozens of times got word that the border patrol was on to him. So he had a helicopter come in and pick up his merchandise. Besides the roads there are small airports where a small plane can land, two Great Lakes and many other smaller waterways.

As I said, the single really bad way to bring narcotics in is to try to hide them on your body. No matter where you put it, in your heel, up your ass, somebody has tried it before. I knew a guy who once tried to smuggle in diamonds by hiding them in specially made false teeth. He didn't make it. These people know where to look, they have the most modern machines to help them, and they are going to find your cache—if they suspect you.

The most ingenious method I ever heard of was a man who smuggled heroin across the Mexican border by homing pigeon. He would take the pigeons into Mexico and tape an ounce of heroin to each one. Who the hell is going to know the difference? They see a flock of pigeons coming in, why bother to look? A pigeon is a pigeon. He had a great racket going and, for all I know, still does.

Two ways you can get caught bringing narcotics in. The first is just bad luck. It happens. You plan carefully and something goes wrong and you're cooked. Nothing you can do to prevent it except get out of the business. The second is greed—somebody else's. Most cops, and that

includes customs people, get their information from stool pigeons. They
have made it very lucrative for people to inform on smugglers, giving
them as much as 25 percent of the total value of the take. One of the great
rackets that Europeans run is to sell a load to some amateur and then
inform on him. That way they make 125 percent of the value of the
drugs. The only completely reliable way to avoid this is to know who
you're buying from and treat them well.

This is a lesson I learned in Mexico. A lot of idiots try to fuck the local
help and end up getting caught. They promise them X dollars for their part
of the job and then they give them half and tell them to take it or leave it.
The Mexicans never complain, because they know the guy will be back for
more in a few weeks. The next trip he tries the same deal, but when he
reaches the border the feds—who have been informed by the Mexicans—
are waiting for him. The Mexicans get paid by him, whatever he's giving
them, plus they get reward money, so they're even. What I did to avoid that
was to overpay them. I worked with a man named Juano Hernandez and I
promised him $500 and his two assistants $300 each. When I paid them off
I gave Juano $700 and his little helpers $500 each. After that I could do no
wrong and I had nothing to worry about. They knew they could make
more with me than they could with the government.

Juano and I got to be good friends. In addition to our narcotics deals we
went into the automobile business. We decided that since I was driving
round trip anyway, we ought to take advantage of it. So a few days before
I was supposed to leave Los Angeles I would steal a car, buy a fake registration, and hide it in a garage somewhere. When Jack told me to go to
Mexico I would drive this car down and leave it with Juano to sell. Meanwhile, he was doing exactly the same thing on the other side of the border.
I would return to LA with the car he stole in Mexico and dispose of it
through one of the biggest used-car dealers in town.

Juano was even more of a friend than I realized. At one point I did a
favor for a lawyer in Los Angeles. A client of his had skipped bail and left
his mother holding a due note with her home as collateral. The lawyer had
gotten word this guy had gone to New York and, when Jack sent me back
there on business, the lawyer asked me to keep an eye out for him. I found

him right away and I told him he could go back to California either on a plane or on a slab. The result was two years in San Quentin, but mama kept her house.

The whole time he's serving he's promising to kill me as soon as he got out. It didn't bother me when I heard it because I figured I would see him as soon as he was released and shut his mouth for him. But when he did get out I started looking for him and I couldn't find him. Nobody had seen him, and now I'm beginning to get a bit itchy. Finally three weeks pass and I'm walking down Sunset and here comes this guy. Both of his arms are encased in casts and he's holding them straight out. I said, "Holy Christ, what happened to you?"

Quietly he says, "Please, tell your friends I ain't never gonna hurt ya. I got nuthin' to bother you about. You the nicest guy I know."

He told me this story. The day he got out of jail he started walking down the road to catch a bus. This big black car pulled up beside him and two guys jumped out and grabbed him, just like in the movies. They drove from San Raphael to Los Angeles and no one in the car said a single word. Finally they stopped in a quiet area in the Mexican part of town and got out. They threw him on the ground and proceeded to break both of his arms. As he was lying there in the dirt in pain one of them leaned over and said, "You hurt my friend, I keel you."

I knew it had to be Juano and I called him to thank him. "Why didn't you tell me about it?" I asked.

He was all apologetic. "Oh, I don't know. I theenk maybe you get mad cuz I interfere with your bizness."

Once you get narcotics into the country it is very easy to move it around. Eventually it is going to reach the street pusher. These street people are very rarely members of the organization. Usually they are drug users themselves, trying to make enough cash to support their own habit. These are the people who run the risk of being caught. And if they are, who cares? They can be replaced within hours.

The people who almost never get bothered are the big operators, the people who set up the operations, or finance them. The bigger a man is in this business the less chance he has of ever getting caught, because there are numerous levels between him and the drugs. He simply hires people to go out and do the work; he never sees the stuff and he never handles it. All he does is give the orders or, if he's at the very top, supply the money.

A deal is easy to set up. An individual will go to a potential banker and explain the proposition; how much cash is needed and what the possible return is. For example, he might say he can get his hands on 15 pounds (the Orientals only sell it by the pound) of pure heroin for $7500 per and he can sell them for $18,000 per key, or a total of $270,000. The banker will either say "Fine, here's one hundred twelve thousand dollars, I want two hundred twenty-four thousand dollars back and you can keep the rest," or he'll pass. If he puts up the money he can usually be pretty sure of doubling it within a month. The guy who set up the entire operation makes a clear $40,000, enough money for him to start a small operation of his own.

Going into business for yourself is not very difficult, as long as you make sure you have the proper permission and you're not cutting in on anyone else's business. If I wanted into this business I could go to almost any city and within a few days stack a warehouse full of as much as I could pay for. I would start with the junkie on the street. I'd lock him in a room, and when he started to bend over with cold turkey he would tell me anything I wanted to know. He would put me onto his connection. I would inform the connection that I wasn't interested in buying from him, I wanted quantity. Because he knows he can expect a small percentage just for making the proper introductions, after checking my credentials he would put me onto his supplier. I'm sure this supplier would have me thoroughly checked out again and then I could get anything I could pay for.

I would have no problem getting rid of it, and getting rid of it in such a way that there would be relatively little chance of getting caught. Most people get caught because they are too greedy and never bother to check on who they are doing business with. If you know who you're dealing with, chances are you won't get in trouble. When I was working for Jack Dragna we knew every individual we sold to. We found out where they lived, who they associated with, what time they went to the bathroom and whether they took a shit or a piss. We checked. I learned my lesson.

If I was selling and you came to me as a buyer, the first thing I would do is deny that I had anything to do with narcotics. Then I would ask you where you lived, what your telephone number was, who your friends were, why you wanted to buy. If you were reluctant to give me any of this information I would buy you a cup of coffee and bid you farewell. I don't need you. But if you answered my questions I would discuss the matter in a hypothetical manner. "If I did have it," I would ask, "how much would you want?" And then, when you left, I would have somebody tailing you to see where you went. Then I would begin checking. Finally, if I came up satisfied I would do business with you. If I had the slightest doubt I wouldn't touch you.

The low man on the pole is my ultimate customer—the street junkie. Junkies come in all shapes and sizes and, in the end, they all die the same way. A great many people have died from narcotics. Billie Holiday, Judy Garland, Sonny Liston, Marilyn Monroe, "Big Daddy" Lipscomb, Janis Joplin. Booze and pills, all of them. And Lenny Bruce, the famous fucked-up Lenny Bruce. I knew Lenny when he was straight. He could have been a tremendous success as a comic but no, he had something to prove. I don't know what, I couldn't answer you what he was trying to prove. But he started on drugs and his mind went. I remember seeing him about six months before he died. I was on the street and he walked by and I said, "Hello, Lenny, how are you, kid?" In a deep, deep, very slow voice he answered, "Heeeyyyy, hello, babeee." He had no idea who he was talking to. He was walking 15 feet off the ground, he didn't even know who he was.

I have to guess that famous people get into drugs because they can't take success. They let the pressure get to them and it destroys them. There is a very famous blind, black musician, for example. The man is a magnificent talent, but up until a few years ago he had a $2000-a-week habit. Two thousand dollars a week! He had to have his connection traveling with him full time. He paid all the guy's expenses plus the cost of the merchandise. This guy was lucky, though; he lived.

Jack Dragna, ironically, died of an overdose. I guess your big writers would call that poetic justice. He supposedly died of a heart attack in a motel. I was in New York at the time and I didn't find out until later that he had actually died of an overdose of drugs. I didn't even know he was taking drugs until a few months before he died. He wasn't an addict and he never lost control of his mind, so he wasn't a danger to anybody, but he liked to take a shot of his own stuff from time to time.

At least famous people and mob people can afford their habits. Most junkies are forced into crime to make enough money to buy their daily requirement. I've used junkies on a number of occasions. I was in the electric-typewriter business; I gave the junkies $15 for a $400 machine and I got $125 for it with no problem. I have no idea how these guys got the machines, but they did. I also did a brisk business in color television sets. Those statistician guys estimate that in order for all the junkies in New York City alone to support their habits for one year, they have to steal over two billion dollars' worth of goods.

Because there is so much money involved you have a great deal of bribery in the drug world. We would simply not be able to operate in this area if officials weren't willing to turn their heads. A lot of money is paid to a lot of people, but your main contacts are always in the local police departments. There are two types of cops working on the narco squad: Those that take and the suckers.

There are a few cops who wouldn't accept a bribe if you dropped a million dollars at their feet. These people are dedicated to their jobs, you gotta admit. To them it's not the money, would you believe, it's the principle?

Other cops I know of joined the force for one reason—to become crooks. A New York City narcotics cop or a Chicago narcotics cop can make as much as $50,000 a year if he's half smart.

I didn't know it was happening but I wasn't surprised to hear that more than 200 pounds of hard drugs had been stolen from the police property clerk in New York City (including the "French Connection" haul). That had to be an inside job. And they had plenty of your leisure time to plan it—like ten years. At this point those drugs have long been recycled and shot into arms all over the city, making a group of New York's finest some of New York's richest.

If a cop is a crook the narco squad is a little bit of heaven. For example, an "importer" I've worked with once got caught with eight kilos. Eight kilos in New York can get you 25 years because this is a felony: possession with intent to sell. The cops had him cold and they hit him for $25,000 cash. He never said a fuckin' word, he just got them their 25 Gs and would have kissed their feet if that's what they wanted. Even your street pushers get hit by cops for $1000, $1500 at a crack, but they're not about to complain. Occasionally you'll really bump into a hustling cop, and he'll not only take your money, he'll confiscate the drugs and sell them himself. But that doesn't happen too often; most cops would rather take the money and run.

There is a tremendous amount of violence connected with drugs. I've never really seen any reason for this, because here too there is more than enough business to go around, but it still happens. The three main causes of violence are moving in on someone else's business, trying to cheat somebody and informing on a deal.

Number one: moving in on someone else's territory. At one point the entire drug trade in Harlem was operated by the organization. But in the last few years the demand increased so rapidly the mob was forced to let blacks and Cubans set up their own operations. The mob simply could not handle all the business and still maintain strict safety precautions. Besides, the drug trade was so open that it was only a matter of time until the police were forced to act—and who better to act as fall guys than the niggers. So they were given some of the business. Not all, some.

A few of the black pushers who worked for white-run organizations saw this happening and began to get independent ideas of their own. They decided to go into business for themselves. Unfortunately, a few moved in on the organization. Two black pushers on 116th Street told their white supplier that they had found a new supplier—themselves— and that he was no longer needed. Actually it turned out to be the other way around, they were the ones who found themselves not needed. They had their heads blown off. That was the last independence movement on 116th Street.

Number two: cheating. If you make a deal with a man you should carry through your end or the other man will get angry. The extent of his anger will probably depend on how much muscle he has backing him up. There are innumerable ways of cheating a man; one that is often used is bringing a gun to a meet and relieving the other man of his cash or drugs. I've known of people substituting flour or milk sugar for heroin, taking the payment and running. I know one guy who decided to make a killing: He pulled this substitution trick nine times in one night and then started running. Sure enough, there was a killing: his. Then there is the simple act of trying to shortchange somebody.

In 1955 I went to Mexico for Jack to pick up 25 kilos of heroin. I arrived at the meeting place and the dealer said, "Give me my money." I told him fine, there would be no problems, I just wanted to count the packages first. I counted 24.

"Hey, babe," I said, "there's only twenty-four here."

He got a little belligerent and started screaming at me and cursing me out. "There's twenty-five," he screamed. "Now give my my money."

"Count 'em for yourself," I yelled at him. Meanwhile I'm getting angry. "There's twenty-four here now and I couldn't have gone nowhere with the twenty-fifth." Then I hit him over the head with something that was lying around, took the stuff and left without paying him a cent. I delivered to Jack and told him what happened. Jack said, "Pay him for the twenty-four." I told him I'd rather put the guy in a river. Jack was adamant: "No, pay him for the twenty-four and tell him I want to see him." So I went back down to Mexico, paid for the 24 and gave him Jack's message. The guy came back with me and apologized to Jack, and Jack accepted the apology and then told him, "You do that to me again and I swear I'll feed you to the sharks!"

Number three: informing. Anyone who informs on a deal had better have a good life-insurance policy. For the most part, narcotics arrests are made through informers. I've found that you cannot operate in any major city for more than 24 hours before some law-enforcement agency tabs you. Someone knows you're coming or hears you're there, passes the word, and the police are out looking for you even before you get established. That's why it's best to make all your police and political contacts before you arrive. This is a kind of insurance that can be provided by the local organization, who you're gonna have to deal with anyway. The penalty for informing is death. I know of one situation in which a New York City narcotics detective turned the tables on an informer. For $5000 he told the mob who had informed him of a shipment. The informer was shortly thereafter found not breathing.

The mob does make an effort to hold the violence to a minimum because it is just not necessary. No one gains anything, and the newspapers always blow it out of proportion. But when it becomes necessary it is used. There is just too much money at stake here.

There are two possible ways of getting organized crime out of the drug trade: completely stopping the flow of drugs into the country, or legalizing narcotics. The only way to stop the traffic would be by picking up every single one of the little pushers in the country and throwing them in jail without bail. Then you go after the middlemen and finally the so-called big fish. You would, of course, have to clean up your police departments, build new jails and have a sweep of the streets like this every two or three months, but if you're not going to legalize it this is the only way to stop it. Remember, a large segment of the public, our customers, supports us, and they are going to do everything they can to stop you from stopping us.

That leaves legalization. Heroin is legal in England, and I'm told you don't have a real narcotics problem in England. An addict can go and get a shot. The profit has been taken out of the drug trade, and once you've eliminated the profit you've eliminated the mob. The only problem then would be to help the people who are already hooked. In the beginning you would have a tremendous rush for free drugs because of all the junkies you've got, but eventually the number would stabilize. And by making narcotics available under controlled conditions to anyone who wants them, you'll eliminate one of the major reasons people start using them in the first place.

Narcotics are forbidden fruit. If I walked out of a room and told somebody, "Whatever you do, don't open that box," I'm not gonna be gone 30 seconds before he's into that box. The same thing is true of narcotics, you tell somebody not to touch and he'll be curious enough to touch. And once he does he's hooked.

Take your pick, you're either gonna make it legal or not. But if you don't, I know where you can get an electric typewriter cheap. Or would you prefer a color TV?

CHAPTER *12*

I CAN GET IT FOR YOU NO SALE

Y ou remember the movie *The Graduate*? Well, Dustin Hoffman's family had a big pool party to celebrate his college graduation. In the middle of that party this businessman took him aside and, very quietly, whispered one word of advice: "Plastics."

Well, almost the exact same thing happened to me. After I got out of the army I was hanging out not by a pool but around the pool hall, running numbers, and trying to figure out which way to go. This older friend of mine took me aside and whispered in my ear the one word, "Shit." Then he added: "Remember, kid, there's more money in shit than there is in gold." Happy graduation.

It was the best advice I ever got. Bootlegging, smuggling, ticket scalping and assorted other small businesses may not sound as exciting as making a hit, smuggling dope or running numbers, but they have been profitable for me for many years. And money—not excitement—is the name of the game. I've made bootleg perfume and liquor, I've duplicated tapes and records, I've smuggled cigarettes and other taxable items, I've scalped tickets and sold cars. Anything to make a fast buck. And, in every single one of these operations, I've had a very important partner: your so-called honest citizen. Your honest citizen is not honest. He may not be as big a crook as me but he's a bigger hypocrite. "We have this terrible crime problem," he says, "and I pay my taxes, but the police still don't do anything about it. What you got to sell me today? Hot TV set?"

One of the more lucrative businesses in this country today is smuggling cigarettes. Not diamonds, minks or watches. Cigarettes. Paper and tobacco wrapped tightly together, to be set on fire. Most states charge a heavy tax for every pack you buy, and that tax just about doubles the price. By going to North Carolina and buying the cigarettes himself an individual can eliminate the tax. Right now, for example, the tax on one carton of cigarettes in New York State is $2.26. The going price for a carton of cigarettes in New York is around $5.10. In Carolina the price is $2.33 a carton, which gives a "salesman" a profit area of almost three dollars to work in. I usually charge $3.50 per carton, which is fair and which gives me over a buck a carton profit. And I never have a shortage of honest citizens willing to cheat their government out of a couple of dollars in tax money.

There are a number of different ways of getting rid of the cartons. I can walk into any office—cold—and say to the receptionist, "Anybody want to buy cigarettes?" She knows what I mean. Five minutes later she'll come back with an order for 100 cartons. I just go downstairs, hop in the back of my panel truck and fill the order.

Or I can find some guy that has a cigarette machine in his place and sell directly to him. If I do that, though, I've got to find out what the tax-stamp number for his area is, have a stamp made (which costs about $50) and make sure every pack is stamped. That way, if the tax inspector comes around, he can't tell the bootleg cigarettes in the machine from the real thing. In most cases the machine owner will mix up packs of my cigarettes with the packs he buys legally because his distributor would know something illegal was up if, all of a sudden, he stopped buying from him.

Or third, I can find a machine myself and pay the owner to let me use it. I can pay him more per pack than he makes normally, so you know he's going to go along with me. The cigarettes are stamped, and the customer never knows the difference. It takes a little longer to get rid of a load by selling through your own machine, but there is more of a profit. You can get as much as 60 cents per pack in most machines, which means you're making a good living.

One of the really nice things about cigarettes and other bootleg items is that you rarely have to put up very much money of your own. At one point I had a deal going with one of the biggest shylocks in the country, a man I mentioned before, Joe Cheese. When New York State first started to raise cigarette taxes he contacted me and told me he had a deal. At that point we were paying $1.65 per carton in Carolina. He told me, "I want you to go down there and pick up forty thousand cartons."

"That is not exactly confetti, you know," I said. "It'll cost sixty-six thousand dollars."

He handed me a paper bag with $75,000 cash in it. "That'll cover your trucks, expenses and give you enough money to make a few payoffs if you get nailed," he said. "If you go down [get caught] you don't have to give me back nothing. If you score you owe me eighty-five thousand dollars." He initiated the whole deal, but I had to do all the work and take all the chances. I wasn't surprised that he called me because we had earned together before and he knew I had never tried to beat him for a dime. So I took the money and went down there and came back up. I got rid of the entire load in ten hours. I sold them mainly to guys who wanted to hustle them themselves, and I charged them $2.35 a carton, which gave me a 70-cent profit. From the original $75,000 I made another $28,000. I gave Joe Cheese his $85,000, which left me with $18,000 clear for myself. This worked so well I was doing it almost once a week for about six months, which was not bad.

I would usually pay him on Thursday afternoons. He has this restaurant and I would walk in carrying a shopping bag, with a towel pushed in on top, filled with twenties and fifties. We finally had to stop because it got too hot. The state of New York got smart and sent tax people down to Carolina to make deals with the agents in the wholesaler's office. They offered them rewards for turning in bootleggers with New York State license plates. The wholesalers would copy down your license-plate number and call the New York people after you left. When you reached the state border the New York agents were waiting, and if they grabbed you, the guy in the wholesaler's office who made the call would get 25 percent of the total amount of the tax value. They could make as much as $10,000 just by picking up the telephone. That's why I had to stop, too many dishonest people to deal with.

I got out just in time. The New York State agents were on my trail and I decided to quit completely. But a onetime numbers runner named Frank talked me into making one last run. He had a good plan, I drove an empty truck down to Carolina and he drove a similar truck filled with furniture. He stopped just over the border and I went and filled the truck with thousands of cartons of cigarettes. I had no doubts that within a minute after I left someone at the warehouse was on the phone to New York State with the license number and description of the truck.

On the Carolina side of the border we pulled both trucks behind a diner and switched the loads. He put the cigarettes in his truck, and I stuffed the furniture in mine. Then I headed back to New York. He gave me a few hours' start and then he followed. Sure enough, a few minutes after I crossed into New York State I heard sirens. They were waiting for me. "What's the problem?" I asked.

"What have you got in the back?" one of them asked.

"Just some furniture. Something wrong with that?"

There were two of them and they sort of laughed. "Open up the back, please."

"No I don't please," I told them. "You guys got a search warrant?" They said they didn't. "Well, if you want to see what's in the back of this truck you'd better get one."

These guys were smart alecks. "No need for that. We are just going to follow you wherever you go. We'll see what you have when you stop."

"Suit yourself," I said and started driving. I drove them in circles for about four hours and then I headed to a legitimate warehouse. I opened the back and began unloading the furniture. These guys couldn't believe it! They knew they had been fooled. But it was too close for me. I told Frank I was through going down and if he was smart he wouldn't make any more trips. "It's over," I explained to him.

Obviously he wasn't so smart. About three weeks later my telephone rang about four in the morning. I picked it up and asked who it was. "Joey?" he said. "This is Frank."

"Who?"

"It's me, it's Frank."

"Who?"

"You know, Frank. Carolina. Cigarettes. That Frank. I'm in jail and I need some help."

"Listen, buddy," I said, "it's four o'clock in the morning and you've got the wrong number." Then I hung up. He was released on bail and came to talk to me. I didn't give him a chance to open his big mouth—I punched it shut for him. "You're an idiot," I screamed. "I told you to get out when you could, but you were too smart to listen. Then you call me from jail! Now don't bother me with your problems, and don't get me involved."

Another business I found to be extremely lucrative is eight-track tapes. At one point bootlegging records was a major business, but since the introduction of tapes most of the action has gone that way. I don't steal tapes, or buy them; I have them manufactured. There is a plant in New Jersey that does nothing but make duplicate tapes. They can duplicate any tape made today and do it with the same quality as RCA, Decca, Atlantic or any of the other outfits. All I have to do is decide what tape I want and go and place an order: 5000 Tom Jones or 5000 Rolling Stones or a few thousand *Jesus Christ Superstar*. I don't even have to bring a sample tape with me; the manufacturer has everything on hand, and his duplicate will be exact down to the color of the cassette plastic. The entire tape, cartridge and everything, winds up costing me at most 40 cents apiece to make. The only other expense I have is getting the labels printed, which is as easy as finding a small print shop, and then pasting each label on by hand.

Normally these tapes go for anything between five and eight dollars. I get two dollars a shot for them, and I can get rid of at least 20 dozen at a clip. I deal mainly with distributors (although occasionally I'll walk right into a store and tell them what I have). Distributors are always anxious to get their hands on bootleg stuff because their customers—the store owners—can't tell the difference. A lot of the time, in fact, the distributor will tell the bootlegger what tapes are worth making up. A distributor can make as much as an additional $2.50 or $3.00 per tape when he buys from me. This becomes a hell of a lot of money after a while.

I have also been involved in the manufacture of perfume and liquor, both high-profit items. In fact, any highly taxed item is fair game. For perfume, all you need is a good dishonest chemist and some materials and you're in business. I know guys who can make Joy, Chanel, Christian Dior, Arpège, anything you can name and they'll make it almost as good as the original manufacturer. Then they buy bottles from France or have some guy in a glass factory make them up, get labels from a printer, a guy to make boxes, and they've got a going business. To put the entire package together costs maybe 75 cents, cheaper if you're dealing in big amounts, and in the store this stuff, or very similiar stuff, is selling for at least $31 a bottle. And the guys making the merchandise are plenty skillful; only an expert is going to be able to tell their stuff from the original.

The sales approach is a little different from tapes and records. Around Christmas is the best time of year for this type of operation because everyone is looking to save money on presents. Whoever is pushing the stuff will contact a number of different businesses and say, "I've got some perfume that is slightly hot. Because of that I'm prepared to let you have it for seven dollars per bottle." Everybody knows that there really is a lot of hot stuff around, so they believe the story. They usually ask for a sample and some time to check the stuff out. So the salesman leaves a bottle, the potential customer compares it to the real stuff, finds it to be just as good and buys maybe 50 or 100 bottles. Everybody is happy: the buyer, the seller and the person who gets the perfume. I have financed a number of perfume deals. The split is 50–50 between the bank and the manufacturer after the cost of making the stuff is deducted.

Once I actually had a still operating . . . in the Bronx! The idea first came to me when I met a guy named Louie Five, who was in the trucking business in New Jersey. He had been a bootlegger during Prohibition, at one time operating a still on Staten Island, and knew the business. "What do you think the chances are of setting up a still now?" I asked him. He said if we found the right location there would be no problem. He explained that the operation had to be set up in an area where there was plenty of running water, both to use in making the alcohol and to carry the fermentation down to a river or out to sea. It also had to be in a quiet area where we wouldn't be bothered by people nosing around.

This is not an easy thing to find in the New York area. I spent four days riding around until I went upstate a little and found the perfect location. It was an old unused storehouse on the grounds of what I thought was a private hospital. The building itself was set back from the rest of the place, and there was a big hedge that separated it from the buildings. There was also a flowing brook that ran right through the grounds.

I took my man to see the place, and he took one look and started laughing. "You know what this place is?" he asked me. I told him I thought it was a hospital. "It's a sanitarium! It's a place where alcoholics come to dry out. The first time the wind shifts, the people here would go nuts." He laughed all the way back to New York.

We settled on an old abandoned brick building up in the Bronx, in an area called West Farms. The building was two stories high but the middle floor had been torn out to make one big room. We never found out who owned it—we had no intention of paying rent—but we found some papers lying around which indicated the last tenant had manufactured coffins.

The place was ideal because it was in a deserted area and there was a little creek out in back that eventually emptied into the East River. It took us about two weeks to get the place set up. We repaired the chain-link fence out in front, bought a lock and hung a "Beware of Dog" sign on the gate. For power we ran a line to a Con Edison power terminal a few blocks, away and I'm sure they never knew we were there. Finally we bought big pieces of sheet metal and copper tubing and everything else we needed to make the vats ourselves. We welded the pieces of sheet metal together, coated the outside with epoxy to make sure they didn't seep, and we had our vats. At the height of the operation we had three full vats cooking all the time.

Once we got the place set up we started buying sugar, sugar and more sugar. You need a tremendous amount of sugar, but naturally you have to be very careful where you buy it. If you buy too much at one time at one place, especially from a wholesaler, you might end up in a lot of trouble. They might take a special interest in you to find out what you're doing with all that sugar. To avoid that we made dozens of trips into supermarkets, buying no more than 10 or 15 pounds at a time. We did nothing else for two solid weeks but buy sugar, going from store to store, throwing the stuff in the back of my van and then on to another store. Along the way we picked up the caramel and coloring we needed.

The only thing bad about the entire operation was the smell. And that was bad. Alcohol has a very strong odor, so usually you have to limit your operation to the winter months and pray for a lot of windy days. But there was nothing you could do about it inside. Most of the people working there wore gauze masks, but even if it wasn't in your nose and mouth all the time, it still got all over your clothes. I remember one night I stopped into Patsy's Pizzeria to see a guy and I was wearing the clothes I had been working in all day. He took one whiff and turned green. "Shit," he said, "you smell like you just came out of a liquor factory." I told him he was exactly right, I had a still operating in the Bronx.

He said, "Sure you do. And I'm Al Capone."

What was I going to do, argue with the guy? To this day I'm sure he still believes I'm one of the biggest drinkers in town.

The key to making alcohol is getting the right guy to brew it for you. If the right guy makes the stuff there is absolutely no way you can tell it from the legitimate. There are a lot of guys in this country who brew good stuff, and I would guess that maybe 15 or 20 percent of all the booze you buy in bars in big cities is bootleg.

A lot of it is made down South and brought North. There is a flourishing market from Baltimore up the coast to Boston. Getting the bottles and labels is easy and cheap. In our still we were making Jack Daniels, which is a very big-selling Tennessee mash whiskey. We would tell people it was hot and ask for six dollars, which is about two dollars below legitimate price. It was costing us an average of 35 to 40 cents per bottle to make it, which means we were making five and one-half dollars per bottle profit. That one winter we made abut 40,000 bottles and more than $200,000.

Of course, if you're making booze you can't do anything else. You've got to work 15 hours a day, seven days a week, and this is ball-busting work. At our peak we had seven men—mostly people just out of prison—working for us filling bottles, pasting labels, loading trucks and distributing the stuff.

There is very little bribery involved in manufacturing because you do not want to let anybody know what you're doing. When you start paying people the word has a way of getting around. And you're violating federal tax laws, which is not a good thing to do. If the feds are so lucky as to catch you they can make you go away for a few years, as well as levy a pretty heavy fine. The key to not being caught is a closed mouth, a good wind and a fast stream.

There is also a booming market for almost every type of bootleg cosmetic. All you have to do is buy one legitimate bottle of whatever you want to make and find a good chemist. He will break down the components and be able to come pretty close to exactly duplicating the original product. I know one individual who is a true genius in this field. His name is John McLellan; at one time he was known as the Acid King because he was one of the country's biggest LSD dealers when it was still legal. I tried to hire him to make something for me but I couldn't pay him enough. He was so rich from working two or three months a year he just didn't have to work anymore.

Another chemist I know got caught making pills and went to prison. The day he got out there were ten legitimate drug companies ready to bid for his services. That's how good these people are.

One item I've never had any trouble getting rid of, when I can get them, is tickets. Football tickets, fight tickets, theater tickets, anything there is a demand to see, people will pay phenomenal prices for. I have made a decent income "scalping." In one instance I got the word I could get 1000 tickets for a professional football championship game. The price was three dollars per ticket above face value. Now, even though this was before the days of the Super Bowl, there was great interest in the championship game. I contacted some of the ticket agencies around town and one guy took the whole load without question and gave me six dollars above face value. A quick $3000 profit with no sweat.

Ticket scalping is not lucrative enough for organized crime to bother with it on a regular basis, but a lot of casual crooks (and who ain't?) supplement their incomes this way. But the guys who make real money in scalping are the insiders.

For instance, there was a guy who worked for the Brooklyn Dodgers, and who is still in baseball today, who used to double his annual salary whenever the Dodgers got in a World Series. He would go from agency to agency with his little black bag and tell them what he had and how much he wanted. I would estimate he was good for about $30,000 each Series, which was a lot more than the players were making.

I'll give you another simple racket. Next time you go into a movie theater, watch the ticket seller carefully. See if she punches you a new ticket or gives you one that is already out of the machine. Chances are, if she gives you one that's already been punched out, she's pocketing your money. It works this way: As you walk in the theater the guy who is supposedly ripping your ticket in half is actually pocketing your ticket and giving you the bottom half of one he has already torn. When he has done this a few times he'll wander to the ticket booth when no one is looking and slip the untorn tickets in. The ticket seller will resell them, without ringing up the money, and split the proceeds with the usher.

One more racket that I am particularly fond of. This individual I know was working for a major distribution company. He was in charge of giving out samples: soft drinks, soaps, anything. Whenever a company came up with a new product and hired this distribution company, he would be sent on a long promotional trip. He would have maybe 1000 cases of soap or 24,000 cans of soda to hand out in maybe 15 towns. What he would do is distribute 200 of the 1000 cases and maybe 4000 of the 24,000 cans and sell the rest to storekeepers at a very low price, four cents a can, for example. That's still $40 a thousand, and he was making as much as $800 a week doing this. I remember he once went to Oklahoma with cases and cases of soap. He distributed a few and sold the rest to people who owned laundromats. Usually he didn't even have to worry about being checked up on, because he was splitting the proceeds with the man who was supposed to be doing the checking.

The system is set up so that anybody who uses his or her head can beat it. A credit card, for example, is money from heaven. There are a number of ways to get your hands on a credit card. A stolen card runs about $50, depending on how glutted the market is. Or if you can get to somebody inside a credit-card company, he can issue a card which can be used six or eight months before you would get nailed.

There are a few important things to remember about using a stolen credit card. Never use it to buy gasoline. Unless, of course, you're driving a stolen car. Because the attendant is going to take your license-plate number and eventually the law will be able to trace the card back to you. And second, never use it to buy anything worth more than $100. If you go to a nice restaurant, you can present the card and have a helluva dinner. You can buy a $35 radio or shirts or shoes, and as long as it is under $100 they are never going to run a telephone check on you, and the list of hot cards is always at least a week behind. The only place you might be able to use a card for more than $100 is at an airline counter because they very rarely check. Just make sure you don't buy a ticket in advance and give them your right home address, because if the card should be reported stolen in the interim you would be very easy to locate.

One company everybody cheats is the telephone company. The phone company is like the IRS—you're supposed to try to cheat them. Phones are great. I know a mechanic who can turn a pay phone into a private phone with a few magnets. You drop one dime in and you can call all over the world. We had him rig our phones once when we had a small bookie operation going.

I've used fradulent telephone-company credit-card numbers for years. A man who used to bet with me works inside the phone company and he lets me know when the credit-card code numbers are being changed. There is no danger involved. If you make a phone call with an old number they just tell you they can't put the call through. You can always hang up and walk away from the phone.

I also make a lot of calls and charge them to a third party, only the third party doesn't know it. If you know the phone number of a company that makes a large amount of long-distance calls every month, all you have to do is call the operator and tell her you want to charge the call to your office. The call goes through and they very rarely check. Their bill at the end of the month is so big they can't possibly pick out the illegitimate calls. I used the number of a large stationery company that has 20 or 25 salesmen calling all over the country trying to hustle paper and paper clips and that stuff.

I saved the best for last—automobiles. This is a little complicated, students, so read carefully. I normally get myself a car every two years or so, a late-model, low-mileage, upper-priced job. What you need to carry out this racket is phony identification, a phony license, a phony job and the cooperation of the credit manager of the place you're buying the car. You also have to know the difference between a registration state and a title state.

In a registration state, like New York, the person who actually has possession of the car is named on the registration. In a title state, like Pennsylvania, whoever is listed as owning the car actually owns it. You make a down payment for the car, usually about $500, and that's all it will end up costing you.

After I buy the car under my phony name and have my phony identification on both the registration and the ownership, I simply drive the car to a title state like Pennsylvania and register the car there under the same phony name. The registration form asks, "Do you owe any money on this car?" and I answer no. Now, the secretary of state, who authorizes the title, states on the bottom of the paper that he certifies that a reasonable search has been made to make sure the facts are true. Bullshit. The paper comes in and they stamp it and ship it back. Now I have the car registered in Pennsylvania under my phony name, and I have free and clear title.

On the front of the same title paper it asks, "Has this car got any encumbrances?" If there aren't any listed, and there never are, you can sell that car anywhere and to anybody you want to. You can also sell it back to yourself, this time using your real name. Now you've got a car worth $3500 and it cost you $500. You can sell it to someone else for $3000 and make a $2500 profit for a few days work, or you can keep it yourself. I get my cars this way and I own them free and clear. If the car dealer has a beef let him go find the guy he sold the car to. And if he does, which we can rest assured he won't, all he can do is sue. No one can repossess this car from me, even if they find it, because I own it. If anyone ever tried to grab that car from me I'd have him arrested for theft. There isn't a cop in the world who wouldn't have to recognize my title as the legal ownership of that car.

Cars, trips, clothes, liquor, perfume—like the man said, the best things in life are free. But sometimes you gotta give the tree a little shake. The fruit don't just fall in your lap.

CHAPTER *13*

THE GODFATHER:
THE WAY THINGS AIN'T

ario Puzo's book *The Godfather,* and the movie they made from it, did for the organization what silicone does for tits. They both make their respective subjects stand out. We needed *The God-father* like Joey Gallo needed another portion of clams. Many people think because they saw the movie or read the book they know everything there is to know about organized crime. This is like saying you know everything there is to know about politicians because you watch "Let's Make a Deal." One thing has absolutely nothing to do with the other.

Don't misunderstand me, I thoroughly enjoyed *The Godfather.* I thought it was a very entertaining, very funny movie. It was also a wonderful piece of fiction. Things just don't happen in real life like they did to Marlon Brando and family.

Let us begin at the beginning. The whole thing starts when Sollozzo goes to see Don Corleone to get financing and political protection for a narcotics operation. He's got the whole fucking mob backing him up, so what does he need Corleone for? The political connections? Any man in his business who is politically connected will help anybody else. That's why it's called an organization. What does this mean to Corleone? The politicians on his payroll do what he tells them to do. Why such a big deal? Besides, Sollozzo did not need Corleone's contacts that badly, he could have gone out and bought his own.

Second, all of a sudden Corleone gets some morals and decides that he doesn't want to deal in narcotics. Ridiculous. When you are controlling a family there is no such thing as not getting involved. Isn't it kind of stupid. Here's a man into bookmaking, shylocking, numbers, fixing, a man who will kill everybody and his brother, and yet he's not willing to sell narcotics. These people are in business to make money, and any man that is a big boss, a controller, he doesn't give one fuck where the money comes from. He'd love narcotics because there's more money being made there than in anything else.

Third, assuming he didn't want to sell narcotics, which no one with his head on his shoulders will believe, he is simply not going to go against a commission meeting, a meeting of the Board of Directors. If a certain thing has been decided there is no reason in the world he's gonna go out of his way to cross them. The commission is too powerful; if it wants something to happen, believe me, it happens.

Next, the shooting of Don Corleone. In every instance I have ever known that a boss was shot, it is because his bodyguard double-crossed him. And a bodyguard does not double-cross him by calling up and saying he is sick. He is there when you get killed. All he does is step aside. He does not leave himself in a position where he will be killed by his own family. Any boss that I've ever known got killed because his bodyguard helped to get him, because he had been offered an improvement in his financial status.

Fifth, the bit about the hired guns "taking to the mattresses." That just doesn't make any sense at all. I couldn't stay locked up in a room with eight other guys for one day, and neither could anybody else. You've got eight tense personalities crammed together waiting for a gunfight, how long can you play gin rummy or poker without going crazy?

During a gang war most people live at home. They just kind of lie low and stay as close to the house as possible. During the Colombo-Gallo War, for example, I met this old friend of mine who was hooked up with the Colombo people. He said, "Why don't you come out to the house for dinner this week? I'm home every night now. But I hope you don't mind if I don't walk you to your car." The home is a sanctuary. You can hit people outside the house, but you can't go inside; it's just not considered proper etiquette.

Even more, no family can afford to keep hired guns locked up in a room for any length of time. An organization that is not earning cannot afford to pay its people, and in order for you to earn you've got to be out on the street. What do you think is going to happen if they stop working and stop earning money? Listen, if people can't earn they leave you. Now, in this so-called gang war they had, these people who "hit the mattresses" were not earning any money. And there is just not enough money to continue paying these men.

Another thing, you are not gonna kill a cop, no matter how crooked he is, and get away with it. No matter how bad he is. There is simply no way in the world the police department is going to allow it. They will hunt you down, they will get informers on the street, they will pay money, they will get you no matter how long it takes. You are not going to kill a cop; believe me, you are not going to do it and get away with it. The cops who get gunned down in the city are hit by crazy addicts, black-power people and other nuts.

Now we come to the murder of Sonny Corleone. To refresh your memory they drew him to a deserted toll-booth area and then about a dozen guys all armed with submachine guns popped out from behind the booth and killed him. Wrong. No way in the world you're going to have that many guys there when a murder is committed. You want as few people as possible to know you're connected with the crime to begin with. Then, if you're going to set up a guy you don't have to go through all that planning, like taking over an entire roadway. There are so many different ways to hit a man. Any professional will pick his time and place; he can sucker you out, find you out or seek you out. You don't have to go through an elaborate plan to hit a man. It's very simple to catch him leaving a barbershop, or catch him coming out of his girlfriend's house or catch him having dinner in a restaurant. Nobody is going to be able to stay behind walls forever, and when he comes out you've got him.

If you remember your book and movie, after Sonny got it the Corleone family killed all the other bosses. No way. It cannot be done. As ruthless as you want to be, you wouldn't last. I don't care how careful your plans are, it is a physical impossibility. And no one can afford to hire an entire army of killers to do the job. The price is just prohibitive. The planning is incredible and the undercover work, getting to every bodyguard, is impossible. When that many people know something is going to happen, it doesn't happen. In 1931 the young turks eliminated many of the old bosses in one day and night. That was more than 40 years ago and simply could not happen again today.

I thought the most convincing character was Sollozzo, the guy who tried to force the issue of narcotics. He epitomized what a man is in this business, completely ruthless, he doesn't give a fuck.

The character of the Godfather himself, Don Corleone, was a composite of a number of people I know. (I personally thought Brando was good despite the line going around that "The Italian who played Marlon Brando did a good job.") But there were some problems in his portrayal. No boss wants to be referred to as a Godfather. Most people prefer to be anonymous. The men in this business who have gone to prison are men who have allowed themselves to become too well known. The quieter a man lives, the better off he is. And when a boss does have an affair, like the Corleone wedding, he tries to hold it in an out-of-the-way place. He does not invite public figures to these affairs, because he knows the embarrassment it would cause them.

Even the relationship between Corleone and his button men, in particular Clemenza, was ridiculous. A button man is in control of an area and he may see his boss once a week, if that often.

I rated it three stars, a great comedy, and almost everybody I know in the mob agreed. For a while the movie was the main topic of conversation. Everybody was running around threatening to "make you an offer you couldn't refuse." The most popular joke in the mob had this guy Funzi asking his friend Tony, "Have you seen *The Godfather?*"

And Tony answered, "No, I went over to his place but he wasn't home."

A big game that everybody was playing was trying to figure out who the different characters were supposed to be. There was one character I had no problem recognizing: the horse who had his head cut off. I think I bet on him out at Aqueduct the day before I saw the movie.

CHAPTER *14*
GALLO AND COLOMBO: THE WAY THINGS ARE

We shall now see how it is done in real life.

Everybody loves gang wars whether via television, radio, newspapers, magazines or movies. Everybody, that is, except the gangs. While the general public finds gang wars exciting and fascinating, the gangs find them expensive and dangerous. They could live without them, so to speak. But they do erupt, and when they do there is little anyone can do but try to finish on his feet.

Gang wars are caused by many things: young hotshots trying to push older people out, personal dislikes and, most of all, territorial disputes. In most cases these wars can be settled relatively peacefully, but sometimes both honor and money are involved, and then you have people shooting other people. The biggest war of all time, the one which set the standard by which gang wars are judged, was Chicago's Al Capone–Bugsy Moran War during Prohibition, which lasted until the entire Moran organization was destroyed. In reality there have not been too many real out-and-out fights since I've been in the business. The last big one, the Colombo–Persico–Gallo War, had all the elements of the classic gang confrontation and made headlines all over the country. As far as I know, the entire story has never been told from beginning to end. I was there, I was approached by all three parties and I know exactly what happened.

This thing had been building for years and there had been some fighting a few times earlier. It actually started in 1957 when Joey Gallo killed Albert Anastasia under a contract let out by Joseph Profaci. As a reward Profaci gave Joey some territory in south Brooklyn. But Joey was very ambitious and wanted a bigger area. In 1959 the Gallo group, headed by Joey and his older brother Larry, broke away from the Profaci organization and started to fight. Although the Gallos were badly outnumbered they fought pretty tough, and bodies kept turning up until 1962.

Actually Joey and his eventual enemy, Joseph Colombo, had started out together in the Profaci organization. They even worked together on a few hits. They both did good work and climbed up the ladder until they split into different factions and organized their own small groups. In 1959 Colombo stayed loyal to Profaci when the Gallos split with him.

At the same time Carmine (the Snake) Persico was also starting to get some power. He was known as a man who could be depended on, even though he blew one of his biggest jobs: Profaci gave him the contract on Larry Gallo and he messed it up. He had suckered Larry into a bar in Brooklyn and was strangling him when a police sergeant happened to accidentally walk in. This was the biggest break I ever heard a man getting. But this attempt caused a great deal of bitter hatred between the Gallos and the rest of the Profaci organization.

Normally the police don't care what happens in these things, unless innocent people get hurt, but they brought this one to a halt by getting Joey on an extortion rap. Peace was more or less made before Joey went to the can, and the shooting stopped. I always felt that Colombo and Persico could have avoided a lot of problems by hitting Joey at this time, which they could have done because he just didn't have that many people. They would have saved themselves a lot of grief.

Of the three of them, I knew Joey Gallo best. Joey was one of the shrewdest and funniest people I ever met, and he was far from crazy. He knew rackets. He knew what made money and what didn't make money.

He knew what he wanted to control. And he knew how to convince people that his way of thinking was best.

He once kept a lion in the basement of his social club on President Street in south Brooklyn. If a guy was giving him a hard time, or if someone defaulted or came up short, he would bring them into the cellar where the lion was tied. He would explain what solution he had in mind and then say, "If it doesn't work out, guess who's coming to dinner?" and laugh like crazy.

Joey was short, about five foot six, and had a medium build, and he was a very violent man. But it was controlled violence; he always knew what he was doing. And he was funny, a lot of laughs to be with, what you'd call good company. Years ago, when I was just getting started, we ran some muscle together. I remember one day I was driving along and I look at him and he's staring into the rear-view mirror. He kept contorting his face into the meanest looks he could make. "Hey, moron," I said to him, "what the fuck do you think you're doing?" He looked at me with a sneer splitting his face and said, "What do you think I'm doing? I'm practicing to look tough!"

He didn't have to practice too hard, he was tough. But his problem was that, from the very beginning, he wanted power. He needed it desperately. When I left New York to go to California he was just on his way up. A few years later he made a big splash when he killed Anastasia. He never talked about the killing, but I knew he had done it.

He had one thing in him that somewhere along the line I've lost: Joey could hate. He was a brutal ruthless man when he hated somebody, and he found it easy to hate anybody who got in his way. I once saw him work a guy over. He really put his heart and his muscle into it. He just kicked this guy until his eye popped out of his head, and then he kicked him in the balls maybe 30 times. He just made himself hate this poor sucker.

We were friendly until the day he died. One of the last times we had dinner together he seemed very wistful. I think he knew he didn't have long to live. "I wish you had thrown in with me," he said. "We could have done some great things together."

I said, "Joey, you went your way, I went mine. You've done good and

I've done good and everybody's happy." Joey never really made it as big as he wanted to; he didn't really control too much when he died. But right up until the very end he was trying. That's the thing you always remember about Joey, he never knew when to lay off.

When Joey went to prison in 1962 Larry took over the President Street mob and the south Brooklyn area. Larry could have handled things until Joey got out because he was tough and smart and people respected him. Unfortunately, he died of cancer and the third brother, Albert, took over. Albert just didn't have the power or strength or the smarts to keep control. When he first took over they called him Kid Blast . . . after a while it became Kid Blister.

Meanwhile, sitting quietly on the sidelines, carefully watching all this, slowly gathering the real power, was Carlo Gambino. He had been in competition with Profaci and when Profaci died in the summer of 1962 he just kind of eased in and took it. He took over whatever he wanted and consolidated his gains because there was no one to stop him—everybody was busy fighting within the mob. Finally it got to a point where it was a toss-up who was more powerful, Gambino or Vito Genovese.

Vito Genovese was the most ruthless man I have ever known. He desperately wanted to be the Boss of Bosses and was willing to kill anybody who got in his way. He set up the Albert Anastasia hit (which helped Gambino, an Anastasia lieutenant, move into power) and also tried to get Frank Costello. Chin Gigante did the job, but his shot just wounded Costello and he recovered. It didn't matter, Frank knew enough to take the hint and he retired, leaving Vito in the top spot.

Even after Vito went to prison for 15 years on a narcotics conspiracy rap he wouldn't give up any of his power. Anthony Strollo, better known as Tony Bender, tried to take a little and one night he went out for a newspaper and never came back. Vito gave the order from his cell.

Anyway, Genovese and Gambino were the big bosses of the New York area in the early 1960s. Between the two of them they controlled everything there was to control. They also had enough influence to make things happen anywhere else in the country, but even they had to first receive the permission of whoever the boss of the territory was.

GALLO AND COLOMBO: THE WAY THINGS ARE

The period just after Joey went to jail saw a lot of power changing hands. Colombo was busy building an organization out of what had been the Profaci family, Persico emerged as the most powerful group within the Colombo organization, with his own men and area, and Vito Genovese went to jail, leaving the active control to Carlo Gambino. Although there was some maneuvering for power, things generally stayed quiet while Joey was in prison.

In April 1970 Colombo's son, Joseph, Jr., was arrested by the federal government and charged with melting down silver coins, a federal offense.

This is where it all started again. Claiming that his son was innocent and his entire family was being persecuted because they were Italian, Joe Colombo announced the formation of the Italian-American Civil Rights League. This idea, this "League," had been discussed beforehand with Gambino, with Buster Aloi (Alloy), Carmine Tramunti, Tony "Ducks" Corallo, and almost anybody else of importance in the New York organization. The deal was that Colombo would be the titular head of the whole thing. The income was to be derived from memberships, which cost ten dollars per person. The idea was to get every Italian in New York to join, which could come out to be a couple of million people, or $20 million.

The $20 million was what the whole thing was all about. The League was more or less a shakedown operation, and a lot of people were convinced to join and pay their ten dollars. The money was to be split among the New York families.

Mr. Colombo's problems began when he forgot that there was a Carlo Gambino, Buster Aloi, Tramunti and Corallo, and he put the money in his own pocket. The newspapers wrote that the mob was angry because the Civil Rights League was attracting publicity to its operations, but that was bullshit. The League was a laughing fucking joke. Nobody cared about the publicity; organized crime had gotten publicity for years, whether we wanted it or not. Anyway this was good publicity, you might say. What got them mad was they weren't getting their fair shares. They were getting double-crossed, and they kept warning Colombo that there was going to be serious trouble if he didn't come through with the coin. While this was going on, Joey Gallo got out of jail.

In public Gallo said he had been reformed in prison, that he had read a lot of books and learned a great deal, and that from now on he was going to play it straight if the mob would let him. In private the first thing he did was go to see Carlo Gambino. "Listen," he told him, "south Brooklyn is mine and I ain't giving it up." He wanted the dock area, the President Street area, the bookmaking, the shylocking, the muscles, everything he had before he went to prison. The old man agreed, and Joe Colombo agreed. Colombo was not thrilled but he had no choice. Gambino said that was the way it was going to be, and you do not go against Gambino and live too awfully long.

The final straw with Colombo and Gambino came when an audit of the League's books showed it was bankrupt. Everybody knew there was plenty of money around and it was obvious that Colombo was keeping it. A meeting was held at Buster Aloi's house and word filtered back to me that Carlo sat there and said very explicitly, "I want Joe Colombo hit in the head like a pig."

Guess who they offered the job to? Joey Gallo would have given anything to set this deal up and so he was given the contract. Joey did not instigate this at all, he didn't have the power. Only bosses can approve the killing of another boss. But Colombo had to go because he had gotten to the point where he believed he was bigger than the mob, that he was indestructible. Wrong.

Hitting a boss is a very complicated undertaking, if you'll excuse the expresssion. In order to get him you have to have people within his own organization who are willing to double-cross him. Joe Colombo's chief bodyguard at this time was a man by the name of Gennaro (Fat Jerry) Ciprio, and he was the man who had to be gotten to to put Colombo in a position where he could be assassinated. He agreed—I assume he was promised more money and power—and the arrangements were made through him. Colombo was to be killed at his own giant Civil Rights League rally in Columbus Circle, right in the middle of Manhattan. They decided on the rally because it was the perfect place to cause mass confusion, which was exactly what they wanted.

Gallo also had to find a man to pull the trigger. He didn't want to use one of his own people because he knew there was no way the killer could get away after the shooting. Through the connections Gallo made while he was in prison he was able to find a black man stupid enough to believe that he was going to get $100,000 or so for committing this particular crime. In reality all he was going to get for his efforts was a bullet in the head. He was dead the minute he agreed to do the job. The mob couldn't afford to let him live, he simply knew too much. It was a real sucker job.

Ciprio, Colombo's bodyguard, was responsible for the actual details of the plan. It took about a month to set the whole thing up. Ciprio had to get press credentials for Jerome Johnson, the killer, to get through the dozens of cops that were in the area. Again, these credentials had to be provided by someone with the organization. And Ciprio had to maneuver Colombo into a position where Johnson would have a clean, clear shot at him. Usually, if you're a bodyguard you shield your man with your own body. If you are out to let him get hit you step aside. Ciprio stayed up on the grandstand and watched the whole thing happen. Colombo should have been killed but he wasn't—although for all practical purposes he's dead because he isn't anything but a vegetable now. Johnson blew the job (the consequences of hiring an amateur) but he didn't live long enough to know that.

The minute he pulled the trigger Ciprio leaped off the stand and headed for him. A New York City cop, who had no knowledge of the plan, wrestled the gun away from Johnson and had him on the ground. The cop never saw Ciprio come up from behind and blow Johnson's brains out. If that cop had been a little quicker, or Ciprio a little slower, Johnson would have lived to tell a very interesting story.

When the shooting took place both Gallo and Gambino were miles and miles away from Columbus Circle. All they had to do was sweat it out that everything went right. Fortunately for them, it did. But there was no doubt who set the whole thing up, and had Gambino not backed Gallo, Joey would have been dead within 48 hours. There is no doubt about that. But the fact that Gallo was seen with Gambino after the shooting was enough to stop everybody. No matter how much people would have liked to take care of Joey they didn't dare. It was obvious he had the old man's approval and therefore had to be left alone.

That didn't mean there wasn't going to be a fight. As I said, some potential wars are settled peacefully, but this one didn't have a chance once Joe Colombo got hit. Forget about it. Blood had to run. It had to.

But not right away. Gang wars are expensive and people go out of their way to avoid them. So a very uneasy peace settled over the New York organization. Joey, of course, started getting more powerful. He was busy pretending he had gotten out of the rackets, he was on parole at the time, which had something to do with that act, and was getting chummy with show-business people. According to newspaper columnists, he was also writing a book. As he should have realized, the worst thing you can do in this business is become publicity-conscious. Unfortunately, Joey Gallo liked to read about himself in the newspapers.

Businesswise Joey started to consolidate his gains. Now he had had a hardon for Carmine Persico ever since Junior (the Snake) had tried to kill his brother. So Joey cried no tears when Carmine got 14 years in a federal penitentiary for hijacking. Now the positions were reversed, Joey was out and the Persico mob was being run by Alphonse Persico and Lenny Dell. Joey simply told them he was taking over. The Persico people realized there was nothing they could do, they weren't strong enough to hold the organization together without Junior. So they went to see Carlo Gambino.

Gambino owed Joey something, so when Dell and Persico went to see him he just shrugged his shoulders and said that this was between Gallo and them. That was his way of protecting Joey, his way of letting the Persico people know that he wasn't going to help them, that Joey would be allowed to do whatever he was strong enough to do. He didn't believe for a second they would be strong enough to knock Joey off and he figured, like everyone else, that they would have to capitulate and give it all up. It didn't work that way.

The Persico people went to Tony Colombo and Joe Colombo, Jr., and acting boss Joseph Yacovelli and explained the situation. The way I understand the conversation, they told the Colombo people that if Gallo took over Persico's organization he would be strong enough to take over the Colombo people next. This made a great deal of sense all around, and both groups went back to the old man. If Gallo took them over, they said, he would eventually have to go after Gambino. And everyone knew Joey was a very ambitious man. They finally told the old man that they were going to fight Joey Gallo and, if they did, they would fight him too. That's when Carlo decided he could live without Joey. Colombo and Persico were threatening all-out war, and since he, Gambino, was fighting extradition at that moment, all-out war was something he could do without. So he agreed to let them kill Gallo.

But the Colombo people wanted more than permission. They knew they were now doing Gambino a favor and, in return, wanted the names of the people within the Colombo organization who had set up Joe Colombo to be killed. This was their price, and Carlo agreed it was a fair one.

I was told Joey Gallo was going to be killed about three weeks before it happened. I was sitting in an Italian restaurant on 86th Street in Brooklyn, and Lenny Dell said to me, "There's going to be an open contract on Gallo. Do you want it?"

I said, "No, I'm not thrilled about it."

He said, "Okay, but then we're gonna need guns, you like to come to work?"

No way. "Look, Lenny, let's be realistic," I told him. "I know you and I know Joey and I know the Colombo people. I've been doing business with you people in one form or another for years. I don't want to offend nobody. If I take sides now, that means I got to take sides for the rest of my life. I just don't want to do it." I had the right to refuse the job, which I did. But it is also understood that I must keep my mouth shut; I can't discuss the fact that the contract was out with anybody. An open contract means that anybody who has the balls can do it, and anybody with brains shuts up about it.

I wasn't afraid to see Joey Gallo, even though I knew there was a contract out on him, because when Joey went out in public he always had at least one bodyguard with him who could be trusted. Number two, I always carried a cannon, and number three, the man was my friend. So what was I going to do? I had dinner with Joey twice between the time I knew the contract was out and the night the actual hit took place. I never even felt an urge to tell him what was happening. I didn't have to, he knew something was up. I just looked at him and thought, "Well, sucker, you took your best shot, now they're going to take theirs." I never even thought about telling him. I figured he had to know they were looking to hurt him, but he made the same mistake Colombo made, he figured he was Joey Gallo and nobody would dare do anything to him.

His real mistake was not keeping closer tabs on Gambino. He figured Carlo was his man, and he was, but Carlo just didn't want a big war breaking out. What Joey should have done was, instead of talking with Dell and Persico, he should have killed them. Had he done that he would have eliminated all his problems. Their people would have either walked away or come into his organization. Remember, all most men want is a chance to earn a living and he really doesn't care much who gives it to him.

Again, if you are going to hit a boss you have to have help. Even if you are going to hit Joey Gallo. Now, when Joey was killed his bodyguard Pete the Greek was with him and made a legitimate attempt to guard him. Pete used to be with Colombo, but since he himself was wounded and did some shooting trying to defend Joey, it's obvious where his loyalties were. But there was a second bodyguard, a guy named Bobby, who had also been to the Copa with Joey and Pete and Joey's family that night. When he was asked to go along to Umberto's Clam House he refused, saying he was going with some broads. I would have to say this was probably when the phone call was made telling where Joey Gallo would be.

To this day I really don't know who did the job. The story seems to be that this guy Luparelli saw Gallo going into the restaurant and went to the social club where he picked up Carmine DiBiase. They contacted Yacovelli, who was running the Colombo mob and making the payment, and he said go ahead. DiBiase, or whoever, then walked into Umberto's, killed Gallo, and shot Pete the Greek. After finishing the job, he ran out and hopped into the car Luparelli claims he was driving. They drove to Nyack, New York, and laid low. Eventually Luparelli got the idea that they were trying to poison him in his hideout and split.

I can't buy this whole story, there are just too many contradictions in it. I'm not saying DiBiase didn't pull the trigger, I just doubt it happened like Luparelli says it did. Believe me, I'm not trying to defend DiBiase. He and I almost had it out in a social club on Mulberry Street one sunny afternoon.

I didn't really know Carmine very well, but we had both been involved in a business deal and it annoyed him that I kept the best piece for myself. When we were making the cash split he made some nasty remarks about my ethnic background and I smacked him in the mouth. Then I went home.

The next day I got a message that Carmine was sitting around his social club threatening to kill me. I could see that if he tried to follow through it would put a terrific strain on our friendship, so I decided to beat him to the punch, so to speak. I picked up my .357 magnum, which is one mighty big cap gun, and I drove down to the social club. I walked in and pulled the gun out of my belt and stuck it right between his eyes. "I understand you don't like me," I said.

One look at Carmine's eyes told me he was upset that this rumor had gotten around and he felt this was the proper time to dispel it. "Like you?" he replied. "Like you? I love you!"

It was nice to know the rumors were unfounded. "Fine," I said, "and if I were you, I'd make sure the romance lasts."

So you understand I never received my membership card in the Carmine DiBiase Fan Club. But let us assume you have a hit going. I'm sitting in my social club and you come and tell me so-and-so is in such a place. Now, I have to get permission before I can go ahead, so I'm gonna pick up the phone and call a man at his home or at his girlfriend's, right? Wrong. Wherever he is, no two ways about it, that phone has got to be tapped. Second, I'm not gonna have you sitting in the car while I go inside and shoot it out myself. Third, I'm not gonna take you to a hideout I got and, all of a sudden, try and kill you. And if I was going to kill you, why would I bother poisoning you? What the fuck do I want to do that for when I can just as easily pull the trigger? I mean, the whole story doesn't hold water with me. But I don't know a better version. It doesn't really matter anyway; the end result was the same. So long, Joey.

The newspapers made a big deal out of the fact that Gallo was hit in front of his wife and daughter, which is a clear violation of mob rules. But they forgot that Joe Colombo was hit in front of his family. Tit for tat. One thing about the mob, they'll even things up, one way or another.

The shooting really started after Joey was killed. I met with one of the Gallo people who asked me if I wanted to throw in with them until the shooting was over. "I turned the other people down," I said, "why should I join you?" I wanted nothing to do with it. What did I need it for? I'm not some young punk looking to make a reputation.

Normally it is easy to recruit guns during a war. First of all, you know the people who have worked with guns before and you contact them. You offer them X dollars to remain with your people for the length of the shooting. It's not going to last more than a couple of months because there is nobody that can afford it; it's a physical impossibility. You hire a good gun and you're going to have to pay him a minimum of $5000 a week plus a bonus for everybody he shoots, $20,000 or so, just to keep him there. No professional will risk his life—which is what he is doing—for less. And business is severely curtailed during the fighting. You have to send someone around to protect your people as they make their rounds, and even then they may see only half their regular customers. And you've got to have some people patrolling the neighborhood, riding around making sure there are no strange faces in the area. A gang war is when you find out who your friends are.

During a war everybody in the organization automatically becomes a gun, even though they really can't handle anything. But on paper they are considered a gun. Plus you have whatever you can grab. You try to have 30 or 40 people who can pull the trigger, and if you're paying them $5000 a week it is going to get very expensive. So it won't last too long.

Once the war breaks out it's easy to see who is siding with who. Just take a ride through their territory and see who's hanging out in the area. And as for the people who have been paying off one boss, if they stop he knows they can't be working with him. That only leaves one other side.

As it turned out the Gallo people couldn't get enough men together to make a fight of it. You have to have something to pay people with, and they evidently didn't have it. There is no longer a Gallo organization. It was completely destroyed when Joey died. It was taken over by Colombo-

Persico. The people in Joey's group were drafted, almost like they do in sports, first one family making a selection and then the other and so on. The Gallo people had two choices: either do business with the new people or be completely cut out. Albert Gallo, for example, threw in with Colombo. Business, as they say, is business.

In all, a total of about 12 people went down. They were turning up in car trunks and vacant lots all over the city. Once they had the names, it was a simple process for the Colombo people to eliminate those men within their own organization who had double-crossed Joe Colombo.

The day before Gallo was killed Thomas Edwards (Tommy Ernst) was shot to death on his father-in-law's porch.

That same day Bruno Carnevale was shot in Queens. He had $14,000 on him when the cops found him.

Ciprio was shot three days after Gallo died. He owned a restaurant in Brooklyn and he walked out one night and was gunned down.

Richard Grossman, who I never heard of and who I doubt was involved in this thing, was found the same day, stuffed in a trunk of an abandoned car in Brooklyn.

Frank Ferriano went down the same day.

William Della Russo went down five days later.

Rosario Stabile was shot in his car a day after Della Russo.

I think you get the point. Gang wars are about as much fun as walking through a plate-glass window. There is no excitement, no adventure, only a lot of time spent laying low. It always seemed to me that, if your average citizen finds them so exciting, he should choose up sides and go at it himself. But please leave me out of it.

CHAPTER *15*

DOING BUSINESS WITH COPS AND POLS

Every October a political ward heeler would come around and give Guido the shoemaker the song and dance about contributing to the party. This time Guido says, "Listen, every year somebody he come around and I'ma give him some money. Now, how about you give Guido something?" The ward heeler agrees and asks him what he wants. "How about makea me assemblyman?" It's done. The next year Guido says, "Why not you makea me a councilman?" Time passes. "I want to be a mayor." Okay, he's the mayor. One more year goes by and Guido decides to be governor. Boom, he's the governor. Finally the politican comes back and Guido says, "Now, you doa good for me, but there'sa still justa one more thing."

"What's that?" the ward heeler asks. "I can't make you the president."

"Oh no," Guido says, "I no wanna be president. I want you to makea me a citizen!"

I love that story, not because it's true, but because it almost could be. Without corrupt politicians and the help of the police organized crime could not exist. It's as simple as that. They are the people who allow us to operate, they are the people who grease the wheels. In return we give them money and favors. In fact, for years I used to think the term "the long arm of the law" referred to the cops reaching out for their weekly payoff.

Now, let me explain that I am not anticop. My cousin is a policeman and he is a good one. He protects citizens from getting hurt, he risks his life in the line of duty when he has to; he does his job to the best of his ability. But he turns his head when he sees the local numbers runner or a neighborhood bookie or prostitute. He thinks the way I do—why bother this guy when he's not hurting anybody?

I believe the police are doing their job the best they can. To me it's very simple. They live on one side of the fence and I live on the other. So we have to try and get along like neighbors.

The only time I get mad at a cop is when he oversteps his bounds and gets abusive. I've spent a lot of time being questioned by police officers, and I know just about every method the cops might use to get an individual to talk. Most of them are fine.

The first trick the police try is to tell you that you made a mistake when you were doing the job. They say they have witnesses or a fingerprint or you dropped your false teeth at the scene of the crime or whatever. Then they offer you a deal: If you'll confess and save the state the expense of a trial they'll talk to the judge and get your sentence reduced. This is known as a "hopefa" case. Actually they don't have a thing except their suspicion to connect you with the crime, so all they can do is hopefa the best.

Then they'll try all the things you see on television. "Listen," one detective whispered to me, "I'm a nice guy but my partner is a real prick and . . ."

I interrupted him. "As far as I'm concerned you're both pricks."

Or, "We've got your partner in the next room and he's singing like a bird."

To which I replied, "I have no idea who you got in the next room, but if he told you he committed a crime, personally I would book him if I were you."

This kind of questioning is fine. Anybody who gets tricked by it deserves to go to the can. Too many guys forget to think positively. They get in a jam and immediately they go for a deal. If they keep their mouths shut chances are they'll walk out totally free.

The only method I really get pissed about is beating up somebody.

They smack you around a few times to see if you'll crack. I took my first beating in a police station when I was 16 years old. The police brought me in to question me about a murder rap. They didn't think I did it, they thought I knew who did. Actually they were right, I did (as I told you, the police are no dummies), but I wasn't about to tell them. They brought me into a dark room in the 41st Precinct station in the Bronx and handcuffed me to a chair. Then they began beating me. This one cop kept driving his fist into my gut, over and over, for a couple of hours. "Talk!" Punch. I might never have gotten out of there if my brother hadn't come looking for me. He had become good friends with another cop, and this guy was helping him look for me. He walked into this room, took one look at me and almost split a gut. He threw the other cop out of the room. Then he took the cuffs off me and sent me home. I spit blood for a week, but I never blamed the police force, just this one guy. I think this is because I knew so many good cops from my numbers business.

The last time a cop touched me was just before the Supreme Court ruled the police couldn't question an individual unless his attorney was present. I was brought into the Elizabeth Street station house because they wanted to ask me some questions about a hit made on the Lower East Side. As usual they put me in a little room and sat me down on a chair. A plainclothes detective asked me where I had been when the hit was made. I said, "I don't remember." The next thing I knew I had his fist in my mouth. "That ain't gonna help me remember," I told him. He gave me three or four quick shots in the gut.

"Does that help you remember?"

I spit in his face. Actually I missed his face but made a mess of his shirt. He knew then he had gone as far as I was going to let him. After that he knew I would fight back. So he quit.

Before the Supreme Court made that decision you would see man after man come into court with a black eye and a bruised face. Every single one of them was beaten up "resisting arrest." Today the police rarely touch an individual. They try the scientific method. As much as I disliked it, a punch in the gut was all the science a lot of guys needed to get them to admit what they had done.

211

Young cops become corrupt because they are joining a corrupt system. You've got guys who have been entrenched in their police jobs for ten years, twelve years, and they are not about to let some two-bit rookie come in and ruin a good thing. So the rookie watches and learns and eventually he gets on the pad and accepts the system for what it is: not perfect but profitable. It is an accepted fact of life in almost every major city I've ever been in that the police will make a contract with you. Chicago, for example, was so wide open that it was known that in order to be a cop you had to put up $10,000—but they guaranteed you that you would make that back within your first six months on the job.

Why make a federal case out of it? Taking money to leave a numbers runner or bookie or shylock or prostitute alone is not going to make a bad cop. He is still going to do his primary job, protect the people, and if he can make a few extra dollars on the side, more power to him.

I'll tell you one thing about cops, they will not take money where violence is concerned. When somebody gets hurt you can't buy the cop. You take the average guy who pulls a stickup and makes some pain, he is not going to be able to buy his way out. You can bet, unless he has some powerful friends protecting him, that a cop will do everything he can to catch him, including risking his own life. In my entire career I have only heard of one case in which a cop took money to protect a killer. This was a case in Harlem and the cop was given the name of the murderer by an informer. Instead of putting a report in, he went to see the guy. He was paid approximately $5000 and never filed a report. Eventually both the cop and the killer were uncovered.

But this cop was the very rare exception. Cops are just not going to jeopardize their careers for a murderer, because there is always going to be a deep investigation. Besides, your normal policeman has the same feelings about crime as your average citizen: He wants his wife and kids to be able to walk out of his house at night and feel safe. But that doesn't stop him from betting on his favorite football team, taking a number or borrowing from a shy. Cops understand the difference between dangerous crime and victimless crime.

I'm a big fan of most cops. I think of them as small businessmen. They got a right to make a living as long as nobody gets hurt, and very, very rarely does a bribe result in someone being hurt. I've made many payoffs in my career, most of them on a regularly scheduled basis as a contract called for. But occasionally I've been involved in a quick shakedown. Once I punched a cop, as I mentioned, in a florist shop and it cost me $1000 to cool that over. And once I got nailed with a truckload of groceries I had just hijacked. It was an unlucky fluke. The police were checking registrations and we obviously didn't have any with us. We had just about talked our way out of it when the report of the truck being stolen came over the cops' radio. We were cooked.

I told the cop, "I've got thirty-five hundred dollars in my pocket. It's yours if you want it. If you take me in all I'm gonna do is hire a lawyer and be back on the street in twenty-four hours. Even if I get convicted I'm only gonna do a short time." He understood the logic of my position. I handed him the money and drove away.

There is no set fee for any type of operation, but when you do business with police or politicians you got to have a contract. This unwritten agreement specifies how much money is going to be paid the police to allow you to operate your business within a particular area. The amount of money to be paid either weekly or monthly depends on the area, the business you're operating, the number of people involved, probably the number of telephones in use, the number of runners on the street and a number of other variables. The amount of money involved is called "the pad." If there is a whorehouse operating, the madam may be down for $1000 a month, a bookie may pay $10,000 a month or $4500 per phone, a numbers controller may pay anywhere from $10 to $25 per runner per week. Whatever it is, everybody is going to pay.

The size of the pad depends on the amount of activity in the area. I can assure you it is enough to make everyone happy. One police lieutenant that I know of (who was recently acquitted on a perjury charge brought by the New York City commission that was investigating the police, the Knapp Commission) was good for between $35,000 and $50,000 a year while he was working in Division. He was shaking down bookmakers, hookers, controllers, anybody who would pay. And that means just about everybody.

The richest cop I ever knew spent 30 years working in the New York Police Commissioner's office. He got caught with his hand in the till and Police Commissioner Kennedy ordered him to put his retirement papers in. When he got the order he barged into Kennedy's office and told him off. "I got half a million dollars in a Swiss bank account for all the years I've been working in this office. All you got is a big mouth." Supposedly Kennedy was stunned, but I don't know how he could have been. Anybody who ever pounded a beat knows what the setup is. It is a routine that has existed in one form or another for 200 years, and I don't care who you make the mayor or who you make police commissioner, you are not going to change the structure. As long as you have laws against things people want to do, you are going to have graft and corruption.

The payoff isn't always in money and it isn't always given to protect some illegal operation. If you have a restaurant the cops come in and eat for nothing; if you have a clothes store you give them a shirt occasionally. Whatever it is, you're paying off. People like to call it a 100 percent discount. The cop might reach in his pocket and offer to pay, but very rarely does that hand come out with money in it.

The Knapp Commission came up with a perfect example. The owner of a small home-delivery fried-chicken store willingly gave the local cops free dinners. Unfortunately the chicken was so good that everyone in the local precinct got to like it, and he was supplying 80 to 90 free dinners a week. This was digging deeply into his profits so he decided to charge the cops 50 cents per dinner and at least cover his own costs.

Not in New York City, you don't! The cops got even by giving tickets to his delivery cars every time they made a move. In one week they issued $600 worth of summonses to his cars. The owner immediately dropped the 50-cent charge and called the police commissioner's office. He never got another summons.

What do these people get in return? Next time you pass a crowded restaurant notice the cars that are parked all over the street without getting tickets. Or check and see where the owner of the clothing store parks his car; I guarantee you he isn't paying for a garage or popping dimes into a meter. At night you know which doors the cop on the beat is going to check, or whose employees he'll walk to the subway after dark, or which burglar alarm he'll rush to fastest. How much do you think these little services cost?

I can recall meeting two, count 'em, two totally honest cops. They just wouldn't take a cent. Now, they also wouldn't squeal on other cops. Let's face it, you're one man and you're facing 32,000 others. Every cop that has ever tried to rat on other cops has either found himself walking a beat among the weeds, picking up phone calls at all hours of the day and night or getting killed.

Remember one thing, a crooked cop has invested his career in the fact that he won't get caught. He's got a lot of time and money invested in his job and his pension, and no desire to go to jail. If you put him up against a wall he's got to hurt you.

A stubborn honest cop in New York named Frank Serpico found that out. He started making problems, problems that resulted in the Knapp Commission, and he got a bullet in the head (from a narcotics dealer, but not without help) for his trouble.

That Knapp Commission was a big joke. It didn't tell anybody anything they didn't know and did absolutely no damage to the mob. Anytime the police are squabbling among themselves you know the mob has got to be helped. As far as we were concerned, all it did was drive up the price of a cop. I was in a bar collecting from the bartender who chose to bet on the wrong teams, and two cops were sitting at his bar watching the hearings on television. One of them turned to me and asked, "How much do you think this will cost you?"

I said, "I don't know. They haven't told me yet."

I gave each of them a new hat, which is what we call a small payoff, and we all sat around and watched the cops on the stand talk about bribery. All the Knapp Commission's hearings did was drive up the price of the payoff. Very few people stopped taking.

Different squads have different rules. There is no pad for members of the narcotics squad, for example; they have to make their money on their own, on any busts they make. A pad in this area would really cause too much heat. One of the people I started in the business with got caught recently with 1000 bags of cut heroin which he was distributing to pushers. He could have gotten pretty well jammed up but he made a deal for $500 right on the spot. But now he's a marked man; these cops will be looking for money in the future.

Setting up a contract is not difficult at all. The boss in your area or his button man will tell you how much the police will charge you to operate. The payment to the police will protect the operation from a lot of different things: Your runners will be left alone and, if they are picked up by mistake, released; and if your operation is going to be raided by the district attorney or the inspector's unit your contact will let you know.

They'll either call the office directly or, if they are being watched and it's too dangerous, they'll call a third number previously agreed upon. That number might be a girl's apartment, for example, and he'll call and ask her out, telling her he'll pick her up at 8 P.M. She'll call you and tell you the raid is scheduled for 8 P.M.

The physical act of making a payoff is easy to arrange. Either the man you're paying off or his bag man meets you on a corner or in the back of a restaurant or wherever he decides and you hand him an envelope. The reason he's called a bag man is because at one point these people used to carry big black bags which they would hold open for you to drop the payoff in.

No one except the people directly involved have any idea how the money is split up, but it goes up as the power of the individual increases. The precinct cop may get $25 a week overall, the sergeant $50, the lieutenant $75 and the captain whatever is left over. Then it goes into the division office, the borough office and finally the commissioner's office. I'm not saying the commissioner is a crook. But I am telling you there has always been at least one cop in the office who was willing to work with us.

As a rule, once you have a contract you are usually pretty safe, but every once in a while somebody makes trouble. If a cop breaks a contract there is actually very little you can do about it. If they fuck you, they fuck you. But if you wait long enough eventually you'll find a way to get even. I haven't heard of more than half a dozen contracts being broken in my 30 years.

As for getting to your federal agents, forget it. It's almost impossible. They're straight. But it doesn't really make that much difference. The people I work with refer to the FBI as the Fumbling Bunch of Idiots. They're great record keepers. They probably have the greatest files in the world on crime, espionage, government workers and things like that. But like any police organization most of their information comes from informers; they very rarely actually go out and dig up their own merchandise. I have a completely honest friend who was dating the sister of an individual the FBI wanted very badly. This man had been knocking over small banks throughout the East for about six months and they just couldn't find him.

My honest friend had a third acquaintance, a college fraternity brother who had become an FBI agent. This agent found out that my friend was dating this chick and contacted him. They met for lunch at a place called Jimmy Weston's, and over dessert the agent said, "You know, we want your girlfriend's brother. I've been authorized to make you an offer. If you can give us information that leads us to him, within five hours of his capture there will be ten thousand dollars deposited in your bank account. It's yours to keep. You won't have to pay taxes on it and you can use it for anything you want. We're eventually going to get him anyway, so by helping us you might be helping him stay out of more trouble. This is the only time I'm ever going to mention this offer. If you tell anyone that I made it I'll completely deny it."

My friend told him he wasn't interested, then asked, "If you want him so badly, why don't you put him on the Ten Most Wanted List?"

The agent smiled. "We can't. We never put anybody on that list until we know where they are."

I have had a few minor brushes with the FBI. Once they stopped me as I was getting into my car and asked me a few questions about an interstate hijacking. I told them I had no information about anything, I didn't read the newspapers, and then drove away. The next time I saw an FBI agent he was at my front door.

A pair of them, very tall, conservatively dressed and very polite, knocked on my door one Saturday afternoon. I let them stand in the foyer. Why not? I hadn't done anything that could interest them in months. One of them took out a photograph that showed me standing in front of a store with a crime boss. "That's a nice picture," I said, "can I order some eight-by-ten glossies?"

They began to ask me some questions about the man. I told them if they were so interested they should ask him. "We only have a few questions," one of them said. "If you cooperate with us we'll remember it if you should ever need some help in the future."

I said, "I ain't interested in what you got to sell."

They understood. "If you change your mind we're open twenty-four hours a day."

"That's nice to hear," I said. "I'm glad someone is protecting my country."

One reason the FBI isn't as effective as it might be is that in many cases they have to work with local police and more often than not they end up fighting each other. There is just no clear jurisdiction most of the time. The federal agents could save themselves a lot of grief if they learned to work with other cops, but they never will and that's why the FBI just isn't that effective.

As far as federal agents go, we fear the Treasury people much more than anyone else because they can nail you on your taxes. Once they know who you are they keep a separate folder on you, which is one of the reasons I don't live big. If they got Al Capone on taxes they can certainly get me. And I don't know one of these agents that has ever been gotten to.

Politicians are tougher to get to than police, which is like saying marshmallows are softer than whipped cream. Lenny Bruce once told me a great story about these parents who wanted to find out what their son was going to be when he grew up, so they put a $100 bill, a Bible and a whiskey bottle on the table. If he picked up the liquor bottle he was going to be in entertainment, if he picked up the Bible he was going to be a clergyman, and if he went for the $100 bill it meant he was going to be a businessman. The child came in and picked up the Bible. His mother smiled. Then he picked up the liquor and took a swig of it, grabbed the $100 bill, put it in his pocket and left. "Well I'll be damned," his father said. "He's going to be a politician."

Politicians are much more important to the mob than policemen because the cops just enforce the laws, while the politicians make them. One of the most important things a politician can be paid to do is help to keep a certain law on the books or encourage legislation for a new law. Legalized gambling, for example. Do you think for one minute that the organization wants legalized gambling anywhere except Las Vegas? Legalizing gambling in this country would kill Vegas; Vegas would dry up like a prune. Take a town like New York City. Half of the people who go to Vegas come from there. With the entertainment and other resources of this city what do you think would happen if they legalized casino gambling? You wouldn't have places to put the people who would flock here, and the city would make a million dollars a day in taxes. The only loser would be Las Vegas and the people handling the action now. How many people would leave New York for Vegas? Only those people who love long plane trips and suntans.

To give you a specific example of the damage politicians could do the mob, the state of New Jersey began a daily lottery in 1972. About three weeks after the lottery started I ran into a guy named J.J. who had a numbers office in Newark. He told me that his business had declined 40 percent in the three weeks the lottery had been operating, and he figured he would have to close down within six months. This is an operation that was grossing $40,000 a day. If the right politicians had been reached the legal lottery might never have happened.

I am convinced that an awful lot of people screaming out against legalized gambling are motivated more by payoffs than by moral scruples.

A man's most important political contact is known as his "rabbi." If you have a connection in city government you would say that you had a rabbi at City Hall. Politicians are elected to help the people, and members of the organization are people. A "rabbi" is a fixer—he works it so you can get a case before a certain judge, or get a license approved, whatever you need to happen he helps happen. He might sit down with a judge he is friendly with and, over a glass of wine, explain that he has a friend who has a problem and it would be wonderful if the judge realized what a good person this is and how any help he can give would be greatly appreciated.

At one point the best-known "rabbi" in New York was a Democratic pol named Carmine DeSapio. An ex-con I know decided to get out of the crime business. He had spent a few years in the can, was married and had a kid on the way. All he wanted to do was make a living, but the only thing he knew how to do was drive a car. So he decided to go into the taxi business. But before he could even begin to look for a cab he had to have a hack license. The first time he went down to the hack bureau they took one look at his record sheet and laughed him out of the office. So it was arranged for him to meet Carmine DeSapio.

"The price," he was told by DeSapio's representatives, "is twenty-five hundred dollars." The contract was made, and two days later he was standing in front of Inspector Irish who at that time was the head of the bureau. I was standing in that room, and Irish, the same bum who had turned this kid down and called him all sorts of names two days ago, was leading him around by the hand. "Would you mind going around the corner and gettin' a couple of pictures taken so we can get 'em on the license for ya?" And finally Irish had to sign a statement saying that my friend had been investigated and was an honest, upstanding young man. Out of that twenty-five hundred I would guess DeSapio probably kept a thousand and the other fifteen hundred got spread around. This is what your local "rabbi" can do.

Years ago it was much easier to place a man in high political office than it is now. At one point the mob could arrange a lot of local and state elections. The best they can do today is actively and financially support the candidate they feel will be easier to work with, and even this doesn't guarantee the man will be elected. To prove my point, Chin Gigante's brother, who is a priest, ran for Congress in 1972. The Chin and all his people did everything they could to help Father Gigante get elected, not because he would help the organization, but because he was the man's brother. But he was still beaten.

The organization contributes to both parties; we do not discriminate. We want to be able to say to whoever wins, "We gave." In fact, if someone comes up with a third party and the mob feels he has a chance, they'll support that party too. The mob does not care who is in office, as long as he's a crook. Personally I am a Democrat, although I'm far to the right of the bleeding hearts. I like the Democrats because generally they've been better crooks than the Republicans, although in 1972 I voted for Nixon. (I figured one candidate was a crook and the other was a jerk, so naturally I'm gonna vote for the crook.)

In spite of the popular notion that the mob is deep in politics, it would be very difficult to find a man, Democrat or Republican, who actually owes his office to the mob. No real mob members hold office. As far as fixing elections go, the mob very, very rarely gets involved. Years ago you used to be able to vote two, three times, but no more. Any fixing that goes on today is done by the parties themselves, and from what I see and hear, they do a better job than we could ever do.

But there are so many elected officials who will do business with us by choice, it's simply not necessary to get our own people in there. Generally fixing starts in your local political clubs with your district leaders. They are about the easiest people to reach because they have a little power and want more. When it has to go beyond them they get in touch with the proper person on a higher level and make the introductions for us.

Now you don't necessarily have to get to the officeholder himself; the people who work for him will do just as well. These people like to think they are the real power, and we encourage them to think just that. Take New York City for example, once again. John Lindsay himself don't look like a thief to me, but he appoints so many city commissioners he has to make some mistakes. James Marcus was one of them. Marcus was an obscure businessman with good family connections (married one of those Lodges from Massachusetts!) who helped raise money for the Lindsay campaign. After his election Lindsay appointed Marcus Commissioner of Water Supply, Gas and Electricity. He didn't have the slightest notion that the high-living Marcus was desperately in debt because of bad stock investments.

Soon after Marcus took over, the city decided to give out an emergency contract to drain and clean a reservoir. The advantage of an emergency contract was that no bids were asked for. It was up to Marcus to award the contract to the firm of his choice. Through a labor lawyer named Herbert Itkin, and with the help of Manhattan Republican Party Chairman Vincent Albano, Marcus made a connection with Ducks Corallo. Corallo arranged a loan for Marcus and offered him a kickback if he would award the almost one-million-dollar contract to the firm of Corallo's choice. Marcus agreed. Had Marcus not made some stupid mistakes, he would have spent the entire Lindsay administration sitting in the commissioner's chair and in Corallo's pocket.

Of course he wasn't the only one. Take a look at the city and you'll see: They don't make bookmaking arrests in New York; they have more hookers per square foot than any city in the world; and you can play a number on almost every corner. And poor John Lindsay hasn't made one penny from it!

One New York City mayor who did work with us was William O'Dwyer. He was very evenhanded; he stole from everybody. Anybody who wanted a contract with the City of New York paid O'Dwyer. I know this for a fact because I made many payoffs myself. I was working in an area in the Bronx they call the Hunts Point section, which goes from 163rd Street to 174th Street and back to the East River, and I used to meet his bag man, a man who is still active in New York politics today as a matter of fact, either right there in Hunts Point or in the Soundview section of the Bronx. He would drive right up to me and I would hand him an envelope. He would say, "Thank you very much," and drive away.

I met William O'Dwyer at a dinner which took place at the Commodore Hotel. We were all there honoring a judge who had been particularly kind to his fellow man—in particular, members of the organization. A mutual friend introduced me to the mayor and told him who I worked for and what I did. "You're pretty young to be moving in that kind of company," his honor the mayor said.

I smiled. "I guess I just learned a little earlier than you did."

He started laughing, then he said, "I've always believed education is important at any age."

New York City has been so full of people on the take I'd need a whole phone book to list them. But compared to the state of New Jersey, New York City is at least careful. Almost every politician in New Jersey seems to be mob connected. The mayor of Newark, Hugh Addonizio, went to jail for taking kickbacks from the mob.

Thomas Whelan, the mayor of Jersey City, went to prison for working with the organization to extort money from companies doing business with the city. The mayor of West New York, New Jersey, went to prison for protecting gambling operations. The police chief in Old Tappan and four cops on his staff were convicted for taking payoffs. A judge in Elizabeth was convicted of trying to bribe a prosecutor to dismiss a case against two mob people. The minority leader of the state senate was barred from practicing law for half a year for helping get a muscleman out of a jackpot. Not one of these people needed the mob, but they were all looking to make some extra money and made it known they were willing to work with us. With people like these so available, why should we bother even trying to get our own men in office?

Probably the most important New York connection was Adam Clayton Powell, the black congressman from Harlem. I don't mean he was getting the most money—I don't know about that—but he was one of the easiest people to deal with. Powell had an incredible amount of influence on the people in Harlem. He was a real power. The big joke among the mob people up there was that NAACP really meant "Never Agitate Adam Clayton Powell." He was big and handsome, he was a preacher, and his father had been tremendously popular even before Adam was born. His people worshiped the ground he walked on. If he had wanted to put a dent in mob business in Harlem he could have done it just by standing up in his pulpit and telling those people. All he had to do was stand on the corner and say, "Go to school. Don't use drugs," and it would have sliced our business, no doubt about that. But he never did, that wasn't his style. Instead, he collected his money. You could not operate in Harlem without his okay, whoever you were. And you didn't get his okay without paying for it.

Somebody up there is still getting paid, and paid well. I could go up to Harlem today and give you 5000 numbers runners or 5000 dope pushers.

Somebody's protecting them, because nobody can operate without protection and everybody is operating.

Some judges can be fixed, but it depends on what the charge is. If it's a violent crime, no, it's very difficult to fix. But if it just involves money, you've got a pretty good shot at least to get the judge to be lenient. I have a relative—let's call him my great-uncle—who is a judge. One thing I gotta say about him right away is that he is totally honest. We were at a family gathering one night and I said, "By the way, uncle, I come up before you for sentencing next week." I thought he was gonna drop the plate. I was just breaking his balls. He knows generally what I do, although he doesn't know I pull the trigger. He knows that I would never, ever ask him for a favor for myself. This man has devoted his entire life to building a clean reputation, he is a distinguished man, and I would never take the chance of ruining that reputation. He told me once, "Look, you may be an embarrassment to the rest of the family, but you're still my kid nephew. If you ever hit a jackpot you know my phone number." I appreciate that, but I could never call him. I get me in, I can get me out.

But one time I did go to him for someone else. An old friend of mine had been convicted in an embezzling case and was due to appear before him. I said, "They've straightened the thing out, the money has been paid back, and he's working." He asked me if there had been any violence involved and I told him that there hadn't. He gave him a three-year suspended sentence. Just call me rabbi.

Some judges are bought and paid for. One New York judge, notorious for his inappropriate friends, used to show up at mob parties all the time. I remember one in particular that was thrown by a delegate of the Teamsters Union. This guy was going up before him to be sentenced so, a little partying, a little money, the guy gets a short stretch. This particular judge was finally nailed and retired, but never convicted.

Occasionally a judge is so deep in the pocket that any crime can be handled. A few years back, for example, Ducks Corallo (he is called that because he waddles like a duck when he walks) had a problem, not a murder rap, but a problem. It was solved by a friendly judge. But Ducks went to a party one night and shot his mouth off saying he had this judge in his hip pocket, and the wrong person heard it. It was finally proved that the judge had agreed to a payoff, and he went to jail himself—but he didn't lose his pension. The state of New York was paying him while he was in jail.

It is always money that is used as a bribe. Women and liquor are just throw-ins. People who accept bribes are described as having "deep pockets."

If the mob needs one politician in particular and that man won't take a bribe, and there are people like that we meet occasionally, the mob will try to get at him another way. But not physically. There is no way on the face of the earth that we will threaten a public official, because if you get him mad he's got the whole city to chase you with. And then he starts blabbing all over the newspapers that so-and-so tried to bribe him, which no one needs. Let me give you a little insight: When you read in the paper that someone was offered a bribe, you can bet 99 percent of the time it was refused. The mob does not fuck with uncooperative councilmen, district attorneys, governors, senators and so on. If they don't want us they let it be known and we stay away from them.

But every once in a while you need a guy, one particular guy, and you've just got to have him. So you begin looking for his Achilles heel. Take the so-called respectable guy, he's got a wife, he's got two kids. And what terrible thing is he doing? Maybe he's making it with his secretary, maybe he receives pornographic literature or films, but chances are he's doing something he doesn't want his wife and children, or the man that appointed him, or the public that voted him into office to know about. We will find it.

We never use blackmail to make money. That's just for the creeps in the street. We use it for leverage. We can make a hundred times more money getting an individual to do what we want, to approve certain contracts, to hire certain construction firms, to use certain trucking firms, to buy certain products, to funnel government money a certain way, than we can by shaking them down for a few dollars. It's a fact of business life: If you try to shake a guy down for money and he doesn't want to pay he's going to go to the law and you're going to jail. For what? For a few dollars?

Five years in prison? Forget it. This type of blackmail is used to get things done.

I'll give you an example. A city councilman in the Midwest was pushing a bill concerning garbage companies. This bill would have cost the mob, which controlled the largest private sanitation company in the city, a considerable amount of money. Certain elements of the organization made it known that they didn't like this bill, but the politician said it would be impossible to get him to change his mind. The mob said, well, maybe it wouldn't be so impossible after all, because they showed him a picture of his daughter. She had been using narcotics and had been to several parties and they had a beautiful picture of her blowing some guy. They just dropped it on his desk. After the guy got through throwing up he went along.

Other politicians have accepted contributions from people they thought were honest businessmen. When they find out different it's too late, and they're smart enough to realize that if the word gets out that they took money from the mob their career is over.

So we have different ways of reaching judges, policemen, politicians, almost anyone we really need. And we do need them because we cannot operate without them. It is their town. They are the law and the lawmakers. They own it. We are just renting certain rights.

Right now, just about the only nonviolent thing I couldn't get fixed is a parking ticket. At one time they were very easy. We had a contact man in the right department. A $15 ticket cost $5 and a $5 ticket was a deuce. He pocketed part, sent part on its way and destroyed the ticket. Today, with the computer system in operation, it is very difficult. So what has this super efficiency forced me to do? Get out-of-town license plates and now I just rip the tickets up.

CHAPTER *16*
FENCES

obert Frost, the poet, wrote, "Good fences make good neighbors," and I agree with him.* We have this guy in our building who is one of the best fences around, and whenever anybody in the place needs something, he can usually get it very quickly. Now that probably is not exactly what Mr. Frost had in mind when he wrote that poem, but if that's not a good neighbor I don't know what is.

A fence is one of the most important men in my business. He is the middleman. He takes stolen merchandise off your hands for a percentage of its value. In turn he sells it wherever he can make a good profit. Lately, thanks to the increasing number of drug addicts who support their habits by stealing, fencing has become one of America's fastest growing industries.

Anyone can find work as a fence. All you need is a source of merchandise and a place to get rid of it. The merchandise can be almost anything: jewelry, clothes, bolts of cloth, electrical equipment, a whole truckload of plumbing supplies, a truck, paintings, money and whatever else you can

*Every book is supposed to have a footnote and this is mine. This line is the only line of poetry I can quote. The reason I can quote it is that a certain fence I knew on 47th Street used to say it all the time. He would make a deal with you and then say, "Remember, good fences . . .," and then he would laugh. He would recite that line at the drop of a two-carat stone. He thought it was the funniest thing he had ever heard.

glom. If it can be stolen it can be sold. The place to get rid of it can be any-where: Legitimate department stores buy from fences, small stores buy from fences, wholesalers buy from fences, rich people buy from fences, and poor people buy from fences.

Since most people in organized crime have the connections to both get the stuff and get rid of it, almost everybody has done at least a little handling in their careers. Generally people within the mob, with the exception of occasional truck hijackings, never actually go out and steal things themselves. Number one, it's risky; number two, the cash return isn't that high for the risk involved; and number three, they don't have to. There are enough full-time thieves around who can steal merchandise of value and are willing to sell it for as little as 10 or 15 cents on the dollar. The middleman, the fence, can then turn around and get as much as 40 or 50 cents on the dollar and as long as there are bargain hunters around he will never get stuck with merchandise he can't sell.

Any deal begins with the actual theft. For example, somebody hijacks a truck with 100 bolts of top-quality cloth on it from a suit manufacturer, the value of which is estimated at about $100,000. Since this is obviously a bulky item it is very tough to keep it hidden, so the man who took it wants to get rid of it as quickly as he can. Either he knows a fence or he has to find someone who can put him in contact with a fence. If he does have to go to somebody else, that somebody is also going to take a cut of the profits. Eventually he finds a fence who agrees to take the stuff off his hands. The going rate is usually one-third or less of the real value, but each deal is separate. So the thief ends up with, at the most, $30,000. Of that he has to give the man who introduced him to the fence at least a third of his payoff, sometimes a half, depending on how badly he has to get rid of the item. The fence can usually get between 50 and 60 percent of real value when he disposes of the merchandise.

Different fences dispose of it in different ways. One fence I know in Manhattan works only through legitimate stores. Another guy up in the Bronx has a miniature department store in the cellar of his neighborhood grocery. When you go to see him it's like shopping in a little Macy's. Only his best customers know what's down there.

When a legitimate businessman buys from a fence he can sell it to his customers for whatever price he wants. I was once driving through the Lincoln Tunnel and, amazingly enough, an entire load of women's slacks heading toward a Korvette's department store fell off the truck and onto the hood of my car. I was incredibly lucky—they fell on the passenger side. Imagine, if they had fallen on the driver's side they would have blocked my vision and I could have been killed. I sold them to a legitimate retailer for $4 a pair. He sold them for $9 per and, had they reached Korvette's, they would have gone for $12 each. So everybody except Korvette's was happy.

Obviously, if you know you are going to be coming into an item it's best to shop around among fences beforehand and see what you can get for it. When you get a good offer you can make the deal even before the item comes in. A truckload of liquor was scheduled to be hijacked, for example, and the guy who was planning the theft was shopping for a fence. He contacted a man and told him he had 100 cases coming in soon. The fence told him, "I'll give you ten large for it," which meant $10,000. The guy said, "Done." Five days later he delivered the truck and was paid his $10,000, or $10 a case. The fence was able to peddle it here and there for $50 or $60 a case.

The only thing a major fence has to have is a place to keep his merchandise while he is dealing it out. Half of the south Bronx and upper Manhattan is crammed with warehouses full of stolen goods just waiting for shipment. I mean giant warehouses, packed from corner to corner with everything from typewriters to tablecloths, millions of dollars' worth of goods.

Although most fences prefer to deal with store owners, some will sell directly to the consumer. This is where a great debt is owed to our old friend, the so-called honest citizen, who is always honest until he sees a chance to get away with a good buy. If you offer a guy a brand-new car for $2500 the guy has got to know it's stolen. But I have heard of few people turning down deals like that.

Even I, a man never convicted of a felony, will buy certain things from a fence when he has them and I need them. About the only thing I won't buy, in fact, is a television set, because there is a serial number on the back. If you ever have a television set repaired the repairman can copy down the number and, if he wants, check it against a list of the serial numbers of stolen sets. It could've been taken five years before, it doesn't make any difference. He'll notify the company and, in return, the company will give him $25 and will try to break your balls when they catch up with you.

There are very few items that can't be sold. About the toughest things to get rid of are easily identifiable art objects, like paintings and sculptures. In the winter of 1972, some guys heisted some paintings from an art museum in New York. But they couldn't find anyone who would handle the merchandise for them. There was absolutely nothing they could do with these paintings but sit at home and stare at them. Art lovers they weren't. Finally they contacted the district attorney and made a deal with him. They returned the paintings and he didn't prosecute. The DA had no choice; if he didn't agree to the deal these people would have destroyed the evidence. The guys hadn't done their homework, set things up ahead of time. Art objects can be fenced; it just ain't so damn easy.

I know of only one man who will handle art objects. He is an art connoisseur himself and he knows collectors who are willing to buy the stuff just to lock it in a room and have it for their own enjoyment. They're nuts, but they're rich, which makes them good customers.

Hot money is one of the easiest things to get rid of, although the movies say differently. Let's assume we have a man who has stolen $70,000, all in fifties and hundreds. Since the serial number of every bill has been recorded, how is he gonna be able to spend this money? The answer is, he can't. So he has a mob connection find a fence who gives him 25 or 30 cents on the dollar, which isn't bad because now he has money he can spend without any problems, whereas before he didn't have a penny. The mob will take the money to South America or Europe and dispose of it there because they don't keep a list of hot money in those places.

Many times a fence has the added expense of disguising an item when he receives it. For his own safety he will make small changes, like removing an identification plate. One day I was down at the docks and I see this buddy of mine walking off a boat with a load of furs. He says, "I

just went into the fur business. You know anybody who changes linings?"
I gave him the address of a guy on 28th Street. The price is ten dollars per
lining. Mink coats in particular are good items because a lot of guys like
to give them to their wives and girlfriends. And you can usually find coats
around for half price. In this particular case the only change the fence,
who was also the thief, made was to change the linings of the coats in
which the previous owners had sewn their names.

Jewelry is another item easy to identify if left intact. One very successful combination burglar-fence I know always takes the stones right
out of the setting and throws the settings away. This guy may throw away
$60,000 worth of settings a year, but he has no problem getting rid of
stones. Unless a stone is 12 carats or otherwise spectacular it's almost
totally unidentifiable. Who's gonna know where a one- or two- or three-
carat stone comes from? They tell you they can fingerprint stones, but
that's almost impossible.

A lot of your legitimate jewelers will take stolen merchandise off your
hands. The only mistake most of them make is after they take the stones
out they leave them lying around. Anytime you leave something lying
around for any length of time it's got to get you in trouble.

The other way you get caught in the jewelry industry is to get fingered
by a thief. This is what happened to Ernie Zimmerman, the biggest jewelry fence I've ever known. Ernie was a very dignified gentleman in his
mid sixties who had half a dozen thieves working exclusively for him.
They would knock off apartments or hotel rooms and bring him the jewelry intact. His office was located on West 47th Street, right in the heart
of the jewelry district. Supposedly Ernie was an appraiser. He would take
the merchandise his employees brought in, break it down and sell it to
legitimate dealers. No one ever realized they were handling hot merchandise. Ernie was good for half a million dollars a year.

He only made one mistake—he hired the wrong kid. The guy got
caught in a hotel room and began screaming his guts out even before
the police arrived. He implicated everyone from Ernie Zimmerman to
the Pope. Zimmerman got arrested; I don't think they bothered the
Pope. He was facing a 20-year rap, but his connections arranged for him

to appear before a friendly judge and he ended up with a much lighter sentence.

I've worked all sides of the fence. I've been a middleman, a fence, and I have fenced goods that I myself glommed. Working as a middleman is always the easiest because you don't actually have to handle the merchandise to make a good profit. All you have to do is make the introductions. I was standing in front of an uptown bar once and a nigger pimp I had worked with before showed me two rings he wanted to dump. I said I would do what I could, but I made him wait outside when I went inside to speak to the fence because then I had a much better chance to cheat him. I went to see my man and he estimated one ring at $2800 wholesale and the other at $5000. I went back outside and told the pimp, "The stones are very bad, they got all kinds of flaws in them. I'll give you $500 for both of them." He took it, and I went back inside and said, "Give me $3000 for both of them and they're yours." I ended up with a little less, but we made the deal.

I didn't feel bad cheating the guy because I've always believed if you're stupid enough to be cheated you deserve to be. Now I would never have tried to cheat a mob guy, or a friend, because I respect them, but what does this nigger mean to me? He's just another thief who wants to do business. If I got a way to best him, I will. Anybody who is an independent thief, he's fair game. Like fences, they'll cheat people whenever they can get away with it. It's the nature of the business: Buy low, sell high. That's their business, and I never blame any man for doing anything he can get away with.

Most of the items I fence I get from junkies who know I'll take almost anything off their hands. I recently did a fabulous business in electric typewriters and adding machines. The only thing I had to be careful about was never taking more than ten at a time. That way I didn't have a storage problem because I could put them right in the back of a panel truck I own. I didn't have to worry about a warehouse.

That panel truck comes in very handy when I have smaller items like cigarettes or cosmetics. I got Revlon hairspray for a nickel a can. Before I took it I asked my wife if it was any good and she told me it was going for like 90 cents a can. So I took it and sold it to beauty parlors at 15 cents a can, but only by the case.

I deal both through the storekeeper and the individual customer. I grabbed a truckload of suits once. I knew it was coming and I made arrangements for warehouse space. We grabbed the truck, unloaded it into the warehouse and drove it off somewhere and left it to be found. Then we took my panel truck and began peddling the stuff. These were good suits, selling legitimately for between $95 and $125 apiece. I got rid of the whole load in two weeks. I can walk into any bowling alley in this country with two armloads of stuff, lay it down, and within an hour the stuff is gone. Any suit: $25. If I don't have your size, wait a minute, I've got one out in my panel truck. I'm very careful when I do glom a truckload to get something that I can sell quickly.

Getting merchandise yourself is not that difficult. There are two ways to go about it. Either hijack a truck off the open road or go directly into the warehouse. If I can get into the warehouse without too much trouble I much prefer to operate that way, because then I don't have to worry about some truck driver trying to become a hero. Recently trucking companies began painting identification numbers on the tops of their rigs, and making sure drivers call in at specific times. If you don't know when the driver is due to call in, hijacking a truck is a dangerous occupation because the numbers on the truck are detectable from the air and if the driver doesn't make his call you can bet police helicopters will be looking for him.

I've been involved in a number of hijackings in my career, the last two taking place in 1969. They were typical of the other jobs. I didn't initiate either one. In both cases I was invited along by the party who organized the expedition. My job was to supply the gunpower.

We took the first one right off the Long Island Expressway. The people I was with had been given the schedule of a truck filled with cases of liquor. They had the plate number of the truck and the color of the cab, and they knew approximately where they could pick up on it. Three of us drove out to Syosset, Long Island, turned around toward New York City and pulled over to the side of the road. Then we lifted the hood up like we were having trouble with the car. We began waiting about 5:45 A.M.

The truck went zipping past us about 6:30 and we took off after it. We finally pulled alongside right near a town called Glen Cove and began signaling to the driver that he had a flat tire. This was a huge van with 12 tires and he could have had a flat without feeling it, so he pulled over. We slipped in right behind him. After stopping, the driver hopped out of his cab and began walking toward the rear of the truck. He was shielded from the traffic on the expressway by the truck. I pulled a gun and put it right to his head. "Don't be a hero," I said.

"Believe me," he answered, "I'm not." We put handcuffs and a blindfold on him and then had him lie down on the floor of our car. We covered him with a blanket so he couldn't be seen. One guy took the rig, the other drove the car, and I sat in back watching the driver. We took him to Staten Island and let him off. The truck went directly to a warehouse in Queens. By noon it was completely unloaded and by six that night the police had found it—empty—parked in the middle of Manhattan's garment district.

The second job was even easier. We parked a block away from a warehouse in the Chelsea section of Manhattan and waited for a specific rig to pull out of the place. We had been hired to pick up a load of appliances that was scheduled. When the truck pulled out we followed it for a few blocks, and when the driver stopped for a light on Tenth Avenue near 18th Street, I hopped up on the side of the cab and put a gun at his head. He just looked at me and sighed, "It's yours. You just saved me a trip to North Carolina." Instead he ended up, alive and well, in Staten Island.

Sometimes the hijackings are set up by the driver himself who wants to make a big score. He contacts the mob, and the job is planned to look completely realistic. When the load is sold he gets his share. On rare occasions owners of trucking companies need help hijacking their own vehicles. The load is insured, so they collect two ways: from the insurance company and for a percentage of the profit from the mob.

I never initiate a warehouse job either. What usually happens is that some guy who bets with me, or who borrowed money from me, will say that he has a key to a warehouse and if I back a truck up to the loading dock one night he'll be there to open the door and settle part of his debt. It's a little dangerous because he may try to settle it by giving me up to the police, but after doing a little checking I usually end up going along with him. I remember one trip like this during which everything went wrong. The guy opens the door and then leaves, and me and the guy I was working with were loading up when all of a sudden this guy freezes. "Don't move," he says. "We're being watched."

I looked. I figured if it's the law, it's the law, we'll just have to see if we can make a deal. There's two pairs of eyes looking at us and I walked over to see what it was. It was two stuffed owls. I threw them at this guy as hard as I could, "Here's what's watching you, jerk," I said.

After we got all loaded up we started driving away and the back tires, both of them, went flat on us. My driver was having trouble handling the truck and he was screaming, "What do I do, what do I do?" and I was screaming back, "Keep driving, kid, keep driving, don't stop now." I wasn't about to abandon the truck with the goods still on it. We drove about 10 miles on the flats, got to our warehouse and unloaded the goods, and then drove that truck about 2 1/2 miles away and dumped it.

We had loaded up with about 4000 pair of men's pants. My first move was to go see some people I knew about taking the whole load. They offered me $2.50 per and I told them I wasn't interested. We finally decided to peddle them ourselves at six dollars per pair. We got rid of them in ten days, and we didn't have to go door to door. I knew a man who managed a supermarket. He sold 20 dozen at $7.50 a pair, which is not bad. A broad I knew worked in an office. I brought up a few pair and offered her two dollars for every pair she sold. She managed to get rid of about 50 pair. Little by little we got rid of the whole load. We just sold them around. I gotta admit it's not the way I prefer to operate. I'd rather unload fast.

Here's a helpful hint if you ever have anything you want to peddle: Two of the best markets in the world are airline stewardesses and girls who work in offices. The chintzy outfits that stews work for want them to wear the latest fashions and have the best cosmetics and yet pay them nothing. Girls who work in offices have nothing to do all day but talk to girls in other offices, and everybody likes to pick up a few extra bucks.

Your so-called honest citizen loves to deal with fences. I was walking on Madison Avenue one day and I bumped into a man who owns a legitimate, well-known top-quality clothing store that sells to your upper-class people. I used to bring him pants that would normally cost him $11 or $12 per pair and he would normally sell for $20 or $22. He paid me $5.50 and sold them below his normal wholesale costs, maybe $10 each. I hadn't given him anything in quite a while. "Joey," he says, "you haven't come around in months, I could really use some of your merchandise." I told him how brokenhearted I was for him. I'm a crook and the guy who sells it to me is a crook, but this honest citizen was begging for our business. It never fails to piss me off.

The penalty for buying or selling merchandise you know is stolen is upwards of five years. It becomes a federal crime if you're caught dealing in interstate transportation of stolen merchandise, so that is something to be very careful about. Because of these severe penalties, every full-time fence I've ever known is paranoid. Fences never look right at you, they keep watching behind you. "Are you being followed? Does anyone know you're here?"

A top fence can make a million dollars a year or more, depending on his volume. My jewelry connection won't even talk to you, for example, unless you've got more than $200,000 worth of merchandise, which gives you some idea!

How can an honest citizen find a fence? If he's looking for a fence, my friend, he is no longer honest.

CHAPTER *17*

GOING LEGIT

The organization has no pension plan, no welfare fund, and most members make no social-security payments. Instead we have legitimate businesses, or what might accurately be described as our antisocial security. The mob is more involved in legitimate businesses than Dean Martin is in booze. The total take from legitimate business enterprises has got to be very close to the take from illegal operations. The mob isn't dealing in millions in this area, it's dealing in billions. If you were to shut down every business which a mob man has a piece of, this country would be hit with the worst depression since 1929.

There are a number of reasons legitimate businesses are so attractive to mob people. They provide a steady cash income; they make great places to hide money from the Internal Revenue Service (who's gonna know if a guy invests money he never reports in a business?); they provide a visible source of income to make the IRS happy; and they give a guy something to fall back on when the numbers stop running so well and there isn't much muscle left in his muscle. Best of all, except for the fact that very little of the money made is reported to the IRS, there is absolutely nothing illegal in this area.

The organization started getting into business in the late 1930s when

Meyer Lansky and Frank Costello realized that something had to be done with all the cash they had floating around. They looked around to see what people wanted. They saw that the average citizen was going to spend his money on transportation, hotels, restaurants, liquor, parking facilities and all the service-type businesses. And then they went out and invested in those businesses.

Smart couple of fellas, in case it escaped your attention.

Costello figured there was going to be a need for parking areas in big cities. He founded two companies that are today among the largest in the field. The mob has gotten into many businesses simply by starting them from scratch, and using their connections to build them up.

Most people don't believe that, they prefer to believe the mob gets into any business it wants to simply by strolling in and threatening to break the owner in half if he doesn't agree to take the mob in as his partner. It just doesn't work that way anymore. Years ago maybe, but not now. There are just too many law-enforcement agencies waiting to knock your brains out. Our money is narcotics, our money is gambling, our money is loan-sharking, our money is kickbacks, and then we throw it into legitimate businesses . . . and make more money.

Today mob members get into legitimate businesses in numerous different ways: On rare occasions they will "assume partnership" of an establishment; or they open and operate the business themselves; mob members become partners in many businesses when the owner can't pay his gambling or loansharking debts; or they might set up the entire business and use a salaried dummy to front for them; they go into straight partnership with some individuals—the mob provides the cash, he provides the know-how and labor; sometimes mob-connected individuals are "invited in" to help operate a business; or they go into business under their own names, and no one knows they are mob people.

The first method, "assuming partnership," is also known as extortion and is illegal. A few years ago this was an accepted method, but times have changed. There's really no percentage in it, and with all the businesses an individual can get a grip on legally, why should he bother taking the chance on some guy running to the police, or to another faction of the mob? The money isn't worth the problems that might result. For example, a few years ago there was a bar up in the Bronx named Richard's Apartment, and some hoods tried to muscle in. They threatened the owner and when he told them to go fuck themselves they beat him up pretty good. So the owner went to a man named Squillante and gave him a piece of the joint in return for protection. This is a perfect example of a legitimate guy "inviting" a mob guy into his business. Squillante did the job and was happily collecting his money until one day he just disappears. Gone. When payday comes his nephew, Jo-Jo Berry, comes in and asks for the money. "I'm your new partner," he says.

By this time the owner is in the middle and he doesn't know what the hell to do. Through an intermediate, he gets in touch with me. I asked him what he wanted. "I just want to be left alone," he said and offered me a cash deal. He had had enough partners.

Before I accepted I went to see Richie Schivone because this was his area and I would have been violating protocol if I didn't talk to him before taking the job. I asked him if he had a piece of the joint and he said no. So I explained, "Jo-Jo Berry is in there and I'm telling you now, if he don't listen to reason I'm gonna break him in half." Richie said I had an open ticket. I made the deal.

That night I went over there and waited for Jo-Jo. When he walked in I told him, "Jo-Jo, you are no longer a partner in this establishment."

He says, "Who says?"

I reached into my belt. "Me and this .357 law firm just drew up a contract. If I ever see you in this joint again, you're dead."

The next afternoon I got a call from Richie. "Jo-Jo was here," he said, "screaming bloody murder. He said that I let you go in there and throw him out."

"Richie," I answered, "you told me you didn't have any of that place."

"Well, I don't," he admitted. "But he wants to give me a piece."

"Don't take it," I warned him, "because then I got to fight you." Richie didn't, because he knew a deal was a deal, and Jo-Jo was out. Eventually Jo-Jo was found in a sewer, which I personally thought was gonna give that sewer a bad name.

Muscle is there, but it's very rarely used for extortion. Every time the mob has tried to muscle in on a legitimate business, where an honest person has been hurt, I would give you odds a mob guy ended up in the can. Recently the owner of a Manhattan bar was killed because the mob was trying to muscle in on his place and he went to the DA's office. He refused police protection, which was stupid on his part. Some hood panicked and thought he was going to be named so he shot him. So far four people have been arrested for participating in this little escapade. Who's the winner? Four mob people have been lost and the public is pissed. Who won?

There are very few businesses that mob people will operate themselves, but traditionally vending-machine companies have been mob-owned and operated. There are very few independent jukebox operators in this country today, and the few that exist are probably partners with the mob in some way, otherwise they would not stay in this business too long. Years ago the jukebox industry was one of the most violent in the country. The strong man in the area had his boxes everywhere he could keep them. But then the mob became fully organized, and it didn't make good business sense to fight with one another.

Today jukeboxes are run on a very businesslike level. When a store is opening up that is going to have a box, anyone who is interested just goes down and makes his bid. If somebody comes along and underbids him, that's the way it goes. This is now a legitimate business, and the only time an individual might get violent is when somebody tries to cheat him, play with the cash register or push your customers around.

Jukeboxes are a quantity business. When you've placed maybe a dozen boxes in one neighborhood, now you've got something. You might have a contact in the license bureau who lets you know where the liquor licenses are going. A $5000 advance against profits for the right to put your box in a guy's place usually gets results. Anybody just going into business can use the money.

A jukebox costs in the area of $1000. You can buy your records at a discount, so that's a minimal thing, you pay a small percentage to ASCAP, and you're splitting the take in half with whoever owns the bar or restaurant. A really good jukebox that gets a lot of play can bring you for your end maybe $125 or $150 a week. Every single week. If you've got ten boxes going you're a rich man.

Cigarette machines are also very profitable. If you have enough machines, and you're smart, you'll mix up bootlegged cigarettes with legitimate cartons. This way you've got an invoice in case an inspector comes around to make sure you're not doing exactly what you're doing. If you buy the cigarettes legitimately in New York you've got to pay 48 1/2 cents wholesale per pack, if you buy them in Carolina you're paying 23 cents per pack. You're mixing them both up in your machine and selling them for 70 cents. Along with your invoice you need a distributor stamp corresponding to the area you're operating in, which you can have made up. Let's assume you move 1000 cartons a week. You'll buy 2000 legitimate cartons and 1000 bootleg cartons and stick them all in the machine. How is anybody going to know how many packs of cigarettes you sell a week? You'll make more on your 1000 bootleg cartons than you will on the 2000 legitimate cartons. This is what I consider good business.

Any time a new bar or restaurant is opening up you try for the linen supply, the jukebox and the cigarette-machine concessions. It doesn't sound like too much, but when you add it all up it becomes a lucrative proposition, and one the mob has been onto for a long time.

Your average organization member gets into legitimate businesses mostly through bad luck. Somebody else's. It is a very simple proposition. A man is in debt and, to settle the debt, he gives a percentage of his business to the man who holds his note. From that point on his new partner, or his representative, will show up once a week to pick up his percentage of the profits.

Say you owe me $15,000. I examine your business and decide it's worth $30,000. I am now your partner. If I didn't have a contract drawn up when I loaned you the money, or when you bet that deeply with me, I have done it now. Nice and legal. Unfortunately, I have to pay taxes on this money because it shows up as income. Suppose a Treasury guy were to get interested in my partner and notices all of a sudden he's only declaring half of what he's declared for the past ten years. Obviously my man will explain he has a new partner, and then they've got to start looking for me. I have no choice, I've got to declare at least part of the income.

A lot of organization people got pieces of the resort hotels in the Catskill Mountains this way. If they had a few rainy summers in a row their banks gave them problems and they would have to borrow from the mob. Once the mob got in they weren't about to let go. The same holds true for the garment industry. A manufacturer needs cash to bring out a new line. The bank has doubts so he goes to the mob. The line ain't all that successful, he can't pay back the loan, and there goes a percentage of his business.

I personally think owning businesses is a pain in the ass. I've got to come around all the time. I've got to have an accountant check the books to make sure my partner ain't cheating me too much. If I wanted to be a businessman I would have sold my gun and bought two white shirts. So I usually find somebody who wants to buy me out. I tell my partner right at the beginning that I'm looking for a buyer or he can buy me out as soon as he gets the cash. That is usually what happens.

Most of my legitimate "business" opportunities have come about because of gambling. Thanks to bad bettors I've owned parts of luncheonettes, florist shops, gas stations, beauty parlors and record stores. As far as I'm concerned the very best of them all was a family-owned Jewish delicatessen. "Poppa" was a horseplayer, so I got a share of this establishment. They had the best lox I've ever tasted, so it was worth whatever the guy owed me.

The biggest business I ever became a partner in was a restaurant on York Avenue in New York City. The owner was into me for $85,000 and I took half his business instead. I never twisted his arm. I gave him all the time he wanted to pay me, and he couldn't do it, so finally I said, screw this, we're partners. He never said a word. I don't think it's necessary to name the place, there is no reason to embarrass the owner, but this place was a gold mine! It was open from 6 A.M. till 2 A.M. and there were always customers. I was in there for over two years and finally my partner bought me out for $125,000.

I once went into a dry-cleaning business that was owned by a guy who went down for ten grand. He was paying me $150 a week for two years, a little more or a little less, depending on how our business did that week.

Then some guy offered me $15,000 for my share. I sold. Why? Because for two years I was making $150 a week, that's $15,000. Plus another $15,000. That's $30,000 for a $10,000 investment that I didn't have to lay out any money for in the first place.

I have never intentionally hurt a business that I was into. In a few ways I can help. For example, there are a bunch of bums hanging around my new store hurting business. My partner has tried to get rid of them by calling the cops, but the cops say they have too many other things to do, so he is stuck with them. Until I come along. I walk in and say, "Hey, bum. Out!" and these kids take a look and they are gone.

Johnny Dio wasn't so good to his partners. In fact he made it a practice to bankrupt the places he went into. Johnny would walk into businesses that borrowed money from him and become an active partner. The first thing he did was reestablish the credit of the business. Then he would start to order goods on credit. He would sell the merchandise, pocket the money and never pay the suppliers. He would also take as many bank loans as he could get against the business, each for as much as he could grab. Then, in a very short time, he would declare bankruptcy. There was nothing the real owner could do about it, not if he liked living. This kind of deal eventually got Johnny in trouble because it was out-and-out fraud. As a matter of fact, Johnny Dio gave the order that had his uncle, Jimmy Plumeri (also known as Jimmy Doyle), killed because he was the one who gave the federal government the information that put Johnny Dio in prison for bankruptcy fraud.

Another guy who did almost the same thing was Joe Pagano. He was named President of the Murray Packing Company in the Bronx when he invested $35,000 in the company to buy a one-third interest and promised to bring in more business. All he did was buy as many supplies on credit as he could and sell them to customers at bargain prices. Then he pocketed the receipts and neglected to pay the suppliers. He must have made somewhere in the neighborhood of half a million dollars before the company went bankrupt—and before he went to jail.

Many times mob people will be the silent money behind a business. They will own the whole operation, but just use somebody else to put his name on a license and front for them. Mob people who have police records can't get a liquor license, or any other business license for that matter, in most states. Most of the big Las Vegas hotels and gambling casinos were built with mob money and front people.

Bars are probably the most popular mob business. I know one guy who was gambling pretty heavy and fell into a deep hole, but the fact that he had a liquor license in his pocket stopped his fall. He didn't have a bar, just the license. I put him in touch with a shy who gave him the money to pay his debts. Then he and the shy opened up a bar. All the shy did was give this guy $50 or $75 a week to use his license and show up once in a while. The shy actually ran the place.

The organization actually prefers people who are anonymous to front for them rather than well-known people. A few years ago a story accusing Frank Sinatra of fronting for the mob was spread all over the newspapers. Now if it had been Joe Doaks, who lived on 32nd Street and First Avenue, nobody would give a damn. Maybe it would have been buried on page 17 in the papers, but Sinatra is big news.

A guy named Billy Whipple was listed as the owner of a bar on West 44th Street. The actual owner of the bar, the man who had put the money up and collected the profits, was Champ Frankel. Eventually the Alcoholic Beverage Control found out about the hidden ownership and closed the place down. It never even made the papers. That's the way it should be.

Probably the easiest way to go into business is in straight partnership with a selected individual. You find a guy, you stake him to a business and you collect profits forever. One man has become a legend in this type of operation. He is known, believe it or not, as The Phantom and he owns a minimum of 400 places in the New York area. Four hundred! Most of the time he's a bookie, and many of them came his way that route—but he has started a large number himself. He looks for young married people and he sits down with them and makes a deal. He gives them proper training, the money to put the place in operation and all the help they need to get it going. This may cost him as much as $15,000 to $20,000. Once the place is open and operating he pays his "partner" a salary, a good one but a regular salary, until his share of the proceeds have equaled his original investment. Then he hands the business over to the man who set it up. He just gives it to him.

He tells him, "This is now yours. Whatever you do with this business is up to you." Then every week, forever, his representative comes around to pick up the agreed-upon weekly draw. It might be as little as $100 or as much as $350. And The Phantom isn't listed on anybody's books, he's paid in cash and never pays a penny in taxes.

The Phantom explained it to me once like this: "I open up a place that will not attract a lot of attention, an ice-cream parlor, a delicatessen, a pharmacy, and maybe it costs fifteen thousand dollars to open the front doors. The guy I put in there works like an animal because the quicker he pays me back the sooner he can start making money. When he starts making it I'm making it too, because I've got my original investment back. More importantly, I don't have to watch over them. These people are in business for themselves, so I know they are going to continue working hard."

Each week The Phantom has four or five guys who do nothing but go around and collect money. These collections are not done out in the open; normally a collector will make a small purchase and the cashier will slip the payment envelope into the bag with the item. Just to avoid temptation, and anyone who might be watching, the collectors are rotated every few weeks. The Phantom must be making between $50,000 and $60,000 every week, maybe one of the richest men in this country, and nobody knows his name!

Mob members will often be "invited" into businesses because they have proven to be good "salesmen." The very late Eugene Catena had a company named Best Sales, for example, which could almost guarantee to greatly increase a corporation's earnings.

Having a mob member on the payroll greatly decreases the chance that you'll be bothered by the mob. I was once working on and off for the owner of an independent supermarket—I could have had a piece of the place in return for my services, but I preferred getting paid by the job—who happened to buy a truckload of hijacked groceries. What he didn't know, because he never bothered to tell me he was making this purchase, is that the load had been hijacked from a mob-owned trucking company. Needless to say, the mob owner was understandably sore. His representative visited the store and told the owner he wanted $20,000 for the load. The owner heaved him out the door and screamed bloody murder. Enter Joey.

GOING LEGIT

I arranged a meet with said trucking-firm owner, and he made it clear he was not going to negotiate: The load was worth $20,000 and he wanted $20,000. The man had a legitimate case, and so I went back and explained to my man, "Listen, I don't want to hurt your feelings, but you're gonna have to give the man his twenty thousand dollars."

He blew his stack. He had paid $10,000 for the load from the hijacker and now he was going to end up paying a total of $30,000 for the $20,000 worth of merchandise.

"That's not all," I added. "My fee for this job is twenty-five hundred dollars."

He couldn't believe it. "For what? You didn't do nothing!"

"I only did one thing." I smiled at the jerk. "I saved your life." He paid, but if I had not been connected with the mob he could have been blown away.

The final way an organization man will get into a legitimate business is to open it under his own name. Assuming, of course, that very few people realize he is mob-connected. How many customers of the G & M Realty Company in Florida, for example, knew that the "G" stood for Carlo Gambino? In many cases a man will appear to be a perfectly honest businessman, but somewhere he'll have mob affiliations and thus be beholden to the mob.

Mob businesses are successful for a number of reasons. Most important of them is the mob's deep and lasting ties with unions. The love affair between the organization and unions goes back a long way. When many unions were first being organized the mob was there with some financial and a lot of physical support. Many high union officials owe their positions to mob influence within the union locals. Mob people take full advantage of their union connections in the world of legitimate business. Any mob member who can threaten potential customers with labor problems if they don't buy from him is going to have a lot of customers. When Eugene Catena wanted the A & P to buy a detergent manufactured by one of his companies he had the heads of two unions—one of which had already struck the A & P and cost them millions of dollars—suggest the company buy the product. I have no doubts the company would have if the detergent hadn't been so lousy.

246

Also any business which knows it is not going to have labor problems has a big advantage over its competitors who have to worry about such things. And this does not include the money a mob man can save for his own business—or for a customer—by using his union contacts to ensure that the union agrees to a contract favorable to management.

One of the first muscle jobs I ever did was in this area. Some truckers had gone on strike and after being out a few weeks they were talking about taking management's offer. I was hired by union leadership to go in and break heads. Easier done than said. Of course, the workers all thought I had been hired by management to break the strike, so they became much more determined to hold out until they got exactly what they were asking for—which is exactly what the union leaders wanted.

Today as much as 40 percent of the trucking industry in New York City is controlled by the mob. And almost every mob-run trucking company does a good business. No one forces people to use mob trucks, but I guarantee you a company that does will have fewer union problems.

The mob is deeply entrenched in the garbage business. This is very lucrative because businessmen in New York have to use private firms to pick up their garbage, and guess who owns the private firms?

The mob is also into the tourist-trap businesses: stores selling cheap souvenirs, cheap cameras, that sort of thing. If you come up with a fad, anything the younger generation will go for, like singles places, mob guys will open stores for you. Take pizza. I would like to have a nickel for every mob guy who owns a piece of a pizza parlor.

The mob recognized bowling alleys were going to be profitable before anyone else and they invested in them. The mob owns many drinking establishments. Surprisingly, a lot of these are fag bars. This is because, as a general rule, fags are not allowed in straight bars. That's not their fault because they give you less trouble than anyone else in the world. It's just that inevitably some he-man is going to have a few too many and start picking on the poor guys. Who needs that? In a fag bar we charge 20 to 25 percent more for booze and stuff, and they'll gladly pay it because it gives them a chance to come and congregate, just like regular boys and girls, among their own kind. It's a form of protection we're giving them.

GOING LEGIT

Occasionally a mob member will work for a legitimate businessman for a salary. He's not going to carry crates or sell shirts, but he might drive a truck if the guy is having trouble getting his merchandise through. He might act as a general troubleshooter, as I did for that supermarket owner. If a distributor is giving him trouble, for a fee he will go and visit him. All he has to do is explain to this distributor that he will never get another delivery if he doesn't start cooperating.

Sometimes I'll do a job like this as a favor, because then I have a favor owed to me and at some point I will collect. I had a friend who was having trouble down at the Bronx Terminal Market. They were giving him a hard time. Why? I don't know, I wasn't really that interested. He just explained to me, "I'm having a tough time down there. Every time I want to buy something they take care of everybody but me." So we decided to go down there together.

One morning we go down there and we're there by 4 A.M. Now this is what I consider early and I am not in what you would call a good mood. Just like my friend says, they start taking care of everybody but him. I finally got pissed off and walked up to the guy and told him, "Hey, fuck, give this man what he wants and give it to him now." Then I told him what would happen if I had to come back a second time. "The rest of your stuff is going to be on the Major Deegan Expressway [which runs above the market] and I'll see to it that there are thirty guys here to throw it up there." He took care of my friend. Now, if he had a mob connection that mob guy would come and talk to me and we'd iron things out peacefully. We got to live with one another, we all realize that.

There are many organization people who are doing better legitimately than they do in the rackets, yet if they gotta make a choice they drop the legitimate end every time. It's difficult to explain why, but there is a point where money is not the important thing. The action is. Why do I play the horses? Because I love it. Why do I play poker? Because I love it. Most of us have been in illegitimate business all our lives. Success really isn't as important as continuing to play the games.

With all the money The Phantom makes he continues to book bets. I asked him why. "Business is one thing," he said, "pleasure is another. Without the action I would go crazy."

CHAPTER *18*
THE GRAYBAR HOTEL

have always looked at organized crime as a game: Sometimes you win, sometimes you lose. When you lose you either die or go to prison. Of the two, prison is better.

I have spent a total of 16 months of my life behind bars, all of it in jails rather than prisons. The difference is more than a little important; jail is where you are put to wait for trial, prison is where you go to serve your time after being convicted. I have spent all my time in county and city jails waiting for my trials to begin . . . because it is almost impossible to get bail on a murder rap.

Once you're inside, though, there is little difference. If you want to know what it's like to spend time in the Old Graybar Hotel, it's easy enough to find out. Just have somebody padlock you in a small room for a complete day. You might even want to make it what we call a strip cell, so take everything out except a mattress and a chair. And then sit there. That's exactly what jail is: incredibly boring.

If you were to rate prisons, the federal ones would get the highest marks. The number-one place in the country is the federal clink in Danbury, Connecticut. It's like a country club. There are no real restrictions on you, except that you have to stay there. You even have an opportunity to go to school and, as long as you don't abuse anybody, you're treated very well. The Federal Medical Facilities in Springfield, Missouri, is also considered a good place. Your southern county prisons are considered the worst, but King of the Bad was Alcatraz. A lot of people were mighty happy when they closed that place down.

Jails are better than prisons because technically while you are there you are awaiting trial and are basically a free citizen. You are just being detained to guarantee your appearance in court. At the Tombs, for example, a jail in New York City, they don't force you to get a haircut and you can wear your own clothes. That may sound like nothing, but it means you remain yourself.

Both jail and prison are better for mob members than they are for your regular run-of-the-mill con. A mob guy is generally treated better in stir than other people because, number one, he can buy favors, and number two, he can make things happen on the outside. As a rule he will end up with a soft job, like in the hospital or the library or the kitchen where he'll eat good, but whatever he's doing it isn't going to be too hard. It's very rare that you see a connected person in there hauling garbage or digging a ditch.

In return, mob-affiliated prisoners are very careful not to cause anybody any trouble. They are quiet guys, don't bother nobody and don't want to be bothered. They stay as far away from problems as they possibly can. They figure they've had the best legal advice and lost, so they're stuck there and they're going to do as little time as possible. Mob people, real organization members, simply accept jail as one of the worst parts of the business.

Thanks to the way the system is set up, though, there are ways of making it at least tolerable. The guards in most places are very crooked. I guess you could say that they really belong in jail. When they see a chance to make an extra 60 or 70 tax-free dollars a week they take it. That may not sound like a lot of money, but to guys making $10,000 a year that's one-third of their annual salary.

For the right amount of money these guys will do just about anything for you. It's public knowledge that in Hudson County, New Jersey, and Nassau County, New York, broads were being supplied to some people. Narcotics? It's easier to get narcotics inside than it is outside. I was in the Tombs and it used to smell like a fuckin' grass factory. You can get anything you want: heroin, coke, hash, grass, you name it. If you can pay, a guard will bring it in for you.

The only rule is you have to pay for everything in cash, no checks and no credit cards in the Graybar Hotel. You get the cash from your relatives or from gambling with other prisoners.

I was 15 years old the first time I spent a night behind bars. The word had gotten out that some guy was after me, I don't even remember what for. Then a very terrible thing happened to this guy: He found me. So after I got through with him they put me in jail overnight to teach me a lesson. And I learned a lesson: Don't get caught.

The only really long stretch I put in was in the Tombs. I spent almost a year there on a murder charge. Normally mob people don't spend that much time before trial, usually they find someone to raise bail and they're back on the streets in a matter of hours. But when a murder charge is brought against you, you sit. If you are eventually found not guilty or the charge is dismissed, as it was in my case, this is all wasted time. Sure, you use delaying tactics, hoping that a witness may disappear, but ten months is a long time to wait for trial.

It's only in the last few years that some states are starting to give bail on murder raps, but when they do, they set it at such a high figure that you're not gonna be able to make it anyway. The bail system in this country really discriminates against the ordinary citizen. But if you're an ordinary citizen they might set your bail at $150,000. You go to a bondsman and he asks what kind of collateral you got. What have you got? A three-room apartment filled with $700 worth of furniture? He'll laugh at you. Bondsmen usually want collateral equal to the total amount of the bond.

Just for your information, there are two types of bonds: a bail bond, which is a bond underwritten by an insurance company; or cash bail, which is generally between one-fifth and one-tenth of what the bail bond will be for. I've seen a guy go to court and have the judge set the figure at $1000 . . . or $200 in cash. But when it's astronomical you can't make a deal so you end up sitting in places like the Tombs.

The first person to contact when the police grab you and the charge is not bailable is your attorney. A good attorney is a rare gem; once you get your hands on one you don't let go. Without a good lawyer you'd be in the bucket so fast you wouldn't know what hit you. I have two attorneys that I use, one in New York and the other in Los Angeles.

I was a kid when I first needed an attorney, and the court was nice enough to provide one for me. He was an older man who had trouble with things like hearing, which is a definite handicap in a courtroom, but he managed to keep me out of jail—he got me into the army.

The next time I needed an attorney a friend supplied one. The charge was assault. I told him the facts surrounding the case, including the fact that the police had confiscated my baseball bat when they arrested me, and he said, "You really don't have anything to worry about. I'll plead you guilty and we'll make a deal."

"*Guilty!*" I screamed. "You're outta your mind. Get outta here right now."

He didn't understand what he had done wrong. "What's the matter?" he asked.

"I don't want to hurt your feelings," I said, "but I don't want a lawyer who says I'm guilty. I want a lawyer who says I'm innocent." I had another friend find a guy for me. He heard what the people I was working for were paying and became convinced I was as innocent as Little Bo Peep. He finally got me off by claiming self-defense.

I always tell my lawyer the complete truth. I don't leave anything out and I don't lie. I give him every gory detail. I'm not worried about this because any conversation I have with my attorney is considered a confidential communication. Besides, this guy is sworn to defend me, and the only way he can properly do that is to know everything there is to know. With my freedom at stake I want to make sure he is aware of anything the opposition could throw at us.

Legal fees are covered under any contract. If a man hires someone to do a job for him, he is responsible for any attorney's fees that may arise. I had somebody fork over $25,000 to my lawyer when he walked me out of the Tombs after almost a year. I have only paid my own legal expenses once in my life. I was having dinner with Tommy Eboli (Tommy Ryan) and some other people in a place called Stella's in Queens; when the cops came in and arrested the entire dinner party for consorting with known criminals. Rather than bother a bondsman and then have to reappear for trial I called a lawyer immediately. He came over and had the charge dismissed on some technicality. The police didn't fight it, they were just trying to hassle us.

As far as I'm concerned a lawyer has one job—to keep his clients on the streets. I knew an attorney who once paid a cop approximately $2500 to get hold of the gun that was being used as evidence against his client and destroy it. I know of other lawyers who have bribed witnesses and paid to have other witnesses intimidated. I don't care what a lawyer does, as long as he keeps me out of jail.

If your lawyer blows his job, or you're killing time waiting for trial, the first thing you have to do when you get inside is establish yourself. Your survival depends on how strong you are, and most of the time you are tested right away. In the Tombs, for example, my first day there I was standing by myself at the end of a corridor minding my own business. This nigger came over to me and all he said was, "Hey, white motherfucker . . ." and I turned around and kicked him right in the balls. He went down and I kicked him in the head about ten times until that boy was bleeding. Then I stopped and said, "If there are any other niggers over here who want to talk to me, he had better say, 'Sir.'" I mean, I was putting on a show and everybody knew it, but it got me respect. From that point on I had no trouble. The guards knew what I was doing and they didn't bother me. Most of them were white and they didn't like the blacks anyway. One guard, a guard I used later to run things in and out for me, he just stood there watching and laughed and laughed. "We heard you were a wild man," he told me later.

There are only two things to worry about in prison: One is the cons

253

around you. You challenge one of these guys without being able to back it up and he's liable to put a knife in you. The other is the guards. You offend one of them and they can slap you across the head with a bat. My fight took care of the other cons, my money took care of the guards.

I was paying them $75 a week, which was split between three guards, and I could pretty much do whatever I wanted. Now, remember, the Tombs is officially a house of detention, not a prison, so things were much looser to start with. We just worked together to make them even easier. The entire time I spent there I don't think I ate half a dozen prison meals. I wouldn't eat slop. I used to have food delivered from a restaurant across the street, or have my wife bring it up. When I really got hungry late at night I would ask a guard to send out for me, but this was a service I had to pay extra for. I was allowed to take showers anytime I wanted and I even had a television set in my cell. Best of all, as long as I wanted it that way, I had a cell all to myself, which was really something, because the Tombs is the most overcrowded jail since the Black Hole of Calcutta.

I would generally get up at 6 A.M. One of the guards would come over and bring me a cup of coffee and take my breakfast order. Then I would wash up and take a shower and wait for breakfast to arrive. After eating I was pretty much on my own. The Tombs had jobs to be done, but there were too many people and not enough to do. How many people can you put to work doing nothing? They would end up taking us out to the recreation area and let us walk around. Big deal, what do you do, smell the fresh air you got in New York City?

My life behind bars has been tolerable, I guess. The only bad part about the whole deal is the time. The hours just don't go very fast. They say after you've spent a year or so inside you pick up a new kind of time and it moves quickly. I don't know, I never really got used to it. To make the hours fade you read, you exercise, you watch television, you swap prison jokes. Examples: This client who was given the electric chair asked his lawyer what he should do. The mouthpiece advised, "Don't sit down!" Or a guy scheduled to die in the electric chair requested mushrooms for his final meal. The warden couldn't understand why, so he asked him. "Up until now," the convict replied, "I've been afraid to eat them." That's prison humor. Maybe now you can understand why the hours go by so slowly.

Some people take advantage of their time in prison to improve themselves. Joey Gallo read a great number of books and all of a sudden became a genius. I had something to do with books in the Tombs: I ran a bookmaking business.

My games started as a joke. I was fucking around, doing absolutely nothing except watching the soap operas, and I said, "Okay, who wants to bet the numbers?" Hands went shooting up. One guy says, "Hey, we get paid?" I said sure. The next thing I knew I was booking horses and football and eventually doing a little loansharking too. It was great fun and very profitable. I was making more than a few bucks a week taking action from the other prisoners, the guards, the people who came to visit. When my wife came up to see me I would just hand her the week's receipts. (She didn't need it, she was collecting every week from the people I was working for.)

Shylocking was the most profitable inside just like out. People needed the money to bet, to buy things, to bribe guards, so they came to me. I considered these people excellent clients and didn't even ask for collateral. I mean, where were they gonna go? They all had family on the outside, and if these guys got in too deep the family always paid. I didn't have to worry about collecting, I was the most exciting thing happening in that place and if you didn't pay me you couldn't play.

The only thing I refused to deal in was narcotics. Not because I'm against it—if there's cash in it I'm for it—but I don't get involved as a peddler. Like I told you, I deal in it as a bulk importer where I can get rid of it immediately, or I will transport it for somebody. Anyway, I didn't need it.

The only good thing that came out of my stay in the Tombs was my relationship with a college professor who was waiting trial for murdering his wife. I met him in the yard one day, one sunny afternoon. Some of the bums there were giving him a hard time. Prisons have a very strong social system. Birds of a feather really do hang together. Your rapists and child molesters are considered the lowlifes and stay with each other; junkies form another group; people with brains, intelligent bank robbers for example, might form a third group; and the mob is another.

One day I was in the yard and I see the little groups together. The junkies and cokies were hunched over planning the great crime they were going to pull when they got out. Over in another corner the speechmakers were sounding off about how the system is stacked against them. (I got into an argument with one of them once. I listened to his crap and finally said, "Listen, ya bum. If you're so smart, how come you're in here?" He asked me the same question. I told him, "Every week I sit here watching television and having the guards wait on me, my old lady is getting two hundred fifty dollars and when I get out there will be a bundle waiting. What have you got waiting?" He didn't say.)

Anyway, they were getting on this professor pretty good about killing his wife and you could see he wasn't taking it too well, so I decided to help him out. He had been married to her for 15 years and I guess she just drove him up a wall. I really felt sorry for this guy because it was obvious he was one of those people who in no way, shape or form belongs in jail. He shouldn't have even been in there while he was waiting trial, and if they had to put him somewhere, they certainly shouldn't have put him in the same place as these animals. He wasn't a violent man, he wasn't going to hurt anybody on the outside, and he wasn't going anyplace.

After I got to know him I told the guard to move him into my cell rather than leave him to the jerks. He had an IQ of something like 160, and we played gin rummy all day. He would, excuse the expression, murder me, but he taught me to play a good game of cards. He also got me on a reading kick. I left school in the fifth grade, the last thing I remember reading there was a pamphlet entitled "Don't Leave School," so what did I know about reading? He said, "Find out what interests you and then read that. Never read just for the sake of reading because, if you get bored, you're just wasting your time." The first book I ever read from cover to cover, right there in that cell, was the novel *The Young Lions*. I liked it, but the movie was better.

At first the professor really didn't care what happened to him. He was sick about what he had done. But then he gradually began to come around.

I think he saw that he was having a positive influence on me and it made him begin to think about going back to teaching. I knew he was in bad financial shape, because he had to use a Legal Aid attorney, and I wanted to help him. Finally I told my own lawyer, "You don't defend this guy, but get him a good lawyer, because I don't think it would be right for this guy to get hung."

He looks at me and asks, "When did you join the Salvation Army?" But he did what I told him and everything worked out. They pleaded temporary insanity, showed what kind of woman he had been married to, and got him off on a manslaughter rap with a suspended sentence and probation. To put a man like him in prison would have been a complete waste. There was no premeditation on his part. He didn't do it because he had a girlfriend or anything like that, it just happened. He's back teaching now in an upstate New York college.

The way prisons are run today no man anywhere is going to get rehabilitated. For me it makes no difference. If I went to prison I would do my time quietly and come out no different than when I went in. But a lot of guys do go to prison and come out a hell of a lot worse for the experience because they are treated like animals. They are caged, they are brutalized, they are given bad food and absolutely no humane treatment. And by the nature of things, they associate with people who are a whole lot worse than they are. How do you expect a man to come out any different—there is nothing to teach him different. Lester Maddox once said that the way to improve prisons is to get a better caliber of prisoners and he's not that far wrong. You take young, naive kids and throw them in with the real animals and that kid is not going to change for the better. I've seen kids 18 or 19 years old go to prison and come out two years later knowing more about crime than I did. They could show me 14 different ways to pick a lock, or 19 different places to hide narcotics on your body. As far as I'm concerned prison is a finishing school for criminals.

Not that we don't need prisons. There are some guys that ought to spend their lives locked up in a cage. An individual who hurts people in the street belongs in prison. Any man who willfully hurts another individual for no reason at all—throw him away. I'm 100 percent in favor of the death penalty because most people are afraid to die. (I don't know what they are afraid of, you've got to die anyway. And how bad can death be, no one has ever complained about it?)

Who should be fried? When an individual is murdered needlessly—for example, an elderly person killed for a few dollars, or an animal comes into a home and rapes and kills a woman—people who do these things should die. Honest citizens have a right to live peacefully.

I also think that killing a cop should be something an individual dies for. It may sound strange that I believe this. A cop is just a man doing his job. A man, just like me, only working the other side of the law. If I can bribe a cop I'm gonna bribe him. But if I can't, am I going to kill him? For what? Cops are people, they want to work, support their families, go home at night to the wife and kids, and make a decent living. What are you gonna do, indiscriminately kill a man because he wears a badge? Anybody who kills a cop should be hung up by his balls in the middle of Times Square. That would make people think the next time they took aim at a cop.

The best stay I ever had in prison was in the Los Angeles County clink. I had been involved in a huge brawl with a professional football player and we both suffered: I spent a few days in jail and he missed two games with the sorest pair of nuts in history. It all started because we were both out of our minds drunk. I woke up in jail with a tremendous hangover. I had been in this place quite a few times before and the jailer knew me pretty well. On Sunday morning, when the religious people came around, he decided he would play a practical joke on me; he directed them to my cell. The joke backfired. One of them happened to be the best-looking woman I had seen in a long time. She started telling me about Jesus Christ and I knew it was going to be an even match. She was going to try to convert me and I was going to try to pervert her. I won. When they let me out I called her up and we started dating. I figure I owe about five months of wonderful nights to our prison system.

CHAPTER *19*

GOOD-BYE

adies, gentlemen and highly esteemed customers of all ages. In conclusion I would just like to take this opportunity to thank all those people who have made my career possible. Without their unselfish contribution there is no telling what terrible fate might have befallen me.

I would again like to thank the newspapers, magazines, television shows, movies and book publishers who have done more to promote the mob than any public-relations agency we could have hired. I don't know where the media continues to come up with its fascinating stories, but they are successfully scaring the living shit out of people.

I was talking with a guy recently about some money he owed me and he was practically on his knees, crying, "Please don't hurt me or send anybody after me." The mob does not like to use violent means and, thanks to the fear you've spread, we don't have to—except on rare occasions. We are business people.

I would like to thank the newspapers in particular for their noble service of providing free advertising for those of us in the bookmaking line. It is with great pleasure I look upon the betting lines that most papers print every day, knowing full well that there is nowhere the reader can legally place a bet.

Although none of us really ever wanted to be celebrities and don't like to see our pictures in the newspapers, I would like to thank the movie and television industry for making us famous as well as respected. Personally, my favorite television program is "All in the Family" (which I originally thought might refer to the Gambino Family, but I was wrong), but I loved that comedy called "The Untouchables." The most important message of the show was: If you don't pay the mob you will be killed. We all appreciate that, even if it is a bit of an exaggeration. What are we going to do, kill a guy for a hundred bucks? Thanks to you TV geniuses, all we have to do is show up and snarl.

I would also like to thank the policemen of this country for their fine work in cooperation with the organization. But I'm sure they could not have done it alone, and for their additional help I thank America's legislators. The lawmakers have done a wonderful job of preventing reform. As we all know, if gambling, numbers and cardplaying were legal, and if this country adopted any sort of sensible narcotics program, the mob would be seriously hurt. So we owe a debt of gratitude to those people who have prevented such legislation.

I would additionally like to thank the lawmakers for making the American legal system one of the most complicated, inconsistent and contradictory in the world. We, the members of organized crime, know and understand the laws. Or our lawyers do. We use the law to beat the law. We know what is illegal in one place may very well be legal in another. If this country adopted a sensible system like England's, in which there is one law for the entire country, the same law in London and Manchester, the mob would be severely hurt.

I would also like to thank the lawmakers for making and keeping the American prison system the shambles it is. Without it we might have problems recruiting new members, and would certainly have to give them the extensive training they receive in prison.

A man may spend ten years in prison and never be taught more than how to stamp out license plates. Then, when he is released, he is denied the right to obtain a license of any sort in most states, and is permanently branded Con. If that man could make a living on the outside we probably would never see him in our business again. Yet our recruiting offices are mobbed.

Somebody told me this great quote once. A sour old guy named H. L.. Mencken said it first, I think. "Nobody ever went broke underestimating the intelligence of the American people."

EPILOGUE

hen first published in 1973 as *Killer*, Joey's book became a best-seller, creating quite a sensation. At one point, my doorbell rang and I buzzed in the man who had been on the FBI's Ten Most Wanted List longer than anyone in history. This 10-year fugitive had been so impressed by Joey's book that he had decided to allow me to arrange his final surrender to the FBI. I did so—and it was nationally televised on the "Today Show."

But the FBI had other reasons to want to talk with me. They asked me repeatedly to tell them Joey's real identity. And repeatedly I told them, truthfully, that I did not know his real name, where he lived or how he spent most of his days. Finally, they told me that they had evidence that Joey was not who he claimed to be and threatened to charge me with mail fraud for sending the book through the mail if I didn't tell them his real name.

If these agents didn't know his true identity either, I pointed out, they would have great difficulty proving anything about Joey at all. I never heard from the Bureau again.

Joey moved in and out of my life, following his own timetable, for about seven years. As time passed, I would get a phone call from him, or he would show up at my front door every four or five months. Gradually, the length of time between contacts grew longer and longer. Then one day I received a call from a newspaper reporter in San Mateo, California. Joey had been shot in the back with a shotgun at close range, she told me. He had lived for several hours, but finally died from his injuries. "Do you have any idea what he was doing here?" she asked.

I took a guess. Joey had been an inveterate gambler. As he might have described it, he'd bet his lungs on a cockroach derby. He loved playing the horses. And he loved the gambling tables in Las Vegas and Reno and all the bust-out joints behind locked doors. He'd rarely bet on sports though—he once told me, "I never bet on anything that talks." Long ago I'd realized that he'd selected the cities in which we'd met based on which racetracks were in operation at that time of year. The places he'd told me to stay were all relatively close to major tracks. If I were a betting man, I would have bet that his killing was caused by large, unpaid gambling debts.

I asked the reporter, "Is there a racetrack near the hotel he was staying in?"

There was.

"Was he leaving just about the right time to make the first race?"

He was.

Well, I explained, that's what he was doing there.

But after his death, I finally learned more about Joey. A detective in the New York City Police Department pulled his rap sheet for me. He told me Joey's real name and where he lived. Joey was Jewish—the reason he was never permitted to become a made member of a Mafia family—and had been born, raised and had lived in the Bronx. His brother was a police officer, a well-respected cop (although Joey referred to him as his cousin in the book, to protect his identity). The detective began interpreting the rest of the information for me. Joey had been picked up on suspicion of murder numerous times without ever being charged. But earlier in his life he had served time in a California prison for assault. Joey was exactly who he claimed to be, a hit man for the mob, although there was absolutely no way of verifying how many people he actually had killed. He was well known to the NYPD by his real name and, surprisingly, to the FBI. Why then, I wondered, had the FBI questioned me about his identity?

The answer surprised me. Joey's identity was known only to a select few inside the Bureau—because he was an informer. That's why his sheet indicated that most times he had been picked up he was released within a few hours without being charged. Joey had his own way of cooperating, I was told. He never volunteered information, he never offered a single name or detail. Instead, he corroborated information law enforcement already had or helped set detectives on the correct path. If asked, for example, whether it was a member of the Gambino family or the Bonnano family, he would tell them, "It wasn't Bonnano." When asked if a specific suspect was responsible for a certain crime, he either would tell the cops they had the wrong guy or just shrug his shoulders in a 'could be' gesture.

Why did he do this, I wondered? It seemed so completely out of character. And then I focused on that exact word, character. Joey was indeed a character created by the person whose name I had so recently learned. But, as I have written, Joey could play whatever role was demanded of him—and find justification for it. The detective offered no reasonable explanation. I suppose a fine psychiatrist could explain this to me—and I suspect the fact that his brother was a cop would prove important. But when I think back about Joey, I remain just as surprised as I was that day.

And that was not the last time Joey would surprise me. Perhaps two years after his death, I received a telephone call from an insurance investigator who explained to me that shortly before Joey had been killed he had taken out a life insurance policy with a double-indemnity clause— a clause that doubled the payout value of the policy if Joey died of various unnatural causes. Ultimately, it would turn out that being shot in the back by a shotgun at close range, when about to get into his rental car, qualified.

But at the time, the insurance investigator explained that on his application Joey had listed his occupation as a 'construction worker.' If the insurance company could prove that the policyholder had lied on his application, that in fact he was a mob hit man, the policy would be voided and the company would not have to pay.

But they had to prove that he was a mob killer, something no law enforcement agency had been able to do. I certainly couldn't help them—I only knew what he'd told me; I had no other evidence. During this conversation, though, I learned more details about Joey's death. The beneficiary of this policy was Joey's sister, whom he had talked about with me. His wife was not mentioned. And then the investigator added, almost as an aside, "and we didn't know about his cancer either."

Weeks before his death Joey had been diagnosed with terminal cancer. Joey's death suddenly took on an entirely new dimension: Knowing that he was dying of cancer, Joey had taken out a life insurance policy and then, very possibly, arranged for his own murder. As with just about everything else concerning Joey, there was no way to ever know if that was true, but it added yet another layer of mystery to the life of this complicated man.

There has been no attempt here to get around the fact that Joey was a cold-blooded killer. Even after all this time, I don't profess to understand his deep motivations, or his ability to live with his profession, even treat it lightly. I should have been appalled by Joey. But I wasn't, at least not after the first few days. Like everyone else who met him, I became fascinated. I was young then, and I had never met anyone remotely like him. I'm much older now, and many have crossed my path. And I can still say I have never met anyone remotely like Joey Black.

—D. F.

A Word About the Collaborator

Since the publication of *Killer* David Fisher has written or collaborated on more than 50 books, many of them best sellers. He is the only author ever to have works of fiction, non-fiction and reference offered simultaneously by the Book of the Month Club.